HIGHWAYS OF THE MIND

HIGHWAYS OF THE MIND

The Art and History of Pathworking

by

DOLORES ASHCROFT-NOWICKI

Foreword by
Rachel Pollack

THE AQUARIAN PRESS
Wellingborough, Northamptonshire

First published 1987

British Library Cataloguing in Publication Data

Ashcroft-Nowicki, Dolores
Highways of the mind: the art and history
of pathworking.
1. Astral projection
I. Title
133.9   BF1389.A7

ISBN 0-85030-554-3

*The Aquarian Press is part of the Thorsons Publishing Group,
Denington Estate, Wellingborough, Northamptonshire, NN8 2RQ, England*

Printed in Great Britain by Woolnough Bookbinding,
Irthlingborough, Northamptonshire

3 5 7 9 10 8 6 4 2

Dedication

To my much loved parents, Jessica and Leslie Ashcroft.
I offer this book with love and gratitude for all we have shared
together.

The Priests of Anubis, by Wolfe van Brussel

CONTENTS

ACKNOWLEDGEMENTS

I have drawn upon many sources for my material and have sought and received help from many people. Therefore to the following people I would like to say, 'Thank you.'

To Sonia Maurice who typed the manuscript and never complained when I changed a page continuously until I got it right. To Dr Deirdre Green who clarified points on the Hekaloth for me. To friend and fellow writer, Neville Drury, who has taken the Art of Pathworking into new areas, and Moses Aaron, once an SOL student who took the whole idea of it to heart and became the first of the modern 'travelling bards' taking pathworking stories into the schools, theatres, television studios and classrooms of Australia and America.

Over the past ten years I have put together hundreds of pathworkings; ninety per cent of them have been tried out by SOL friends, students and tutors, most of the time with wry patience as they often came back with more than they bargained for. To all of you my love and thanks.

PREFACE

Unbeknown to myself at the time, I first learnt to pathwork around the age of 4 or 5, but it was not until the war years that I began to use it with the intention of actually 'going somewhere'. Along with thousands of others, my whole family had fled the island of Jersey where I had been born and brought up, when it became obvious that the German Army would soon invade the ancient Duchy of the Channel Islands. The same small boats that had fought so tirelessly to save the British Army at Dunkirk now turned wearily to the task of ferrying men, women and children to the mainland. Once there, most of the men joined up leaving their families to swell the thousands of refugees crowding beleaguered Britain.

On a warm June day in 1940, hundreds of us huddled together on the deck of a tiny Norwegian coal boat, with many more below. Dangerously overcrowded, it took us sixteen hours to reach Weymouth on the Dorset coast, shadowed by U-boats every step of the way. On reaching Britain, we headed for the north-west, to the town of Wallasey where my father had been born and where we still had relatives. There we prepared to wait until we could return home again. We had, or so we thought, reached safety but we had not reckoned on the fury of the *Luftwaffe*. During all that long summer and into the autumn, the whole of the Mersey River became a nightly battlefield of fire, explosions, death and destruction. At school the classes dwindled as whole families were killed in the almost non-stop bombing of Liverpool and its adjacent towns. For a child of 10 the days were filled with an apprehension almost as bad as the terrifying nights; one never made plans to meet and play with friends on Saturdays or Sundays, it was all too possible that neither you nor your friends would be alive by then.

Most of our nights were spent in a bleak air raid shelter where, terrified by the bombing, I would bury my head in my mother's lap and stuff my fingers into my ears, hoping that if we were hit I would neither hear nor feel it.

One night during a particularly bad raid, I became so frightened that it produced an almost trance-like state. Without any warning I found myself somewhere quite different to the air raid shelter that had almost become home. I was in a small valley among very high mountains with distinctly shaped peaks. Somehow I knew that it was very cold, though I felt nothing of the icy wind that blew down from those white peaks. In front of me, around a large fire sat seven men, all of them wrapped in what I took to be woollen blankets of dark red.

After the scream of bombs and the clatter of anti-aircraft guns, the sudden silence was shattering. I stood there, a 10-year-old girl whose nerves were stretched to breaking point after months of terror. Then one of the men turned and beckoned to me, making a place beside him. I sat down, becoming one of the circle around the focal point of the fire. No word was spoken, indeed I never heard any of them speak in all the time I was to enjoy their peaceful company during the worst of the 1940 blitz. There was only the utter peace and quiet of the high mountains, while the feeling of being safe from all harm, and the calmness of my companions was like a balm to my shaken mind.

I could feel no heat from the fire, just as I could feel no cold from the wind, but at the back of my mind I knew that both the fire and the wind were *real*. I was fully aware that this place existed far away from where my body, rigid with fear, was crouched in a concrete shelter. All this had form and meaning, and deep inside me I *knew* it was no dream.

The monks, for so I took them to be, remained silent yet alert, but the silence contained words that comforted and reassured me until I relaxed. Then, when I was able to concentrate, came the stories. Stories that explained, taught, and formed the beginnings of the future. Stories that awoke memories far older than the ten years I had lived. It never occurred to me as strange that I should understand what was obviously a foreign language; the knowledge was passed directly from their minds to mine.

It seemed like hours before one of my new-found friends raised his head and smiled at me. He appeared to be about 25 years old, yet with so much wisdom in his eyes that he could have been as old as the mountains that surrounded us, and as strong. Then I was back in the cold dampness of the shelter with my mother shaking me, telling me that the raid was over and we could return home.

I said nothing about my experience. Young as I was I had already learnt the dangers of appearing to be different. Besides, I felt that this was for me alone and not to be shared even with my parents. For some time we had trouble-free nights, then came another raid and we hurried to the shelter. I waited in an agony of suspense for something to happen but nothing did; the raid was a small one and we soon went back to the house. During the following months I was to learn that I could only reach my circle of companions when the raid was a really bad one; at other times I had to rely on my own store of courage.

For almost a year I had the security of these new-found friends. Then we moved out into the country where it was more peaceful, and air raids were a rarity. There the whole thing came to an end. But I did meet my companions once more. It was long after the war, and I was now married with children of my own, and had begun serious magical training under a much-loved Master Craftsman.* We were sitting meditating together, when, as suddenly as it had happened all those years before, we were in the same place, with the same circle seemingly unchanged during the intervening time. I took my old place and basked in the feeling of coming home. My teacher and another member of the circle seemed to know each other well and 'conversed' in the same wordless way that I remembered. It lasted only a short time, then we were back in the old Tudor cottage where so much of my training was to take place.

I had told my teacher about my wartime experiences some time before, and now I questioned him. He told me that mine was not an isolated case, that many others had had similar experiences. In most cases it occurred where a person had past ties with an Inner Plane Order, and this kind of pathworking was used in times of stress by the Brethren to reach those with the ability to use the inner pathways of the mind. It gave them a breathing space and saved the hard pressed personality from cracking under severe mental stress. Bringing a book from the shelves, my teacher opened it at a photograph of a mountain range, asking if I recognized them. I certainly did. They were, he told me, part of the Pamir range. He had heard during his time in India of a monastery high up in a mountain valley at the point where India, Pakistan and Afghanistan meet. It was and still is a place where borders have little meaning. Where, even in this day and age, there are hidden places where time flows slowly and hearts and minds can be trained to a high degree of perfection.

If I had any past connection with such a place, my teacher told me, it was entirely possible that they would have protected me during my time of fear. He had no doubt that at some time in the future, some form of confirmation would be given to me. As in most things he was

* W. E. Butler.

right. A few years after his death I met with someone who had been in that part of the world, and he told me a strange story.

High up in the Pamir range he had heard of an unusual monastery. I queried his use of the word 'monastery', surely it should be 'lamasery', but he was adamant that it was a monastery, where many of the inmates spoke a patois of the local dialect and an archaic form of Greek. Although he had not been there himself, he knew someone who had stayed there for some months, a German who spoke fluent Greek. He maintained that the monastery had been founded by Alexander as the young conqueror had forged his way into India. The lamas say that Alexander took with him some of the local priesthood, and left in their place some of his own priests. The monastery was said to hold many early Greek manuscripts and artefacts. What interested me most, however, was a photograph of the mountains some miles east of the location. I could never forget the shape of those mountains – they were the same I had seen so many years before in childhood.

I am a lot older and a little wiser now, and the art of pathworking is, among other things, part of the occult teachings I have tried to bring out into the open in the past few years. The realms of psychology have tried to claim them for their own, and they are appearing in many guises and under many descriptive names, but I hope to show that they are as old as man himself, and that the term path *'working'* is very apt, as they do indeed require a great deal of work. They are part of a much greater structure in the make-up of man, and pertain to his dreams and hopes, and his ability to make those dreams come true. Used with purpose and by trained minds, the pathworking becomes a series of controlled thought patterns, and thought is the basis of creation.

Dolores Ashcroft-Nowicki
Jersey, 1986

FOREWORD
BY RACHEL POLLACK

We live in a culture that considers the imagination of no great significance
in human life. We teach our children the difference between the 'real'
world and fantasy, saying 'It's only a story', and 'It's just a dream',
whenever they appear to take their imaginations seriously. If they continue
to play 'let's pretend' games past a certain age we worry about
psychological troubles or immaturity. As adults, we all daydream, or
fantasize about the future (fear fantasies as well as hope). In fact, life
is not possible without imagination. And yet, we pride ourselves that
we do not take such things seriously, that we pay no attention to 'idle'
fantasies.

This division goes back to the roots of our Western religions. Judaism
began a campaign against story, against myth, insisting that all the events
described in the Scriptures were historical facts, and that this alone gives
them value. Despite a long tradition of storytelling in Judaism (the
Midrash, as it is called, runs into many volumes, expanding and
improvising on Scriptural 'events'), stories were seen as somehow minor,
even suspect, compared to the Law.

Christianity carried this denigration of the imagination a step further.
While constructing a clearly mythical story about its central figure, Jesus,
Christianity has adamantly insisted on the 'historicism' of every event,
every word, described in the New Testament. Even today, educated and
intelligent people will attempt to find 'scientific' explanations for the
Biblical miracles, as if this will make them acceptable. We read of great
amounts of money being spent to try to find a boat on top of Mount
Ararat, and so 'prove' the historical validity of Noah's ark. If some
important person, such as a bishop, mildly suggests that maybe some
of the things written about Jesus didn't actually happen, Christians send
furious letters to newspapers and radio stations, calling for punishment
or resignation.

Occultists, too, suffer from this dismissal of the imagination. In her many years dedicated to teaching the occult, Dolores Ashcroft-Nowicki has observed that students love the glamour of rituals, with their costumes, their powerful words and gestures, their lighting effects, the summoning of powers and forces. But many of these same students will ignore what Dolores calls 'pathworkings', the use of the imagination to create and enter an archetypal world, a literal *path* through the varied energies of the unconscious. Sometimes, Dolores comments, students will advance to high levels, memorizing systems, serving in rituals, only to find that they must go back to the level of a beginner and learn to work the pathways. For without the ability to experience, say, the sephiroth and their links on the Tree of Life, all their knowledge remains outside them, and their rituals will not lead to transformation.

Because our culture relegates the imagination to childhood we tend to think of fantasies as childish amusement. But a properly constructed pathworking will resonate through many levels of the personality, bringing unconscious energy into conscious form, opening up a person's life as well as awareness. In my own experience I have known people to make major decisions after undergoing such journeys as climbing the World Tree from the Earth to the stars. We tend to think we can only deal with our problems through sober analysis of all possible choices (as if such a thing were possible). Often, however, a guided fantasy — a pathworking — will confront us with the choices in a non-rational way that can lead to greater understanding and a firmer decision.

With the influence of modern psychology as well as the occult, many people have begun to recognize the value of a particular programme using the imagination. However, we still set these things apart, something we do in therapy, or occult training, or in weekend workshops. Dolores Ashcroft-Nowicki knows that imagination permeates our lives. It is a particular value of this book that it brings us to see the connections between a journey in the worlds of the Tarot and a businessman fantasizing about building a commercial empire. *Highways Of The Mind* brings together such things as daydreams, childhood imaginary friends, ancient mystery religions, television shows, cave paintings, occult teachings, psychotherapy, masturbatory sex fantasies, and literary criticism. Dolores does all this with the sharp earthy humour that fills all her work.

If daydreams of success and romance come from the same faculty as pathworkings, that does not make them as true or powerful. Someone like Dolores, experienced in the ways of the imagination, sensitive to the images of myth, will know how to construct a pathworking that opens up levels closed to the normal uses of fantasy. The pathworking brings us to 'archetypes'. This word has been much abused, but we can define it as essential images or stories which affect us in ways that defy rational explanation. They give shape to unconscious experience. In our society most people rarely meet such powers, even in church, for the major religions have demythicized themselves. Through a carefully led pathworking we not only experience these archetypes but act within their worlds. We not only *see* the lion in the Tarot card of Strength, we *do* something with it. And that doing can lead to practical steps in a person's life as well as changes in consciousness.

Highways Of The Mind gives advice and instruction to those who wish to create a programme of pathworking. The founder of an occult school, Dolores knows that nothing can substitute for a teacher. At the same time she tells us how to form a group, how to begin a series, how often to do a fantasy, how to separate the worlds, and so on. She describes the two basic sorts of pathworking, the active, in which a leader takes her or his listeners step-by-step through an imaginary journey, and the more complex passive, in which the leader sets a scene, and the listeners allow their own stories to emerge. And she tells us as well how to set up pathworkings on our own.

Dolores knows the importance of training. She stresses the 'work' in pathworking and reminds us again and again that this work requires skill and practise. People who first try visualizing some simple image, such as a gateway, will discover how difficult this can be. Similarly, the first time we enter an imaginary world, we will find the attention wandering, going off into street noises, plans for lunch, physical annoyances, judgements about how well we're doing, even daydreams external to the fantasy. As with meditation, pathworking can teach us, first of all, about our own appalling lack of concentration. (Children, interestingly can concentrate much better than adults. We think of children as having short attention spans because they get bored in school. In fact, in their own games and fantasies, children can focus with an intensity very few adults could emulate.)

For proper pathworking, then, we need to learn discipline. Dolores also stresses the need for knowledge, research. The more you know of something the better you can conjure it in your imagination. Do you wish to experience shape-shifting, becoming a tiger or a bird? Then learn all you can about these animals, go to the zoo, take photographs, read about their habits. The more concrete reality you absorb, the freer becomes the imagination. Pathworking helps to break down the artificial distinctions between the outside world and the world of inner creation.

Dolores stresses the occult discipline of pathworking, but she never neglects its many other uses in daily life. She shows us, for instance, how creating a pathworking out of a poem can give us a greater understanding of the poem's truth. She then demonstrates such understanding with an original interpretation of Coleridge's *Rime of the Ancient Mariner.*

In one of the book's more courageous passages Dolores defends the value of sex fantasies for people without partners. Elsewhere she looks at religious mystics such as St John of the Cross and shows how religion at its most intense joins with the imagination. And finally, never neglecting the ordinary, she advises parents on how pathworking can improve a child's performance in school.

In discussing the imagination Dolores Ashcroft-Nowicki speaks from long experience. Listening to her can open up an essential yet neglected part of our own lives.

Rachel Pollack

CHAPTER ONE

The Nature of Pathworking

Pathworkings are an ancient and valid form of occult training, but it is only in recent times that they have been made available to those outside the magical fraternities. Even within the schools and Orders of the Western Tradition they have been neglected and their full value in the mental and spiritual training of students has been and still is very underrated. Nor is this entirely the fault of their teachers, for many who eagerly apprentice themselves to the Path of High Magic prefer to press on to the more glamorous ritual work until they gain a little wisdom and begin to see the value of such training. Then it can mean months of back-tracking and the acquiring of the acute sensory perception that accurate pathworking needs if it is to be used correctly and to its full potential. Did they but know it, it is the training gained in the art and practice of this kind of work that opens the doors of the mind and gives full access to the inner universe that lies within. Moreover, it lays down the important basics of the higher levels of symbology without which it is almost impossible to penetrate the Greater Mysteries.

Science tells us that we use only a fraction of our brains' potential, but that is because the mind using the brain as its tool has so little training in the use of such a complicated piece of machinery. If you put an unskilled person in front of a computer they will only be able to switch it on so that it ticks over. In a few weeks, and with the help of a basic primer or two, the same person will be able to use the computer well enough to program simple instructions into it. In a year, even with no further teaching, a reasonably intelligent person will have figured out a lot of quite complicated procedures, but the machine would still be working at a mere fraction of its potential. If, however, that person had been trained from the start, learning what the computer could and could not do, then learning to control its mechanical functions and direct them according to what was needed, gradually a high degree of skill would emerge and the computer would be used almost to full capacity. It is the same with the human brain; unless the brain user, that is, the mind, is well-trained, much of the brain's ability will never be put to work.

There is no doubt that the long months of practising visualization, and of simply walking round and really *looking* at things in order to be able to re-create them in the mind's eye, can get boring. Books of a certain type, containing highly descriptive writing must be read and a data bank of images has to be built up gradually and this takes time, so many people prefer to move on to the more exciting ritual work.

Rituals are important, of that there is no doubt, but they have been given an air of glamour that cloaks the hidden dangers lying in wait for the unwary and the ill-trained. All rituals should be approached slowly and carefully and with due respect for their unpredictability. This is where pathworkings come into their own. Though they do have levels where they become mental rituals of the highest and most taxing kind, they should also be seen for what they are, as the beams and struts, nails and screws that hold occult training together. Learning one without the other is to leave half your training unaccounted for, yet even today few students are competently trained in their use and meaning, or even in their basic construction, let alone their deeper and more mysterious uses.

I hope this book will remedy the neglect and put the art of pathworking where it belongs as one of the oldest and most important methods of occult training.

Pathworkings are not new, in fact they are incredibly ancient. They were used in early Egypt and Sumer. Chaldea made use of them in her fabled star magic. Others can be discerned at the heart of the old rites that have come to us via the oral tradition of folklore, fairy-tales and nursery rhymes. Some are hidden among old papyri and dusty vellums in libraries that rarely see anything more than the occasional scholar, or which are forbidden to the general public by ecclesiastical decree. They fell into gradual disuse as newer, though not always better, methods of training were introduced over the centuries by those whose work it was, and is, to keep alive the teachings of the Mysteries.

Such things are the normal hazards, new ways grow out of old ideas and rightly so for, without change, all would become stagnant and die. But in the search for those new ways we sometimes lose sight of solid and well-tried methods of training that need only a little adaptation to keep them serviceable.

When the sciences of psychology and psychiatry became part of our modern world, the old pathworking techniques were rediscovered and given new names such as Visual Experiences, Mind Games, Guided

Meditation, Altered States, Thought Building, etc. The intelligences ancient man had contacted when he used them were now termed Archetypes, while the inner universe, used by the temple neophytes of long ago, became the Realm of the Unconscious. Today most psychologists employ the use of such techniques as a matter of course and it has even become a money-spinning game called Dungeons and Dragons that attracts young and old alike. But how many people realize that they are methods of mind control thousands of years old?

The Therapeutoi of ancient Greece, the priests of Aesculapius, used both dreams and pathworkings as a means of healing, and found them very successful. Earlier still in Egypt the priests of Anubis, whose task it was to guide the dying across the dark waters between life and death, used them in a way that has remained unchanged in the Mysteries down to the present day. Waking dreams inspired the earliest biblical prophets, and the basic idea behind all pathworkings can be found in the oldest examples of all, the art of the cave-dweller painted in the dawn of pre-history.

They are not, as many believe, an invention of modern psychology, though to do them justice many eminent psychologists are aware of the debt owed to the old traditions. Neither are they a product of the Order of the Golden Dawn, though they figured prominently in their training methods and they probably saved the idea and method from total extinction. But we must now ask ourselves the first question . . . What *is* a pathworking?

A pathworking is a journey between this side of the mental worlds and the other side. One of the most exciting journeys mankind can take because it offers a path, a map through the landscapes of the mind, landscapes that are as yet barely explored and offer one of the last great frontiers. They are Doorways between the known and the physical and the unknown and the non-corporeal. They accomplish their work through the medium of the creative imagination, which ability is the seed from which everything made and produced by mankind has sprung. They can and do cause actual physical effects in the everyday world in which we live, which is one of the reasons why they have been held in secret for so long. (I have spoken of this in my book *The Shining Paths*, Aquarian Press, 1983.) This fact is behind the statement that rigorous training and control of this imaginative faculty is the most important work students of the occult will undertake during their period of study. Without it all other abilities will work at only half strength. A sweeping statement, but true.

Every man, woman and child has this talent to a greater or lesser degree, but however little you may have, it can be trained. If you have a real gift for it, you need, above all, people to train it long and hard, for it can change your life, heal you, guide you, teach you, and when the time comes, lead you gently from this world to another, where strange suns go down over unexplored mountains. They are the portals to that strange world known to the ancient psychopompoi, the dual-natured gods who walked freely between the lands of the living and the dead and those that lie between them.

Some people are born with the gift of imagination falling out of their ears, others barely know it by name let alone by acquaintance. We use it every day of our lives, asleep or awake, knowing or unknowing. With it we can bring into being things as grandiose as a plan for a cathedral, or as ephemeral as a love poem. Incredible though it may seem, the imagination – which is a talent possessed only by humankind out of all the life forms on this planet – can and does bring about everything we can claim as man made. This includes the works of Shakespeare, the paintings of Leonardo da Vinci, the power of a Rolls Royce engine, the exquisite detail of old handmade lace or the recipe for a new cocktail. *Everything* is thought about and imagined before it can become a reality. This fact is one of the most important keys of magic. Used by a trained and balanced mind the imagination can literally move a mountain – simply by designing a bigger and more efficient mechanical digger.

The imagination is used in different ways and for very different purposes, all of which have vital and far-reaching effects in our everyday lives. It works for instance in conjunction with memory and together the two faculties enable us to recall on our mental TV screen everything we have seen, known or experienced in our lives, though most of it is stored in the subconscious and can be reached only through a series of triggers, or medically through the use of drugs in cases of amnesia, or sometimes through shock. It is the combination of memory and imagination that enables us to recall the layout of streets and recognize faces of old friends when we have been away for many years. Without memory we could not learn or store knowledge, without imagination we could not recall the faces of loved ones or even find our way home from work. We use this method of recognition connected to the inner eye when we give instructions to a stranger who asks the way to the post office or bus station. As we give precise directions we mentally take the route we are describing. We point out various landmarks as a guide to certain streets and actually re-create within our mind's eye the way to be taken; a pathworking functions in exactly the same way.

In this modern world where we tend to crowd out the imagination in terms of pictures and substitute the symbols of letters and numbers, there are some people who find great difficulty in recalling or creating inner images. We use the spoken word as a means of communication now, and do not need to draw vague shapes in the earth with a bit of stick to explain ourselves, so we are in danger of losing something of great value unless we cultivate it. In the past we have tended to train the imagination out of our children, especially in school, with words like – 'Don't daydream, James, or you won't pass that exam.' (The longer James daydreams the better chance he stands!) Another favourite was – 'Don't sit around daydreaming, do something useful.' Later, the same children were blamed for not being able 'to see the opportunities of life'. Of course they couldn't, the ability to 'see' had been ironed out of them.

Happily this kind of teaching is on the way out, and more and more schools are actually encouraging children to use their imagination in their work both in the school and outside. There is also the fact that many occult-minded parents are encouraging their children to meditate from quite a young age, using the techniques both actively and passively. This means that a whole new generation is growing up with a stronger and clearer inner vision than at any time since the days of the great Mystery schools.

We have seen that pathworking is a term used to describe the trained use of the creative imagination and that such journeys within the mind can inform, calm, heal, relax and train the mind and its tool, the brain. We know also that it can cause events to happen in accordance with the will, not always as precisely as we could perhaps wish but, given training, time and the all-important mental discipline, an occultist can expect a reasonable amount of success. A few people can do it with no training at all and absolutely no idea of what it is or how it works. They are the success phenomena, men and women who seem to do everything right first time off. They are in the right places at the right times with the right contacts and they have the ability to grasp the situations and make them work. Why? Because they have subconsciously caused those events and have already prepared themselves to deal with them beforehand. As I have said in *The Ritual Magic Workbook*, the ability to imagine events and play them out in the mind *according to your desires* is the basis of every book on personal success ever written.

If this is so, why isn't everyone a successful millionaire? Simple. You have to want it, want it with every atom of your being to the exclusion of everything else until that goal is attained. This takes a single-mindedness of purpose that very few people possess. Most of you reading this book will know at least one fairy-tale about a poor man being offered three wishes and, although this represents a once-in-a-lifetime opportunity, he makes a complete mess of it because he cannot make up his mind what he really wants. At this point it is time for our first pathworking.

Imagine that you are walking along a deserted beach. The day is warm and sunny and the saltiness of the sea air is making you feel really good. The tide is coming in and, as you walk along near the edge, that magical place where it is neither sea nor sand but a little of both, a bottle is washed up at your feet. It is made of dark-green glass and there is something inside that sparkles and glitters. You look around but there is no one but you on the beach. The bottle is closed by a silver-topped stopper over which wax has been poured. In the wax you can see the faint imprint of a seal.

You peer into the bottle and see something moving about inside. You shake it and there is a squeak as if something is protesting at such rough treatment. Gingerly you prise off the seal and work the stopper out of the bottle neck. A thin plume of smoke emerges and rapidly spirals up into the air, taking on a human shape as it does so. Soon there stands before you one of the ancient djinn of the East. For a moment you think about running, then realize that it is very unlikely you could get away from this supernatural creature, so you stand your ground, albeit shakily, and wait for it to speak. This is your lucky day. It is so happy to be free after several thousand years that it is prepared to overlook the shaking and even to reward you . . . with the traditional three wishes. *Only* three and you cannot change your mind once a wish has been made, and will you do it right now because he wants to get home to Damascus and the wife and children, always assuming djinn have them.

At this point your mind would most probably go completely blank. You may think it would be easy to reel off three wishes, but is it? Health, Wealth, and Prosperity I can hear someone say – true, except that as prosperity by and large means the same as wealth, you would have wasted one wish. Health certainly, but whose health? Yours? In magic the first thing a student learns is to be absolutely specific about wishes, etc., otherwise you can get things you would rather not have, simply because what you asked for was not fully explained, for example, a new coat . . . of what? Paint? What colour, what size, what material? So whose health are you wishing for . . . just saying 'Health' could mean anyone's, even the djinn's. And if you say *my* good health, will you have any guilt feelings about not wishing for the continuing health of your children, wife, parents, or the little girl down the road with leukemia? You are already getting confused.

Wealth next . . . how much? Don't say 'As much as I need'; what the djinn thinks you need and what you think you need could differ quite a lot. Remember it has been in a bottle for thousands of years and inflation has set in. What currency? Do you want it to come as a big win with all the resultant publicity or quietly so you won't get any hassle?

You still have one more wish and it is my bet that you have already got a list as long as your arm, but which one do you make? No matter what you ask for you will wish you had asked for something else later. That is human nature. There is the rather nasty little story about the man who, having been given just one wish, thought he would be clever and wished for a thousand-dollar bill under his pillow every morning for as long as he lived. He got two bills before he was knocked down by a car and killed! Or the man who wished for immortality and forgot to ask for eternal youth with it! On the whole, it is the fair sex who seem to know just how to go about getting what they want - like the lady who, having conjured up an Elemental Being, and been granted one wish, said simply: 'I wish that you would fall hopelessly in love with me and be unable to refuse me anything.' Now *that* was a well thought out wish.

All this is leading up to the fact that to use pathworkings to cause events by which you may prosper, you must have a one-pointed mind about the results of that event and go for it. If you do this, it will work. If you dither about, forget it. So to use pathworkings on the physical level and for causing events on that level, you must first develop your powers of concentration, self-discipline and your visualization ability.

We now know what a pathworking is and what it can do, but how do they work? Every moment of our existence we are surrounded, encompassed by energy and matter. It is what we, ourselves, are made of along with everything else in the universe. This basic life stuff is highly impressionable. It will take the shape, form, colour or imprint of anything that hits it hard enough, and what hits it hardest is thought. As I have already explained, everything ever made by mankind since the beginning was thought about first. Perhaps long ago one of our ancestors hit his hand with a sharp stone, making it bleed. The 'thought' registered that the same thing might happen if you hit a bison with a stone. Along with this thought came pictures of himself hitting the bison and the animal falling down. Until that moment the flint was just a piece of stone. Suddenly it became a weapon. It took a while to seep through the rudimentary brain man was using at the time, but when it did the first axe took shape and the Stone Age was born. Everything we make, from works of art to weapons, from textiles to books, music and dance, is born first in the realms of the mind via the creative imagination. To realize this fully is to take the first step towards understanding the potential divinity of mankind. But it is just that, the first step on a long, long journey.

Like everything else, this power of the mind can be misused and often is by those who have little concern for others – another reason why the art of pathworking has been kept hidden in the inner courts of mystery schools for so long. I have said elsewhere and will continue to say as long as I remain a teacher, that ethics *must* be taught to every student who comes to the Door of the Mysteries; without them the students and the training can go disastrously wrong. There are rules laid down in such a school and they must be obeyed for the good of everyone.

Once the invisible life-matter is impressed by a thought, idea or a deliberately built sequence of events, the pressure must be kept up. The idea must be gone over again and again. The sequence must be run on the mental TV screen until it becomes a reality for you on that level. There will come a time when the mind accepts it totally as something that has already occurred. That is the moment when it starts to work towards the physical level and the idea, invention, event or desired article starts to materialize. Now, more than ever, the continued pressure must be kept up and suddenly, everything starts to fall into place.

Sometimes the desired thing takes years to manifest because there is a subconscious block preventing it. When this happens the desire often seems to disappear and one gives up hope and forgets the whole thing. However, life never gives it up, it can lie dormant for years and then spring into being when you least expect it. You only have to look at grass growing through the concrete of deserted landing fields to understand this phenomenon. You impress basic life-matter with an idea and it will work its way towards you even after years and years (see Chapter 3), *providing* that first impression was strong enough.

You may think that making pictures in the mind's eye is child's play. It is and children are far better at it than adults. Children have the ability to see clearly, adults see only what they want, or expect, to see. This means that when it comes to imagining something in precise detail, adults find it very hard to do. Imagine an orange right now. Look at what your mind has offered you. Unless you have a naturally good inner sight it will look like a round, orange ball, but very little like the fruit it is meant to be. Try again, but this time before you do, get an orange and look at it closely for a few minutes. Try to imprint on your mind every detail. The dimpled skin, the shades of colours, for the deep orange shade is very slightly paler top and bottom. Look at the base where it was taken

SANKALPA

from the tree, and where it may still have the remains of the stalk, then at the other end where you will find a tiny indent of deeper dimple. Scratch the rind and smell the sharp zest of it, then close your eyes and build it in your mind's eye a second time. Different isn't it? That is what you will have to learn to do with every pathworking if they are to be successful. That is the kind of detail you will need to know.

People who have the most difficulty with visualizations are those who have either lost, or have never cultivated, the art of observation. In order to utilize your imagination to the fullest extent, you must fill the mind with data it can draw upon at will to provide your inner world with shape, colour and information. It is no use sitting down to do a pathworking based on a medieval jousting tournament if you have no idea where and how such an event would be held; how the people would dress, what procedures would be followed by the knights and their esquires, or not even the vaguest idea of armour, weapons or heraldry.

To fill the mind on the scale needed for good visualization techniques takes time and effort. Pictures, films, exhibitions, museums, theatre, old photographs, maps, posters and travel brochures and, above all, the right kind of reading. The right kind will not always be on things magical. Just about everything will offer rich pickings for the mind that needs to fill its data banks. Look along the bookshelves of a practising magician and you will find, besides the occult section, a motley line of travel, historical novels, books on art and antiques, music, poetry, and costumes/weapons through the ages; all these will be cheek by jowl with others on archaeology, architecture, anatomy, gardening, herbals, and the odd one on dress- and mask-making.

In the fiction line any author with a particularly descriptive style will provide a mental file on which the mind can draw time and again without exhausting its repertoire. Writers like Anne Macaffrey, Ursula Le Guin, Susan Cooper, T. S. Eliot, C. S. Lewis, Maureen Peters, Marion Zimmer Bradley, Katherine Kurtz, André Norton, Arthur Machen, C. S. Forrester, Robert L. Stevenson, Olaf Stapleton, Algernon Blackwood and Rider Haggard may seem unlikely bedfellows but all have a style of writing that causes images to rise in the mind without effort. They are not the only ones, there are many, many more. The myths and legends of the ancient world will also provide a good source for this kind of work, and on this kind of foundation you can build continuously with no limit placed on the range of your imagination.

Let us recap on our question of 'What is a pathworking?' We know it is of ancient origin, that it is a journey taken within the mind and that to use it well we must fill the mind with images, but we can expand on this. It is also a journey that moves between two specific points in the form of Doorways, Gates, or Symbols such as the I Ching, or the Major Arcana of the Tarot. Once given an entry the imagination does the rest, it will act as transportation and building material for landscapes, events, experiences, and even companionship along the way. Pathworking, in fact, is the main key to the inner universe that every human being carries within them.

To get the best possible results from such inner journeys obviously requires training but even a beginner can benefit a great deal from them, providing common sense is used and the rules laid down by one's teacher are obeyed. But what results can we expect from these inner journeys? They can be used to increase one's knowledge of the inner self, the prime requisite of any occult scholar. Or, to learn of certain aspects of the Mysteries long forgotten. They can be used to heighten psychic abilities and change levels of consciousness, to trace symbols to their source and discover their primal meaning. To contact whatever aspect of the Godhead you worship, to promote health, scan the body for disease or simply to relax and take pleasure in beautiful surroundings which are as real on their level as the Tower of London is on ours. Under certain very stringent conditions they can be used to gain admission to what is known as the Akashic Records.

A word of warning here. This last has become one of the most glamorized and abused reasons for pathworking. Let me state here and now that a very high degree of training in the Mysteries, plus a very deep understanding of the responsibilities involved, is needed to be allowed to approach the Hall of Records, to say nothing of exceptional ability as a Mediator. Permission has to be sought and obtained before entry is granted, and that permission is most often refused. Despite this, I know of a case where someone with all of six months training, most of which was in vain, set himself up as some kind of filing clerk of Akashic Records to the world at large. Untold damage was done to several families and a lot of heartbreak was endured because of this. Such a one is far along the road of self-deception and would do well to retrace his steps before it is too late. There are circumstances when entry to the Records is permitted, but only to one section and for a short time. There are certain types of people whose specific work it is to read these Records at certain times, but they are chosen by the Inner Levels and take their orders from Them alone.

What a pathworking is *not* is almost as important as what it *is*. It is not a day-dream, though this passive hypnogogic state is a close relative to it. A day-dream is used mainly to gratify a fanciful desire, or to create a state of affairs that is unlikely to be fulfilled in real life. In this way day-dreams are important to our well-being for they enable us to be contented in situations and environments that are not always as good as we could wish. Thus they act as a safety valve for pent-up emotions.

Sometimes a day-dream goes beyond its normal boundary and becomes a pathworking because of the overwhelming desire that underlies it. When emotional need overrides all else, it demands – and gets – fulfilment. This can be disconcerting to the dreamer, who is usually unaware that, by sheer fluke, they have hit on the fuel that a genuine pathworking needs to push it from the inner level to the physical one. That fuel is one of the basic drives of mankind: emotion. This too is something that is strictly trained in a Mystery school for, without it, no magic can be entirely successful. Imagination plus emotion, combined with a specially designed ritual or pathworking, can quickly cause very real results to appear on this level.

A pathworking is not an astral projection, though it has some similarities. A projection can be either voluntary or involuntary, but with one single exception a pathworking is never involuntary. That exception is the Death Path, which will be discussed in a later chapter. A projection can take place in the physical world or in the world of dreams. In the former there have been many cases where the subject has travelled over actual terrain and brought back information that later proved true. In dreams projections often carry the day's pressures and stresses into the dreamworld and sometimes offer a viable solution.

Active meditation is sometimes confused with pathworking but lacks the carefully worked out scenario that a good working needs. Childhood fantasies are subject to the child's whim of the moment and, therefore, cannot be counted. Only the sexual fantasy, because it nearly always has a carefully worked out central theme, comes close to being a real pathworking, and because it is fuelled by highly volatile sexual emotions, it can become a very powerful experience, sometimes too powerful and there follow repercussions that are difficult to control. In rare cases it can result in an encounter with an incubus.

Lucid dreaming has been the subject of reports by the media of late due to the work of Dr Celia Green and Christopher Evans.* Lucidity in dreams is far more common than one would think and seems to be even more common in women than men. Waking up inside one's dreams and learning to gain control of them has some similarity to a particularly vivid pathworking, but while the latter has a great deal of power when

* Dr C. Green, *Lucid Dreams*, and C. Evans, *Landscapes of the Night*, Gollancz.

performed by an expert, the dream remains a dream.

When working under a strict training programme a student of the Mysteries will learn over a period of years to experience all forms of astral working, including those we have mentioned. Emphasis is laid on the distinction between them, and students are encouraged to experiment for themselves, for, in this kind of work, there is no substitute for personal know-how.

But is there any danger in such experimental work, or indeed in the practice of pathworking itself? Since there is no kind of work without its attendant pitfalls the answer must be yes, there are indeed certain specific dangers but they are easily avoided with some common sense and a little self-discipline.

The main danger is one of over-indulgence: pathworking can become very addictive. When Fantasy Role Games first came on the scene they became an instant succcess, especially with young people at college and university level. Headmasters and tutors grew increasingly worried as more and more of their students became immersed in the game of Dungeons and Dragons. It got to the point where many young people were completely taken over by their 'characters' in the particular game they were playing. Sometimes actual (and extremely dangerous) locations, such as old mineshafts, sewers, condemned buildings and natural caves were used and costumes worn to heighten the effect on the mind. Because of the amount of time and energy involved in working through a game, grades and exams suffered in consequence, but the worst outcome was the effect on the minds of these young people. They began to exhibit symptoms of withdrawal from the everyday world, they no longer wanted or felt the need of companionship outside their fellow players. Ordinary things like bathing and clean clothes, regular meals and day-to-day interaction with other people became burdens from which they sought to escape. The drug of astral glamour had drawn them over to the thin line between the worlds. In older times they would have been described as 'pixie-led'. Our legends are full of such tales where young people are enticed into fairyland, or under the hill, there to dwell with the elves and fairies. Later, when they finally come to their senses, they find themselves old and forgotten and their surroundings unfamiliar.

Another effect of pathworking on return to full consciousness is to find yourself bemused and disorientated for a few minutes. One can imagine that after a Dungeons and Dragons 'game' lasting, as they can, for several days, the same problems would become magnified many times over. Because these games were shared and became overfilled with intense emotion, they turned from daydreams and 'let's pretend' games into fully fledged pathworkings. They became 'Close Encounters of an Unknown Kind' and highly dangerous.

Unfortunately, in this day and age, when the planet has been mapped and explored almost totally, there is little adventure and excitement left for young people to experience. We stand between times. That of such adventurers as Marco Polo and Livingstone is over, the time of exploring other planets is yet to come, but the urge to discover, explore and experience is still within, making its presence and its pressures felt and bringing a sense of frustration with the world as it is. Is it then any wonder that we turn to the unexplored country that lies within each one of us to satisfy that longing for the unknown: But remember the rules?

1. Be aware of and check constantly for the twin dangers of over-indulgence and self glamour when practising the art of pathworking.
2. Listen to the advice of your tutor or take to heart what is written about the frequency with which the work should be undertaken.
3. Remember whatever happens within a pathworking, *you must come back to face full reality at the end of it*.
4. Don't let yourself become 'glamoured'.

If you obey these simple rules you will become master of the art, and not its slave. Because of its ability to spin seemingly real events out of the astral, pathworking can become addictive to those with little willpower, or an easily inflated ego. One comes across cases where several workings have been undertaken in a single day. This is not only stupid, it is asking for trouble when one realizes that each path can and will cause its own kind of effects on the physical level, and *all at the same time*. The whole purpose and value of this work is its ability to cause changes, not only in the state of mind, but in the everyday world. But to overcome the mind on these levels will speedily bring its own kind of retribution. One working every ten days is quite enough for a beginner, one a week for those who know what they are doing, or who are working either alone or with a group under a competent leader. The word *working* means just what it says. It is not an excuse for ego-boosting, nor does it make you an adept in a few weeks.

Brought to a peak of perfection pathworkings can be utilized in many ways to enhance other aspects of occult work. A ritual in full ceremonial robes with lights, colour, incense and well-trained officers and brethren can be breathtakingly beautiful, as well as breathtakingly powerful! But no physical lodge can compete with the 'Temple not built with hands', the Temple of the Mind that is used in high-level ritual pathworkings. At certain levels ceremonial is largely phased out and its place taken by mental rituals of such high intensity that a non-participating member (there is always a Doorkeeper on hand whose responsibility it is to prevent interruptions and to stand guard over the physical bodies when the minds are elsewhere), can easily tune in to what is taking place.

One advantage in taking pathworking to this high level is the convenience of being able to perform ritual work anywhere, at any time, and with no physical equipment. As training progresses even higher, one learns to work with abstractions, and eventually the temple, robes, ritual implements and all the outward trappings of magic become outworn symbols and are laid aside. Magic then becomes part of the natural way of life as indeed it always has been, but now it is recognized and fully integrated into the physical plane.

As training proceeds and, depending on whether your school professes one tradition only or has a wider viewpoint and encloses many traditions within its scope, you will be taught many variations of style and procedure in pathworking. The difference between active and passive, between the Orphic, sometimes called the Mythic, the Hermetic, the Mystical, the Magical, and those undertaken for relaxation and pleasure. Within all of these you will find further divisions, and points where they tend to overlap. All of them, or as many as may be possible, should be explored, and at least two fully mastered, as part of a true magical training. We will look at each one in greater detail beginning with the difference between the active and the passive types of pathworking.

In the active type a definite path or scenario is followed and followed exactly with no deviations, unless one is an experienced student and has permission from one's tutor to vary the pattern as it is laid down. The reason for this is simple. All such paths are worked out along astral leylines to safeguard those new to the inner levels. By staying close to the path, you are protected from anything untoward. What is there to be protected from, you might ask? First and foremost from yourself. Most of the 'nasties' you come across on these levels come from within and not from without, but they can only cause trouble if you deviate from the pattern laid down. Against the protection that a well-devised pathworking puts down, your inner Furies cannot prevail, but once outside that protection, you are a prey to your own inner fears. When you have gone further along your chosen path of study and have faced those fears and defeated them, then you can leave the well-worn tracks that have been your safeguard and strike out on your own.

Besides the inner dangers there is the fact that other people's nasties are always floating around on these levels and, although they are unlikely to cause permanent damage, they can give you a very bad fright from which it takes a time to recover. As you gain more experience in the occult arts you will be able to deal with such things, but until you gain such proficiency, better safe than sorry, and that means keeping within the patterns laid down for you.

An active pathworking usually follows an Orphic or Mythic pattern using symbols, personalities and creatures from any and all traditions. If you are of sufficient level to build your own workings you may choose to re-enact an entire mythological sequence taking it first from the point of view of an onlooker, and then from that of a participant. Both offer much in the way of knowledge and realization of the underlying truth of that particular myth.

This is a good time to emphasize the importance of the dual approach to the active working. By first watching the myth or working as an onlooker several times, you gain much insight into the reasons behind certain actions of those involved. You will also have the opportunity to build up the landscapes in which the action takes place and to enhance your observation regarding things such as costume, head-dress, vocal tone, weather, scent, etc. - in fact, watch it as if you were there but taking no part in the ensuing drama.

Once you have done this several times the storyline and background of the working will be firmly fixed in your mind and you will have no need to refer back to the story or increase your awareness of certain parts of it; it will be second nature to you. Now you are ready to undertake the same working but this time actively taking part in it, 'being there' in fact. This is much harder and you will find yourself slipping back into the observer mode several times before you find the knack of keeping your astral self actually within the working. *Do not* take the part of one of the mythic characters unless you are close to the completion of your formal training. This comes under the heading of the Assumption of Godforms and needs a fair amount of experience before it is attempted. If I seem unnecessarily cautious please remember that complete beginners will be reading this book besides the 'old hands'!

When following an active working in the Hermetic tradition there is even more need to keep to the path. Within this tradition you will find Geometric workings. These are pure sound, colour, and abstract form. They are very hard to hold on to when working in the active mode and it is easy to lose your grip on the entire working and find yourself back on the physical level with a thumping headache. The Mystical Tradition, for the most part, uses the deeper levels of Christian and Jewish symbolism ranging from the exercises devised by St Ignatius of Loyola, which we will discuss in a later chapter, to traditions associated with the early Celtic Church, the Arthurian cycle, especially where it concerns the Holy Grail, and to a certain extent, the alchemical symbolism, particularly that of *The Chymical Marriage of Christian Rosencreutz*, and finally the Midrash of the Jewish Tradition.

Magical pathworkings are those that are used mainly in place of ritual or for special reasons, such as the obtaining of certain facts hidden with the memory of the World Soul or the almost impossible task of researching Akashic Records. It is a sad reflection on this modern age that few people will undertake the long, hard and dedicated training that bestows the right to such levels of work and knowledge, but many will claim that right and boast of it when, in reality, they come nowhere near it. To deceive oneself is foolish, to deceive others requires that the Scales be balanced at some future date.

There is no reason at all why a pathworking may not be used for recreation and pleasure, and magic does have its lighter moments. Lying in bed and building a sundrenched beach complete with sound-effects of seagulls and waves is child's play for any competent magician. Equally so is lying in the bath and making the warm water into a swim in the Mediterranean. In fact, if you are the kind of person who mimes to operatic arias in the privacy of your tub, or cannot resist 'conducting' the London Philharmonic when no one is around (even to taking a bow at the end of the symphony), if you get uncontrollable longings to do a Gene Kelly down the High Street in the pouring rain, you are probably a born pathworker. A few weeks after Torvill and Dean won the Olympic Ice Dance Championship with their Bolero routine the manager of a suburban ice-rink put Ravel's seductive piece on the loudspeaker one afternoon. Within seconds everyone had paired off and started giving impressions of the famous duo. As the music came to its emotional end the entire rink-full of people flung themselves flat on the ice in that last dramatic pose. That shows the power that a pathworking can have when there is emotion and imagination behind it.

In the country of the mind the sun is just as hot, the water just as inviting, the landscapes as exotic, life as adventurous as you will find in everyday life. The difference is that *you* can be more than you are anywhere else. What does it matter if you are near retirement age and have two left feet? In a pathworking you can dance like Nureyev, skate like Dorothy Hamill and look like a pin-up!

Passive workings can be used in all the foregoing categories. It is only the actual technique that is different. Whereas the active working uses a well-defined 'plot', the passive working allows the images to rise from the deeper levels of the subconscious mind. A similar start or Doorway is used as a means of entry into the astral world but, thereafter, you take what comes and follow it to a climax, then you reassert your own will and make your way back to the point of entry.

Obviously you need some form of lifeline to save you going round in circles and this is usually in the form of a guide, animal or human, or sometimes a combination of both. In fact, five times out of ten the guide is a centaur! The Door or Entry must be built with great care and have some outstanding feature that will make it easy to distinguish again. Never allow the guide to come through that entry point and into your own level; keep all that belongs to the inner world on the other side of that Door. This applies to all kinds of pathworkings, active, passive, magical or for pleasure. Always keep the worlds separate. *You* can come and go; *they* must keep to their own plane.

Once you pass through the Door or Gate and your guide has made contact, you might find it useful to visualize some sort of mist that shrouds the landscape for a few minutes. This will give your subconscious time to come up with something. Remember this type of working acts rather like a dream, so the subconscious mind will take the opportunity to show you symbols, images or events that it thinks are important for you to know. As in dreams they may not be in the right order and could be jumbled up, but there is a message from your inner self in there somewhere, it is up to you to record the results of the working and fit the puzzle together later on.

You may impose your own landscape on a passive working and then allow images to come into that landscape or you can use the symbol of the mist and walk into it, and through it, to find whatever your subconscious mind is offering for your consideration.

It is a good idea, until you gain more confidence, to have someone act as a watcher when you enter a passive working. This has two advantages. First you can relay what you are seeing, speaking out loud and having the watcher take it down and, secondly, you have someone who will *gently* wake you at the end of a specified time. There is a marked tendency for people to lose their sense of time when working in the passive mode; with a working laid out as in the active type you go a certain distance and then return using the same route. With the passive you have no time-limit and this can lead to your spending too long on the inner levels.

With experience you will learn to set your internal clock to warn you when it is time to return and, instead of a watcher, you can use a cassette tape to record your journey. Remember, you will not have the same amount of control over the working as with the active type. So you must take more care in your preparation and especially in the recording of the journey and the realizations that come from reading them later on. Record the events on one side of the page and your interpretation of them on the other, and never be tempted to leave it until the morning, for then the finer points will have faded from your mind.

Try to observe all aspects of the landscape, people, animals or events that form part of the working. Look for clues. Scents, flowers and trees will often give you some idea of where you are for remember your subconscious mind will use images and places that it already knows. Look also for landmarks of an unusual nature and try to draw them when you return. Take particular note of anything that is said to you or to another person; symbols on walls, buildings or hung around the neck; books especially when they are open. All these will give you a lot to work with and mull over later on.

Above all, whatever type of working you undertake, remember to curb your initial enthusiasm. Don't be tempted to rush off onto the astral level every day and twice on Sundays. Once a week will be more than enough for quite a long time. Every action has a reaction, and that includes pathworkings: *each one you take will cause an effect on you and your environment for good or ill.* Take a leaf out of the Boys Scouts manual. Be Prepared!

CHAPTER TWO

Everyday Pathworking

The human brain is gradually giving up its secrets; in the last ten years we have learned more about this superb and complex organ than we have in the preceding one hundred and ten, and yet we still do not understand more than a fraction of its powers. The ancient world did not have our medical skills or such things as X-rays it is true, yet they managed to train their priests and priestesses in mental techniques that leave us standing still. Unhappily, only a fraction of that knowledge has come down to us, most went up in smoke when the great libraries of the world were destroyed by those who have always been afraid of the power of truth. Some small part may still be lying in dusty forgotten corners of monasteries that themselves will soon fall into total decay.* Some may be crumbling away in the great Vatican Library, condemned as 'dangerous reading' because they contain wisdom that was old centuries before Peter was born and, perhaps, because they might prove that much of the so-called New Testament was, in fact, already part of the teachings of the ancient world. But to all intents and purposes they are lost to us; we must learn to do the best we can with what has survived.

Napoleon once said 'Imagination rules the world.' Believe it. You will find throughout this book an oft-repeated maxim: 'The creative imagination is a priceless gift given only to humankind.' I make no apologies for saying this over and over again because it is vital that those reading these words fully understand them. Anyone can 'know' something, but to 'understand' it fully requires time and effort. With this gift we can see things that are, as yet, no more than a dream. We can imagine what a finished building will look like and make a detailed drawing of it, we can imagine what we will do on our holiday in six months time. We can create a finished image inside our heads, change it if we are not satisfied and then manifest it on the physical level in

* See Morton Smith, *The Secret Gospel* (Aquarian Press, 1985).

metal, wood, stone, gold, silver, wool, cotton and even flesh, for we can imagine what a much-longed-for child might look like when it is born. Yes, thought is creative and fantasies are thoughts that need only a strong emotional push for them to become as real as the hand that carves or shapes the dream into reality. The story of Pygmalion takes on a very different slant when this is realized, for the myth is telling us the same thing, only in a more fanciful and time-distorted fashion.

We all need our fantasies, though many will deny emphatically that they use them, and regard them more as perversions or delusions. They do not understand the miracle that is occurring within their minds, or the godlike gift they are pushing away. Sometimes fantasies stem from needs within us and the stress involved opens the gateway to an inner world into which we can escape when the need is great. This happens more often than one would think, and to people from all walks of life from the highest to the lowest, and whether they are involved in the occult or not, as the case may be. To deny ourselves the use of this faculty is to cut ourselves off from the creative riches that lie deep within us, something that the ancient Greeks knew about when they named their God of the Underworld Pluto, meaning riches. For them Hades was no flame-filled hell, a place of punishment and torture, but a land of dreams and of the heart's desire, words echoed in the Celtic Land of Tir-Nan-Og.

There is no one who has not at one time or another used a dream fantasy to satisfy an inner need. Those needs are not always what one might term highly spiritual either. Who will deny they have ever dreamed of getting their own back for some slight, real or imagined, or thought up a whole scenario where they win fame and fortune overnight. What girl has not fantasized about a pop or film star becoming her husband and lover? The poet knew about the effect of spring on young (and old) men, when their fancy . . . 'lightly turns to thoughts of love'. The power and urge to dream within the inner self is inherent in mankind. It has always been and always will be a gate that opens a way of escape for stressed and troubled minds as well as those for whom the beliefs of childhood have never faded.

The teachers of the ancient world knew this and used the inborn ability to train the will and the mind to a finely honed peak of perfection. We can do the same by following their lead and learning to build deliberate logical sequential dreams instead of simply allowing them to manifest as they will. In this day and age, with so many people living on the earth, there is more loneliness, depression, boredom and hopelessness than ever before. Is it then so improbable that many of them will turn

to their inner world for some kind of fulfilment? Before we can begin
to understand how we may use pathworkings as a means of actual,
spiritual and mental growth, we must first learn to understand their
role as emotional safety valves.

There are some people to whom reaching the top of whatever profession
or whatever line of work they have chosen is a challenge they cannot
resist. It is not always the money angle that drives them but a need for
perfection in themselves. Many a successful businessman owes his success,
albeit unknowingly, to his ability to pathwork. He would probably call
it 'thinking things out', or 'looking at all the angles' . . . Whatever name
he puts to it, it will more often than not involve him putting his feet
up on the desk, his head back on the chair, and closing his eyes . . .
and woe betide the secretary who disturbs him during that time. What
is going on behind his closed eyes? He is reviewing different situations
one by one, each in its own section with the consequences neatly mapped
out. He will go over each one, acting it out with full panoramic
technicolour and all-round sound-effects. He will note the reaction of
his opponents to what 'he' is doing and saying, and then, having squeezed
all he can out of that situation, he will try another one to get a different
set of reactions, and so on until he finds one that is right. That is the
scenario that he will choose to bring into the physical world.

All this is done at a speed that, in real life, would make everything
a blur of sound and colour, but this is the normal speed at which the
brain works when put on to automatic. That man has little or no idea
what he is doing. If you told him he was using a technique thousands
of years old to accomplish his plans, he would laugh in your face. Two
of the oldest games in the world owe a great deal to the ability to 'see'
future situations in your head and make your move accordingly: both
chess, and *wei-chi* rely on the use of detailed visual planning inside one's
head in order to forestall the opponent. Good generals and tactical experts
have the same ability. In fact, there is any amount of professions for
which inner visuality is of vital importance. Architects, interior designers,
dress designers, landscape gardeners, cartographers, animators (very
important here, how else does the artist know just what a lovesick Donald
Duck looks like?), film directors and film editors, to which one could
add floral and textile designers, window-dressers, stage-designers and
many more. All of these must be able to see clearly with the inner eye
just what they want the end product to look like before they make a
start. To do that they have to time-travel into the future and look at the
finished product, then come back and put it together. Pathworking can
accomplish this with little or no effort. But, as I have said, few would

call it that, or even admit to doing it on that level.

But there are some areas where the modern world is making full use of the ancient ways. Apart from the spin-offs from Dungeons and Dragons, the role-playing games in the form of a storyline which is worked out via your choosing one of several options and abiding by the results, there are other more realistic uses. Have you ever watched a golfer or a snooker-player go through the motions of a shot several times before actually playing? Ever wondered just what they were doing? They are pathworking – playing the shot in their heads, watching the ball roll towards the hole or the pocket, judging by the force they had, in their imagination, put behind the shot, how far it will go and/or what course it will take. They can then, having already 'seen' it played, adjust if necessary the force needed to play a successful shot.

Some of the more astute sporting coaches have taken this ability ahead of time and made it into a new and very exciting form of training for many different sports. A tennis-player will often come to grief against an opponent time after time because of that opponent's strength of attack in a given area of the game. With this new form of coaching the player is encouraged to lie back and actually play a whole game in the mind, going through it stroke by stroke and hit by hit. Time and again, as the opponent comes in for the kill, the player 'sees' the attack successfully beaten off. Soon it becomes a habit. The feeling of apprehension begins to diminish and the player gains confidence, and when at last a real game is played and the moment, once dreaded, comes into reality the player is prepared. He has beaten it many times inside his head, he can beat it now. This form of pre-playing a game is helping a lot of players who suffer from nerves over an opponent's ability to knock them out in certain areas of the game. Once the losing habit has itself been lost, the player gains confidence in his own ability. It does not mean he will always win against that opponent – chance and free will come into it too; but there is every reason to suppose that he will win more easily and more often in the future. In a 1955 article in *Reader's Digest*, Joseph Phillips tells the story of a chess master Capablanca whose game was so superior it was believed he would not be beaten. But he was; by an obscure player who for three months beforehand *played chess only in his mind*.*

While monitoring the players during their sessions one thing became noticeable. The muscles normally used in a game were still being used during the imaginary game, although very minutely. Players were ending their pathworking match sweating almost as much as if they had played

* Quoted from M. Maltz, *Psycho-Cybernetics*.

a real game. This brought an interesting piece of information to light, the fact that when the mind was engaged in imagining a sequence of physical activity, the muscles normally used in that activity were working as if it were for real. In turn this led to the discovery that has been clinically proven, that the human nervous system cannot tell the difference between an actual experience and an experience *imagined vividly* and in detail.

To demonstrate: think of your favourite dessert. Imagine it as strongly as you can, recall the smell, the flavour, the aftertaste, the colour, everything about it as strongly as you can. If you have done it right your mouth should by now be watering in anticipation of a delicious treat. The fact that there is nothing in front of you does not mean a thing to the mind. As far as it is concerned, you are seeing a banana-split with vanilla ice-cream and hot chocolate sauce or whatever it was you were imagining right there in front of you, so your mind is sending signals to the brain to get ready to eat. This is known as a 'synthetic experience'.

This gives a lot of food for thought – if you will pardon the pun! If you need to diet can you trick your stomach into thinking that you have just eaten and you can barely manage to nibble those three limp lettuce leaves on your place? Yes, you can. If you go about it the right way you can eat your way through a five-course meal in your imagination – a sort of culinary pathworking – and get that full-up feeling. However, having tricked your mind into feeling full, in turn your mind will trick your body into doing what it would normally do with a five-course meal, i.e. plant it firmly on your hips. Everything has a plus and minus!

Healing also has a place in the art of pathworking and there is some evidence to the fact that vivid visualization can help to inhibit the growth of tumours. There are several 'self-help' groups working in the UK at the moment that use guided meditation, pathworkings and visualization to retard the growth of cancer cells. The evidence seems to prove that determination, plus the use of creative imagination, can achieve healing when doctors have given up hope, especially in cases where there has been damage to the spinal cord.

There is no doubt that the mind, in conjunction with its tool the brain, is capable of far more than we can possibly know at this time. But every year brings more evidence and new possibilities of using this fascinating combination of mind and brain in new ways. The ancient teachers intuited much of what we now know for certain. Who are we to say that their knowledge has no foundation because they acquired it through dreams, omens, intuition and inner silence and ours is gained through more 'scientific' means?

The Therapeutoi of the old world knew more than we realize. The embalmers of ancient Egypt were the forerunners of today's pathologists and it is to the detriment of modern medicine that much of their teaching has been lost to us. To the priests of Heliopolis, the Star Chamber of Isis, the Halls of Anubis and Thoth were not just fanciful terms applied to mythological locations; they were places within the living brain where, so the teachers taught, a trained priest or priestess could meet, talk with, and be taught by, the Gods themselves. Listen to the description of the Star Chamber of Isis given by a priest of Isis undergoing the Rite of the Meeting of Mind with Mind:

> The corridor is long and narrow and gleams like the inside of a shell drawn from the depths of the sea. The curtains that guard the entrance are of the softest linens, so fine that they seem like mist on a dawn river. They part before me that I may enter and thus I come into the place and presence of the Great Goddess. The walls are of silver and give off a faint silver light that illuminates this holy place. Beneath my feet is the sandy silt of the sacred Nile, and all about me I hear the heartbeat of Isis. Behold She comes, my Beloved draws near and I shall be made welcome in Her Arms, an Osiris the people shall name me for have I not dwelt in the Star Chamber of the Goddess.

The pituitary was at one time thought to be the master gland of the body, though new discoveries now place more emphasis on the hypothalamus. The pituitary can be described like this: it is about the size of a small nut and hangs suspended by a short stem from the underside of the brain. It is a part of the mid-brain or limbic system and is the gland concerned with sexual development, the growth of hair and of the body in general. It also controls, among many other things, the human appetite for food and drink. It has a pearly iridescence, and *gives off a faint phosphorescent light*. It often contains grains of a sandy substance about which we know little as yet.

This recalls the passage in the old text quoted above in quite startling detail, even to the description of the long narrow corridor (the stem) leading to the Star Chamber itself. In the limbic system we are coming close to the source that has influenced much of the teaching of the ancient world. This small, but vital, part of the brain is the receiving station for all sensory input, both external from the physical world and internal from the solipsistic universe we all carry within.

Man has more than one brain and as he has climbed the evolutionary tree, has overlayed one brain with another. The first, which we share with all animals that have backbones, is the primitive reptilian brain. This governs all our instinctive, automatic responses. We also have the cerebellum which came next, followed by the mid-brain or limbic system, which was enough for mankind for a very long time, then finally came the neo-cortex containing the right and left brains. But the mid-brain, deep within the head, protected and almost cosseted, remains a very important link with our inner self. The more we learn about it the more we learn about our secret selves, following the injunction above the doorway of the great temples of old, *Gnothi Seauton*, Know Thyself.

The mid-brain is the coordinator of the whole thinking process as well as taking care of the growth and well-being of the physical vehicle. It works closely with the right and left brains and monitors everything we experience through our senses, the five we know about and the others we have reason to believe we possess but do not always know how to use to their fullest extent. Among these extra senses we may count those we term 'paranormal'. This includes the power generated by a pathworking, and the influence it exerts upon both the inner and outer life.

The limbic system could be seen as the original Sleeping Beauty lying in her protective enclosure waiting for the enlightened higher self to awaken her. If that seems fanciful you should read the alchemical texts and those early medieval documents that tell of the 'fallen' Sophia, the allegorical term for the lost wisdom and innocence of mankind. There have always been such stories that tell of a lovely and innocent maid locked away in a tower from which only a prince pure in heart may rescue her. Someone once remarked that only seven basic literary plots existed and all stories were either derived from one of them or a mixture of several. On the face of it that seems a simple statement but when you come to think more deeply it throws a lot of light on the fact that many of the ancient tales and myths hold the same basic ingredients, and they must have had the same source.

In some people this sleeping princess is only half asleep and wakes up very quickly if the right approach is made. One such approach is through the sense of smell. The olfactory sense is the only one that connects immediately with the mid-brain with no kind of transformer between the particles coming in and the actual organ of scent. Much has been written about the memory stimulation brought about by different smells. It is because of this direct contact with the hidden 'Halls of the Gods' that incense has always been of the greatest importance in magical work. Its use, in conjunction with pathworking, has not been so widely advertised, simply because it enhances the effect of the working by as much as 50 per cent using just an ordinary mixture; if you use one that has been blended to stimulate certain areas you can raise that another 25 per cent at least.

This links in with the fact that the jackal-headed god, Anubis, is also one of the god-forms linked with this area, and the jackal is said to have the most acute sense of smell in the animal kingdom. He was also the Guardian of the Threshold, one of the Psychopompoi or Conductors of the Dead and, therefore, fittingly placed here where the conscious and the unconscious minds touch, and where the mystic find their sleeping princess, the fallen Sophia of ancient times.

The ability to form mental images relies upon being able to recall data from the memory; storing images, details, experiences etc. is the job of another part of the limbic system, the hippocampus. This curious structure looks uncannily like the pages of a book seen end on. It is here that we store all the knowledge we have ever acquired. There is a section for short-term memory and one for long-term memory, and both are needed in the use of pathworking. With a well-adjusted long-term memory, one can cross-index and file an incredible amount of knowledge. Equally, one can recall any part of that knowledge with amazing speed and correlate it with new information coming in, adjust the memory to include the new data in future and file it away until needed. Mathematicians say the human brain can store up to a hundred trillion bits of information; the largest existing computer can manage only a billion!

Though familiarity with the working of the limbic system is not a requirement for being able to pathwork, as I have said elsewhere,* a magician needs to have a certain amount of knowledge about an amazingly large number of subjects; and a little know-how about the working of the brain will not come amiss, especially as it is almost certain that much of our so-called occult powers lie in the mid-brain area.

A leading American psychiatrist once wrote: 'Beneath man's thin veneer of consciousness lies a relatively uncharted realm of mental activity.' Another psychiatrist, Eugene D'Aquili, writing in an article in *Science Digest* (August 1982), talks of experiences that he calls Absolute Unitary Being, brain-flashes that strike in one of two directions. One goes only through the neo-cortex from right to left across the linking corpus callosum. This gives a short-term uplift of feeling, but occasionally the flash gets routed from the right brain down into the limbic system, and this results in something far greater. The emotional force supplied by the mid-brain boosts the flash into an Altered State that can result in a permanent spiritual conversion. D'Aquili feels that this is what happened to William Blake during his visions and perhaps to St Paul

* *The Ritual Magic Workbook* (Aquarian Press, 1986).

on the road to Damascus. The 'fuel' in these cases is the all-important emotional boost, something that is vital in any pathworking undertaken for spiritual or mental training.

All this may seem to have little to do with pathworking on the face of it, but in actual fact this is the *root* of it all. So many people regard these things as extended day-dreams, or as a simple, easy-to-do mental ritual. Nothing could be further from the truth. The deeper meanings behind the pathworking experiences touch the depths and the heights of the human psyche, as we will discover in later chapters. If, therefore, this book is to do its work in a competent manner, it must make certain that not only the surface data are presented and dealt with, but that the physiological aspect is also made clear. Since the whole idea of pathworking became 'popular' too many people have dashed off books on guided meditations without bothering to find out what else they stimulated apart from the emotions, or even how the brain and endocrine system came into it. Preparation is the first step to success. Once you know about the beginning, you can look forward to the middle and anticipate the end. Once and for all remember this, where pathworking is concerned, it is not for nothing that the second half of the word is *work*.

There are several books I would recommend that will explain in far greater detail some of the things mentioned in this chapter. For the workings of the brain, although it is not a medical book, the one that helped me most when I was researching the mid-brain theory was *The Dragons of Eden*, by Carl Sagan (Hodder & Stoughton, 1977). Another was *Breakthroughs*, by C. Panati (Pan, 1980). With regard to healing, *Imagery in Healing*, by J. Achterberg (New Science Library, 1985), distributed by Element Books. *Science Digest* and *Scientific American* are both good magazines that often publish articles on new discoveries in neurobiology and psychology and I have drawn on my own files of their articles for some of the information offered in this chapter. I am by no means scientifically minded but have come to such books and articles firstly through curiosity and then with the firm conviction that the physical basis of the pathworking experience must be included in any deeper study of the subject if it is to be used to its greatest advantage.

CHAPTER THREE

Gently into that Good Night

We have established the fact that a pathworking is an enactment within the mind of a theme which can be extended by a written or spoken narrative and that theme can include amongst its many gateways the art of painting. The earliest examples of this can be seen in the cave paintings of early man. Many of these display a high standard of both skill and observation, talents that are basic to the art of pathworking. At their best they offer a combination of ritual behaviour, magical correspondence and a primitive but working knowledge of the ability of thought to affect circumstances.

A visit to Les Eyzies in the Dordogne will confirm the fact that so-called primitive man had an artistic ability comparable to any impressionist of modern times. Among the most well-known is the so-called 'magician' from Les Trois Frères and the magnificent running boar from Altamira in Spain. This latter is painted in such a way that the animal can be seen standing still and in the act of charging according to how one looks at it. But it was not just single figures of animals and human beings that were depicted but whole scenes that carry the eye from the first sighting of the herd through the actual killing and on to the celebration of the hunt afterwards, with the dividing of the meat and even in some cases a sort of formal dance with men and women separate from each other.

Sometimes it is a single animal pierced by an arrow or a spear, the blood flowing freely and the hunter standing close by. The fresco of mammoths painted during the Magdalenian period must surely be one of the most outstanding examples of cave art anywhere in the world, and the treasures of the caves of Lascaux will show the range of imaginative visualization possessed by Neolithic man. At Castillo a group of crouching bison is shown 'stamped' by overlayed palm-prints, as if the long dead artists were claiming their imaginary kill, while a rock drawing in a cave in Upper Egypt shows a group of female figures linked by lines to strange half-animal-like shapes behind them as if they were in the act of transition from one form to another, shape-shifting in fact.

From the earliest times wherever there has been a suitable flat surface men have drawn, painted and written on it, recording their thoughts, dreams, hopes and wishes. The beautiful copper-skinned ladies captured for ever on a rock at Jabarren in the Tassili Hills of North Africa show that early man had an appreciation for female beauty even then. Most of these paintings are hidden from casual sight within deep caverns that mean, in some cases, over a mile walk to the actual sites. In addition, the way to them is tortuous and frequently not without considerable danger. We cannot but assume that their construction was not just one of pleasure, but had a much deeper significance in their lives, that they were not meant to be seen or used as everyday things but as sacred objects, something hoped for or invoked as a necessity of life. To make their needs more directly known, clearer in the mind, they set them out and in doing so *worked through the desired scene with emotion*, making it the earliest form of pathworking.

The light of day would not have penetrated so far underground and the minute oil lamps would have offered just a mere flicker of light. It is highly possible that they would never have seen their work in its entirety, stretching as some did for many metres. Certainly they could never have known of the staggering size of some of the subterranean halls which their magical artwork has decorated. Some of these chambers must be approached on hands and knees; others require squeezing oneself through tiny fissures in the rock. Only after a lot of difficulty and not a little danger are the best and most magnificent examples of cave art to be seen. All this to satisfy an artist's need to paint? No, only those who painted them, the first shamans, priests of mankind, were meant to see and understand their meaning and their use.

Such is the power of these ancient magical doorways that even today they could be used as pathworkings providing the person doing it was trained to keep the balance between the ancient past and the present. The locked-in power of such things is so primitive that the mind could well be swept into a time vortex from which it would be both difficult and painful to escape.

This type of working in time moved on, from cave walls to those of the temples and tombs of the early Mediterranean cultures, and of course pottery. The great temples were decorated with the legends of the gods for each particular god or goddess had their city, site and temples dedicated to their worship alone and around the walls were their stories so that the ordinary people who had little or no learning could follow the story in picture form. All ideographic languages stem from the same basic idea to lead the eye and the mind from one action to another causing images to rise in the mind as they did so.

The same idea was used in the tombs of the nobles and the rich, only here the idea took on a different meaning. The walls would be covered with scenes of everyday life with the deceased included in them, portrayed behaving and living in the afterlife as they had done during their worldly lifetime. In this way it was hoped to secure the same prosperity they had enjoyed before. But in the actual burial chamber the scenes were altered. Here would be depicted the death, burial and judgment of the dead person before the gods of the Underworld. By painting the scenes they saw the dead as acting them out in the Land of the Dead. The sacred words and emblems of power, the supporting presence of the local god-forms on each side - all were set out stage by stage in precise order, with as much attention to detail as we give to the building of a modern pathworking. In this way the dead were enabled to pass safely through the terrors and dangers that beset them on their way to the Land of the Blessed.

Sometimes, as in early Chaldea and Sumer, the pathworking took on a more sinister aspect for it was acted out in truth and royalty went to the tomb surrounded by everything they would need to reign in the same kind of state in the afterlife: gold, silver, furniture, jewellery and armour; chariots with grooms and horses, servants of every kind from cooks to musicians; hunting dogs and favourite carvings, gaming sets and clothes, sometimes even favoured wives and concubines, all went down into the darkness to serve their masters on the other side of life. All this spectacle helped to concentrate the minds of the ordinary people and enabled the priests to strengthen the magical effects of the death working. Most of the servants and slaves went to their deaths quite happily believing that, in doing so, they would share in the benefits and honour that would be shown to the king or queen in the Land of the Blessed.

Nowhere has the ritual of death been more carefully preserved than in the tombs of the Pharoahs. The artists caught with perfect clarity the rich detail of ordinary life as it was lived thousands of years ago and left it for us to marvel over today. The Pharoahs believed passionately in the afterlife and their beliefs demanded a highly complicated set of actions for the soul to go through before achieving the status of an Osiris.

The Book of the Dead was first discovered painted on the tomb walls of the Pharoahs of the fifth and sixth dynasties at Sakkara. There are, in fact, some five different versions of which the Papyrus of Ani is the best known and the one most offered in print. During the actual burial long prayers and litanies were chanted by the priests on behalf of the dead person, putting words into the mouth as it were, in some cases literally for copies were actually placed in the mummy's mouth. All the required passwords, actions and responses were there painted on the walls of the tomb for the soul to read, and in the outer chambers the scenes from everyday life were set out so that it could remember and re-experience the joys of mortal life.

The Book of the Dead itself can be used as a source of pathworkings for each of the vignettes or little pictures is accompanied by a description of what is happening and a translation of the text. Using these as a base one can write out a short working incorporating the hymn or invocation given. Some of these are very beautiful and full of clear and detailed imagery and, because they are not very long, they can be used without undue strain. The actual papyrus itself can be seen in the British Museum and is well worth visiting.

For those who were not of noble rank and who could not expect a painted tomb and all the pomp of a royal burial, there were other ways of crossing over the bridge between life and death. The god Anubis was the psychopompus of the Egyptian pantheon and the Walker in the Two Worlds. He is synonymous with Hermes or Mercury in the Greek and Roman pantheon and it is the work of the Priests of such gods to accompany the dead on their journey. When summoned to their task they would come in pairs, one to describe the journey and the other to provide companionship and safe conduct as far as possible.

When priests arrived the family would gather round and the journey would begin. One priest, or sometimes a priestess, would lie down beside the dying person and take their hand and, after a few minutes, the other priest would begin to describe the journey that the soul would soon be taking. As he did so the family would watch the event in their minds, going with the one departing as far as their imagination would allow. The dying person would sometimes be conscious, or nearly so - and one should remember that the sense of hearing is the last to fade, even when undergoing a general anaesthetic the last thing of which you are conscious is the voice of the doctor or nurse reassuring you. It is the first thing of which you are conscious on coming round, the voices around you. So it is with death and the one departing would have heard, even subconsciously, the voice of the priest of Anubis describing the Path to Amenti, and felt the comforting pressure of the hand in his.

They would have walked along the familiar paths and seen familiar scenes, perhaps coming to the great river where a barge would be waiting. Its helmsman would be wearing the ceremonial mask of Anubis - only this would not be a mask as in the temple. Anubis would perhaps acknowledge his presence with a nod and the priest would help him aboard and follow him. The barge would move out into a river curiously empty of other craft, for already the soul was moving into the higher realms of existence. Gradually, he would become aware that he was not the only one on board, that there were many others, men, women and children all taking the last journey into the western sun. The priest would be there until the last moment, then would be recalled by his companion back in the little chamber of death. In this way death became a gentle friend, a short journey into a different environment, away from pain and fear. The ancient Egyptians did not fear death in the way the modern world fears it. They accepted it as inevitable, something that would happen, and prepared for it while they still lived. Even the peasants would have access to the priests and their help. The nobles and the royal household would have their personal priests but everyone had the right to go into the adventure of death with the comfort of Anubis and his priests.

Since earliest times there has always been some form of ceremonial departure at the end of life and mostly it has been a preparation of the departing soul for the journey ahead. Whilst still alive, or just after death, the priest or shaman would describe the journey and its attendant dangers, speaking the rhymes and spells that the dead must know in order to pass them safely. All this would have been assimilated during life, watching the ceremony for others, so when their own time came it was a well-remembered story or pathworking that they could, and did, identify with and experience as they gradually eased out of this level and into the higher one.

This was what the Book of the Dead was all about, preparation for death and the journey to Amenti that lay beyond it. In later times other ideas and ways were adopted, some not quite as elaborate maybe but all designed to prepare and comfort. The Last Rites of the Catholic Church serve the same function today, and the devout can leave their bodies with the same warm safe feeling that the man of ancient Egypt felt as he slipped away down the river with the great god-form of Anubis guiding the Death Barge through the currents towards the setting sun.

The many myths and legends surrounding death and the afterlife show that mankind has always feared being unprepared for the transition from life in the physical sense to life on another level. To overcome this fear he has built around death a whole mystique with many themes leading to and from its central idea of another and greater existence. The idea of eternal punishment for the ordinary little sins of life was not accepted by ancient Egyptians. That kind of punishment was kept for the really big crimes like disobeying the gods in some fearful way, but the ordinary people living ordinary lives looked forward to Amenti, or the Elysian Fields. Granted one had to pass certain tests before entering. In the case of the Egyptians it was the Forty-Two Assessors. These judges were lined up, each asking the deceased a question,* and of course there were always two, three, maybe more to which one's answer would be less than desirable, but the priests got round this with the question put by the last assessor: 'Is there one person upon the earth who is glad that you have lived?' Even the most hardened criminal, the sharpest-tongued woman, the loneliest child, has known someone who is glad, and so they would pass into Amenti and peace.

The Rite of Departure has been part of the teachings given to initiates down the ages. 'Ye know not the time and the day of your departure,' they were told. 'Prepare yourself that ye may pass gently and with honour.' In those schools that still hold and teach the sacred ways this rite is still part of the knowledge passed from teacher to pupil. In this age of fast travel and uncertain events such as terrorism, to say nothing of the stress of modern living, it would be foolish to ignore the fact that death may come at any time. But the Rite of Departure allows one to build a pathworking to the location of one's choice and to seal it with a kind of astral time-lock. This means that, should you pass on quickly with little or no warning, it will start automatically and you will find yourself in the pathworking and heading for your destination. If you are given the grace of time to prepare, it can be worked over and over again until, finally, you slip away taking the journey in reality – the true reality. It may happen that you have a particular friend who is willing to act as your 'Priest of Anubis' and who will talk you over as it was done in ancient times. Then you are indeed favoured among men for it is a mark of the highest respect and honour.

Some years ago such an event was enacted within the Servants of the Light group in Germany. The lady in question, 'R', had been ill for some time and she and everyone in the group knew that it would soon be time to leave. My husband had been to Germany on one of his frequent visits as the teacher and head of the group. In talking to 'R' he found her quite ready to leave but a little apprehensive as well. He began to question her gently about her earlier life. 'R' had never married but had always been a person with a lot of love to give out. Gradually Michael drew out the story. She had loved and been loved by a young officer

* See Appendix to *The Shining Paths* (Aquarian Press) for list of questions.

and on the eve of his departure for active duty they had celebrated their engagement with a ball. 'R' remembered every detail of that night, her dress, its material and colour, the way her hair had been arranged, the uniforms, the flowers her fiancé had given her and the ring, the music and the laughter. He had never returned and 'R' had never loved again.

From all this Michael reconstructed the evening in the form of a pathworking which was then recorded on tape. However, instead of the evening ending with the last waltz and the parting, this ended with 'R' and her fiancé dancing out through the french windows into the night-scented garden, and on.

The group was given precise instructions and arrangements were made for the time when 'R' would have to go into hospital for the last time, then Michael left for home having done all that he could. The time was very short and soon 'R' was taken in and placed in the terminal ward. The group rallied round and with the doctor's agreement there was someone with her almost all the time. When they were not there, the tape was placed by her head and played softly time and time again. Each member of the group took turns to be with her and when they were, to talk quietly through the pathworking that had been so lovingly prepared. Her mind filled with her memories, 'R' needed far less in the way of pain-killing drugs, much to the interest and amazement of the hospital staff. While she could talk she was encouraged to do so and often spoke of the days leading up to her engagement ball. Now she was living almost entirely in the past when she was young and pretty, in love and without pain or fear of the unknown. She began to speak of her fiancé as if he were near, or soon to arrive; the Rite of Departure was now quite ready.

We got the phone call in the early morning from the group member who had been the last one to render service. 'R' had seemed very lucid and had talked happily of getting ready, her dress and her hair must be just right, then after a while she seemed to sleep, waking to say, 'Oh, it is so beautiful, the music is so lovely, so lovely . . .' and she slipped quietly away through those french windows of long ago, with the one man she had loved for so long.

The shock of losing a much-loved member of the group was greatly minimized by their involvement with the whole process of 'R''s death. They still grieved but it was not an unhealthy grief that sought to hold back the soul, but allowed it to go with love knowing that it was not gone for ever, but that when the time came they too would take the same kind of journey and that, without doubt, 'R' would be there waiting for them.

The hospital staff were greatly interested in the whole situation and approached the group to organize similar assistance to other terminally ill patients, work that they did in fact take on and did for a considerable time until, as is the nature of groups, it changed. People left and others came in but the seed had been sown and out of all this had come people willing to sit with the dying and talk with them about their youth and especially their 'golden days', days that were special in some way and thus could be used as a departure point.

There are some groups who do a similar kind of work in some of the big hospitals, though for the most part they do not know how ancient is their calling, or how it can be made even more useful and more gentle. For those that do know and do understand, the Rite of Departure can be prepared for others ahead of time, even if those departing know nothing of the inner work of the occult. It is a way that much-loved parents and other relatives and friends can be eased over and sent on their way gently. It will also ease the pain of parting for those left behind for a while.

It is not hard to do but it must be built with care and attention to detail, and it must have a symbolic barrier that will activate when the person goes on alone so that there is no returning through that door. A death-working for yourself will, of course, be quite different to one built for another person, especially if that person has no knowledge of the inner meaning and purpose of such rites. But because of their nature they can be constructed in such a way as to sound like a reminiscence of some happier event in the past when people who have already left this level were still alive in the physical sense. In this way they can be summoned to await the arrival of whoever is preparing to go over. Let us first look at the building of such a pathworking destined for one who has no occult knowledge, but whom you would like to ease over gently and with love.

For an older person, one that you know well, it is easier. You can start to ask questions about their early days, searching for the times when they were happiest. Perhaps a dead husband or wife or mother was alive then, or a brother perhaps lost in the war will be recalled. Try to find a particular time, day or event that seems fresh in the memory. Older people often remember the past with far greater detail than the present. As soon as they say something like, 'I remember one time when we all . . .', then you can start to build the working. Get them to repeat it as often as possible until you know it by heart and can fill in the details, time of year, weather, who else was there, what they were wearing, etc. If there are others you can ask about that event, get a different look at it from their angle. Remember one important thing: the other people in this little scenario do not need to have already passed on, though it is easier if there are one or two who already know, as it were, the lay of the land. But those angelic/devic forces, whose work is concerned with such times, can be invoked to take on the appearance of those still in the physical world so as to make it more welcoming.

When you have enough data, build the working as far as possible just as it happened, with two exceptions. One is the approach; use one the person knows, or knew well, preferably some quiet country lane or road, or maybe, for instance, you could build up a coach full of people they have known and loved, even a few that they perhaps did not altogether get on with. It will all add to the authenticity of the working. Talk to the person just as they are falling asleep or just waking from a nap and go through the working quietly just above hearing level so they will catch it on both the conscious and the subconscious levels.

Go through the event calling their attention to the people and the details you have worked out. Then gradually bring them back. Try and time it so that they just come into consciousness, for people at this stage pass in and out of full consciousness very easily. Then when it becomes evident that the time is getting near, instead of bringing them back, leave them there, and tell them you will see them again soon. When the working is done for the very last time, take them as far as the barrier, which would be something like a gate that you have built into the working, a point at which you can say, 'You go on from here, and I will see you again later on . . .' Once they are past the gate, close it and seal it with either the closing pentagram or a seal of your own devising. Then you can let those waiting on the other side of the gate take over from that point.

If they are occultly aware then of course things are much easier and they can cooperate with you in the building and working of the rite and they will be able to go over in almost full consciousness, which is the right and privilege of all true initiates. This is what I personally have arranged with my own parents who are initiates in their own right. I will try to make it as good a going away party as I can, and I will know that they understand fully the part they must take. We all know it will be for just a short time, for time is a very different concept on the other levels.

When building a Rite of Departure for yourself you do not need to be tied to an event in the past, unless that is your preference. You can build a location that is the sum total of your dreams, with an approach path that is distinctive and has the all-important *gate* dividing this world from the others. You may choose those you will want to be there to welcome you, and perhaps a much-loved pet to add to the happiness.

Work on this location until it is just right.* Then work on the approach
to it, put the two together and add the gate. All you have to do now
is to wait.

When your working is complete and you are satisfied that it is as good
as you can build it, then work it one more time, but now lock the door
behind you and place the key somewhere where you can see it clearly.
Then take the path back to the gate. Close it firmly and mark it with
either the closing pentagram or the sign of infinity which is like a figure
eight set on its side. Now make the rest of the journey back to your
own time and place. The path is now set. If by any chance the change
comes suddenly, the pathworking will snap into action at once without
your doing anything. You will find yourself standing by the gate, it will
open and close behind you, and you will know what it means. It will
be important at this moment not to give in to the temptation to try and
get back. Make the break there and then, it will be easier for you and
those on the other side of the gate.

Follow the familiar path, you know where the key is, and you are bound
to find someone there already, waiting for you. Place yourself in their
hands and rest. Remember you are only a dream away from those you
love. You may have very definite ideas concerning life after the change
of body, in which case build the path and its goal according to your
beliefs. If you want a flight of steps and a large pair of gates, that is
your privilege, you can have them. What matters is that you build
something in which you can believe and place your trust. Without
something to hold on to the time immediately after can be needlessly
traumatic and lonely. Pathworkings have a serious role to play besides
being used for training, teaching or pleasure. They can offer insights
into every part of your life both on the inner levels and the outer. Work
the path until it is second nature to you, but always leaving the gate
wide open. You can amuse yourself by decorating the house, cottage,
or whatever and filling it with the things you love most - from books
and records to the lopsided vase that was your son's or daughter's first
attempt at pottery. This is where you will spend your time immediately
after your passing, where you will sleep a lot and relax and prepare for
the next step, a halfway house where you will go over the life you have
just left, remembering, recalling, reliving the joys, being wise after the
events that caused sadness or heartbreak, and even anger. Here you will
have a chance to meet those you have wronged and who may have
wronged you. It is a time for letting go of petty things. This, in fact,

* See *The Ritual Magic Workbook* (Aquarian Press, 1986), page 237.

is the equivalent of the Forty-Two Assessors, for you will be going over all your actions and judging them yourself. When this is done, there will come a time when you know it is time to move on, to leave this haven and seek new adventures.

Does it seem strange that this is part of both life and death? It should not feel so, for they are the same, just opposite sides of the barrier. Such practices as these have been an important part of mankind's beliefs since the earliest times. The stone age chief lying beside his rough pottery bowl and flint knife took the same journey that we will take when the time comes. 'Death is my Beloved,' sang a poet in ancient Egypt. 'I look for her at each new turn in the road of life./ Her arms are gentle and her lips warm.' As seekers after the eternal truth we should have the same faith in Her.

To initiate and student alike a working knowledge of the inner worlds is of vital importance. It must be mapped as far as possible and that can only be done on a personal level because it is your world and no one else's. The mind is an enchanted loom on which we may weave throughout our earthly lives our hopes and dreams. We may choose which of them we will bring to full life on the physical plane and which we will keep as dreams to be enjoyed with the bitter-sweet knowledge that they should not be fully materialized. Thus a woman may dream of a lover quite different from her gentle dependable husband, knowing all the while that she would never exchange the dream for reality, and a man may happily plan the house he would build if he became a millionaire, but remain content being a nine-to-five office clerk.

Without our dreams we would not, could not survive. They are essential to our happiness and even to our mental well-being. Scientists tell us that without dreams during sleep our mental state would suffer. But unless we dream during the day we cannot build our hopes and plan the future. However, if we are to use those dreams to help us grow in every sense of the word, the mind must be trained to separate the serious pathworking from the day-dream, must be trained to exercise discipline and discrimination in their selection and use, must be trained to use ancient methods for the purposes for which they were designed, that is to bring the mind and spirit of humankind into the realm of the gods, and onwards, higher still to the point of Creation. With a trained mind there are no limits, no barriers, no end of time or space, just a wonderful infinity of 'possibles'. Who in their right mind would want it any other way?

Pathworking is the key to this mastery of the inner world, but as a key it is also a two-edged sword for it is perhaps the most tempting of all occult practices. It offers an escape from dullness and poverty, age and ugliness, loneliness and despair. However, what the trained mind realizes and the untrained mind disregards is that sometimes these things are placed like hurdles before us so that in learning to scale them we learn to overcome things on the physical level by physical means. This is the difference between dreams and pathworkings: like fairy gold, daydreams can melt away with the coming of sunlight, but a well-constructed pathworking can bring about just the change of direction that particular hurdle needs. With such help we can find inside ourselves courage and abilities we never knew we possessed. In his book *The Magic Power of Your Mind* Walter Germain tells the story of Swaboda, a young coloured boy of 15. He was found eating his fill at a free lunch counter in a saloon in Omaha, in the early years of this century. He had 'hopped' a train from New York after his parents had died of tuberculosis. Swaboda himself was a victim of the same disease. He obtained a job at the saloon sweeping out and running errands, then a few months later, much strengthened by regular food, he moved on. Some years later they met again in New York, but now Swaboda was healthy and robust, and cured of TB. He said that he had seen a man sucking a lemon and the mere sight of this soon had him drooling. He reasoned that 'just thinking' could influence both the mind and the body, and from this developed a method by which in time he cured himself of TB and in the process brought his body to peak physical condition. It is quite possible; even cell structure can be renewed through the power of thought. It is this power that is drawn upon by those running self-help cancer groups. We still do not know just *how* it works, but sometimes, just sometimes it does, and the renegade cells begin to shrivel and disappear. If we could learn to control this more precisely, many cancerous growths, and in particular those of psychosomatic origin, would perhaps become things of the past. There are many people now running such groups who are doing all they can to promote this kind of self-healing. There is, after all, nothing to lose and everything to gain.

It would have been techniques such as these that the Therapeutoi of the ancient world used to combat disease in their time. They were well aware of the healing quality of sleep and relaxation and these, combined with dream therapy and visualization, would have made up a large part of their healing methods. Herbal remedies along with manipulative practices are still with us and used, not only by those our critics would term 'cranks', but by people from all walks of life.

A serious and in-depth study of the Mystery religions of the ancient world will soon dispel any idea that these sages and philosophers are to be despised and looked down on. Yet, it seems that even today there are those who find such things as the ability of the mind to heal the body unacceptable, and all forms of 'alternative' thought purely for cranks with an IQ lower than their shoe size. If they were to look deeper, further, they would find that a high proportion of those who actively study and use such ideas are not only healthier both mentally and physically but hold university degrees such as the PhD and MA. My own school, and it is not alone, numbers doctors, professors, psychiatrists, neuro-surgeons, teachers, university lecturers, airline pilots and research fellows, clergymen and publishers among its students. One can hardly call such people cranks!

Mesmer found the same difficulty. Highly praised at first, his methods later fell into disrepute due to the machinations of his critics but, in the years following his death, much of his work was vindicated. Mesmer was helped in his early work by a Jesuit priest with the intriguing name of Father Hell. In fact the Jesuits have figured on more than one occasion in this kind of study. A devotee of Paracelsus, another Jesuit, one Father Kircher, used ground-up magnetic lodestone and gave it to his patients to swallow. He then applied a poultice of iron filings over the affected area, assuming that when a magnet was over the spot it attracted the filings, lodestone and disease all together, thus ridding the patient of his affliction. Much later another Jesuit, a Father Gassner, experimenting with Mesmer's ideas, achieved some spectacular results proving beyond doubt that 'suggestion' was a power to be reckoned with. Jesuits are not noted for their lack of mental abilities – far from it since their founder built the whole training programme of the Society of Jesus around the ability to concentrate thought to induce altered states of consciousness, and we will be taking a closer look at these exercises in a later chapter.

But never forget that within every man and woman is a God-given gift, the power of creative thought. It can be used for good or ill as can any talent, but with the right training and application of self-discipline, it can change your life in any way you want it to change. Those who want to scoff can do so; let them stand and watch as you pass them on your way up!

'Anybody can do anything' was a piece of advice given to me when I was much younger. Is your ambition to skate like Torvill and Dean? Well, you may not achieve their standard, but you can certainly learn to skate with some degree of style and grace. Do you think you are too old to do things? Think again. Men have climbed mountains in their sixties, started new businesses in their seventies, married and raised a family when they were older than that. Remember Grandma Moses.

She didn't start painting until she was over 70, then she became world-famous. Mistinguet was still starring in the *Folies Bergères* at 67 and had the best legs in the show, *and* the youngest lover. She was more fascinating at 60 than she ever was at 25. Edith Piaf had nothing going for her in the way of conventional beauty, but men fell over themselves for her. All these people had one thing in common. They believed in themselves, and they 'thought' power, beauty, charm and success into their lives. Day after day they saw themselves in the mind's eye as successful, always hoping and looking forwards and up, and they made it. Creative thought is the building block of the universe, any universe (did you think there was just the one?) including the one inside your head. When you get something clear in your head it is half-way to materialization. The more detailed the thought, and the more you build it, the closer it gets – it is no harder than knitting a jumper or putting up a shelf.

CHAPTER FOUR

The Light Fantastic

In this chapter we will see how important the creative imagination can be in the life of a child and to the development of the adult hidden within the child, like an oak tree secreted inside the acorn.

It is only within the last decade that teachers and teaching methods have really taken notice of what children *need* to learn as opposed to what adults *want* them to learn. Children of pre-school age are, in one respect, little primitives. They operate on 'self' and what that self needs and wants. It is essential that they learn to coexist with other children and indeed with the adults around them. Of late there has been far too much emphasis laid on reasoning with a child instead of applying a discipline. Children of pre-school age do not reason – unless it is how to get your own way, a subject on which most are experts by the time they are 2. But a child with no discipline in its life is a desperately unhappy child because there is no 'edge' around its actions. A tantrum allowed to go on and on eventually reaches a point where the child becomes terrified of its own temper but does not know how to stop. With a sensible discipline that is adhered to by both parents and not overruled by one or the other, the child has a Ring Pass Not beyond which it knows it cannot go. It feels safe and guarded. Parents lay too much onus and blame on teachers who get the child only when its character is already three-quarters formed, but they are expected to iron out all the bad habits already acquired, usually by copying the parents.

The amount of energy put out by a child is nothing short of phenomenal. If one could figure out a way to tap the output of a whole group of them the National Grid would never need a boost. Such energy can and should, if channelled in the right way, last a lifetime, slowing down a little at full maturity. But on the whole we *expect* to slow down, and hang on to the images presented to us as children that getting older means less energy, less enjoyment of life, less interest in what is going on around you. If you think that, I can only say that at 56 I work a

sixteen-hour day at least six days of the week and often seven. In between
running a school, lecturing and travelling, writing books and coping
with a busy office, I also run a home – and without the help of anyone
else I might add. The same thing can be said of my parents, now in
their eighties and looking every day of at least 65! It is how you think
of yourself and your energy core that holds the key, and this starts in
childhood.

It has been proven that elderly people, especially those living in
residential homes, gradually grow apathetic and rapidly become senile
when they have lost interest in themselves and their surroundings. If
given a stimulus and the opportunity to plan ahead for events and
occupations that really interest them, they perk up and take on a new
lease of life. Children do not need stimulating; their interest is fully locked
in to the process of living and learning and, so long as they are shown
how to use their inner resources to the best advantage, this energy flow
will last for life. Contrary to opinion, old people do not always want
to sit around and doze; the majority would enjoy a weekly trip to a concert
(and *not* necessarily chamber music but light classics and even 'pop')
or lecturers giving talks on everything from butterflies to bee-keeping
in Outer Mongolia. Most have lost the ability to energize themselves
through an interest in the world around them but, if they had learned
to exercise their creative imagination in childhood, they would never
have lost the child they once were. It is a curious thing but when we
are little we hold within the adult we will eventually become and it often
shows itself in fleeting moments of unexpected maturity. When we are
old, if we are lucky and know the secret, the roles are reversed and the
adult can still contact the inner child that he was long ago. The child
can be taught how to contact the older part of itself when young; the
older person can reach inside and retain the youth that was theirs, in
mind and spirit, if not in body. 'Those whom the gods love die young'
goes the quote but, like all Mystery sayings, its real meaning is hidden
in the play on words. Read it again. 'Those whom the gods love die
. . . young in heart, mind and spirit . . .' Those in whose darkened depths
the child is forever hidden will always be old; the child we start out as,
if kept alive through the creative imagination, makes us all the once and
future king of the inner world.

The mind of a young child is at first concerned only with images
and pictures, then gradually it begins to understand the concept of words
and their meanings. By the time it goes to school it has acquired the
basis of abstract thought. Nowadays very young children are given visual
things to do, painting and using aids like the Cusenier rods to learn

about numbers, etc. But not so long ago there was almost a deliberate blocking out of visual thinking. Nowhere is this seen to more advantage than in the kind of books we give our children. When they are young we give them picture books full of lovely coloured images that encourage them to look and store those pictures in their minds. At school there are more books but with less pictures and more diagrams. Finally, come books that are all words; the pictures have gone. If the children have been encouraged to use the inner eye, a book, if well-written, will not need illustrations; the mind will provide its own images. Sadly, few books are written in this way and the inner eye becomes dim and clouded.

When they turn to the television for visual stimulation, do-gooders scream about the amount of time children 'waste' by sitting in front of the screen. 'They should be outside playing sports and building healthy bodies', they cry. Maybe, but what about building healthy minds? Television in moderation never did anyone any harm. As an educational tool it has enormous potential, and as for the violence and sex arguments, there is always the off switch at the side and there is always the word 'No'.

Children thrive on fantasy and contrary to the narrow-minded opinion of some, it does them no harm at all to follow the adventures of Star Trek, or Hill Street Blues for that matter. *Some people interfere in the lives of others mainly because their own lives are so dull!* But left to their own devices children are quite discriminating in their viewing and their reading and can distinguish between the real and unreal very well. Given the opportunity and the right building materials, they can create a full and abundant world within themselves that can enrich their whole lives be they long or short.

All fantasies stem from inner needs that cannot be met in any other way, and such stresses open the gateways to the inner worlds and we escape for a short while to a place where the world cannot hurt or torment us. Small children learn about the inner world very early in life, for they are close to it when they are born. If encouraged to do so by understanding parents they can keep that door ajar for ever. Unfortunately, all too often the sheer pressure of everyday life clouds the entrance and it is lost, sometimes for ever, or until a chance word, meeting, or even a stray memory of childhood uncovers the secret entrance once more.

Fantasy friends, pets and even places are common among children. Usually it is an only child or one that finds it difficult to make friends, but sometimes a happy, well-integrated child born into a large, noisy and loving family will produce a 'phantom friend' and woe betide anyone who does not take it seriously. Many children, due to circumstances, cannot enjoy the sheer bliss that comes of owning a puppy or a kitten, growing up together and experiencing life and all its ups and downs – even learning gently about death, through the pet's shorter life span.

Then they will invent a pet, talking to it, petting it, demanding that a bowl of water or food be put down for it and so on. It is wrong to assume the child is lying, or disturbed; for them the animal is real and they need its presence for a while to ease them through some inner need. Go along with the fantasy and resign yourself to taking a non-existent puppy for a walk and putting down bowls of milk for invisible cats. Talk to the child about the animal, asking what it looks like, what its name is and so on. You are not condoning a falsehood, you are saying to the child, 'I understand, for a while you need this friend. I will be here when you feel you can let it go', and indeed it will go, when the time is right. Sometimes it will surface again, inherited by a younger child in the family. An imaginary friend like this can be a very real comfort when a move is made to a new town. With a new school and the need to establish new friends and contacts, life can be very difficult for a child, especially if the other children make fun of you for your size, shape, accent or appearance. Having been in this position more than once, I can say from experience that the only escape is to an inner place of one's own.

More rare is the imaginary place, and often a child will find a small space where he or she can curl up and slip away into a world of its own making. Trees with wide comfortable forks well off the ground, attics with their wealth of fascinating debris of bygone years, or dilapidated garden sheds are the favoured places, less often the child's own room for, all too often, an adult cannot understand a child's need for privacy and will barge in without knocking, breaking into the 'dreamworld' with a shock-wave that can cause a physical upset to a sensitive child. Yet the same adult insists on the child knocking before entering their own room. If a child shows signs of wanting or needing a private place of its own, allow it. Put a small bolt on the inside of the bedroom door, clear the garden shed out and make it into a hidey hole with an old bolster, some blankets, a box large enough to hold books, a biscuit tin, and a bottle of coke. Real furniture would spoil the fun. It has to be a tiny 'nest' in which the child can curl up and opt out of the real world into the world of the heart and mind. We all need places where we feel we can sit undisturbed and get in touch with the inner self. Those who cannot stand being alone, or who find the soft, warm darkness of the night to be something menacing, people who cannot tolerate silence, these are people with deep problems.

All these things, invisible friends, pets and secret places, are forms of pathworking. The doorway into the inner world has, under pressure, opened wide enough to allow full access and occasionally the denizens of those regions that border the inner landscapes slip over the threshold and onto the physical level. A child has its own protection from anything that might harm it. There is little within the psyche to provide a basis for anything nasty unless there is a genuine psychosis already building up inside, but that is so rare in the very young that it may for all intents and purposes be discarded as a danger. This being so, a fantasy friend will be more of a help than a hindrance. Of course, you will get a few strange looks when the vicar, canvassing for the local charities, is told with suppressed fury that he is sitting on the cat, or your little darling insists on the 'friend' taking up a seat on a crowded bus! A small box with a blanket in a child's bedroom provides the 'pet' with a bed and can help with things like nightmares and a fear of the dark. Where my own children were concerned, although we included both a dog and a cat in the family, I went further and gave to each child a small glass animal and in talking with them showed them how, in dreams, these tiny figures could grow to lifesize and act as guardians, going with them into their dreams at night and guarding them from anything scary. With these under their pillows they slept like tops. Some years later my daughter came to me with her little glass cat and asked if it could be placed in the temple. 'I don't need it anymore but I would like the elemental in it to have a nice place to rest after all it has done for me', she said.

Such imaginary helpers/pets/companions can help a child over many difficult times, of fears, illnesses, or traumas but they will also accept that one day these invisible presences will leave them. A parent can gently encourage in a child the idea that the 'friend' has a home of its own that it will eventually want to return to in the future. This will help the child keep things in perspective. Such companions rarely last beyond puberty and in most cases will have disappeared long before then. Where the companion is another child it can be pointed out that it has to go home at night to its own bed but that it can stay for the odd weekend, just as a school-friend might sleep overnight on special occasions.

This instinctive pathworking by children is something quite natural for them and nothing for parents to worry about providing a few precautions are observed. If the companion starts to encourage the human child into acts that are wrong and anti-social, such as stealing, telling deliberate lies, and causing hurt to others, then something has gone wrong. The first place to look at is an influence within the house itself. If the house is an old one it might be that the child's need for a companion has encouraged a presence already lying dormant within the house area to take the form of a companion for its own ends. Or if the companion has lingered over the age of puberty there can be the risk of a poltergeist. However, such things are extremely rare. If it should happen, a firm hand with the companion is needed. 'Show' it to the door in no uncertain manner and forbid it to re-enter. Once the child knows it is barred from the house it is more than likely its influence will fade.

Sometimes you will come across a child happily talking to itself in a quiet monotonous tone, often swaying slightly to and fro as they do so. In point of fact the child is building up a scenario in its mind and working it out in words and mental images. If you could hear what is going on it could be something along the lines of . . . 'and then there's this big white gate and a path that goes into the wood, there's lots of trees and green things and flowers you can pick without getting shouted at . . . and there's a little house in the wood just big enough for me and the door is painted blue like the curtains in my room. It has tiny windows with criss-crosses all over them and a big shiny door-knocker. There's a little kitchen, and a front room with a big fireplace and the fire keeps me nice and warm but it won't burn me. There's a little bedroom upstairs with a bed like mine and a big rocking chair and this is all mine . . .' The child is here building what it sees as the ideal place to live, preferably without any grown-ups around to spoil it all.

Such a place is very real to a child although it is more than likely the venue will change the day after into a pirate ship in which to sail far away from mothers who make one go to bed at seven o'clock every night. Every child should be allowed such a secret place either in the imagination or in real life. When you live in a tower block or a council estate that is tantamount to a war zone, there is no place to build a tree house, no room to make a hidey hole for yourself, and if you are sharing a bedroom with brothers or sisters your imagination is the only place to go for a bit of peace and quiet. In this way the inner world of the mind provides a safety valve that is desperately needed to let the child keep its sanity. It can be a world rich in possibilities.

When I was a child before the last war the thing I wanted above all else was to travel around the world to see people and places that I knew only from books. But in the thirties only the very rich travelled and even going to a neighbouring island was a dream. I pored over maps and books showing the great cities of the world, dreaming of adventures in far-off places. With mounting excitement I would await the arrival of the summer holidays with its long days of sunshine and freedom to indulge my favourite fantasy. The first task was to acquire several shoe boxes and these would be fitted out with the aid of scraps of material, cardboard, anything useful I could lay my hands on or cadge from parents, grandparents and shopkeepers. With all this I would transform the boxes into first-class state rooms on an imaginary liner. Small dolls about three inches high would be bought from Woolworths with money saved up for weeks. They cost, I remember, three for sixpence and were called Paradise dolls. These dolls were my alter egos and were given names that I thought sounded sufficiently glamorous, like Camilla, Adele, and Penelope.

The biggest and most enjoyable task and one that occupied a good two weeks was the plotting of the cruise itself. Much writing of lists ensued with a great deal of crossing out and adding of new places as the course was changed again and again. Mileage, times of travel between ports of call and estimation of the length of the cruise were all part of the fun. Once the itinerary was established the next phase started, the fitting out of the dolls for the clothes they would need for all these exotic places. As my mother did a lot of dressmaking this presented no problem and each doll was carefully fitted with a whole wardrobe. I even thought out a way to make tiny shoes for them. Each wardrobe was different and no doll was allowed to wear the dresses of another. The next list was an important one, the list of all the presents they would bring back from their journey. Each place would be looked up in the battered set of encyclopaedias and their exports and specialities mulled over until a choice was made.

For the better part of the whole summer holiday I would plan and plot, seeing the dream materialize in front of my eyes. (Nowadays I prefer to travel by air, hating the idea of going in a ship, but that too has its cause, which story is for another time). There remain some places as yet unseen, but they will come. Dreams fed by emotional need become pathworkings, and pathworkings become fact.

This is one of the powers of pathworkings, that they can cause reality to materialize on this plane. Imagination, desire, emotion – these are the raw materials of manifestation. The teachers of the ancient world knew this very well, and because they knew also that such knowledge could be abused, they hid it from ordinary people and taught its use only to those they had trained to follow them as teachers. The exercises with which they honed the mind to total obedience are still a part of the Mystery training. Concentration to a high degree is needed, and of course the ability to see with accurate mental imagery. All of which is natural to the one-pointed, self-centred mind of a child whose whole attention is focused on its own needs at that moment.

The occultist says 'As Above so Below', and we must always be conscious of the fact that there is only a thin veil between what is visible to our physical eyes and what is not visible but which still has a valid reality on its own level. Human beings are not bound, as many think, to time and space as we know it, but belong to and are part of a much vaster universe which harbours things, places and beings that we as yet know nothing about.

Colour is a magical thing to a young child and it is essential to see that the strong primary colours are part of the formative years. Focusing on such things as brightly coloured balloons and balls helps a child to fix coloured shapes in the mind. Stimulation of the senses is the key to helping a child find its way into the inner world. Later on these are enforced by the age-old games of childhood, especially the round games that use song and dancing movements and which have their origin in ancient cult rituals of the sun and moon.

Music too plays its part in the imaginative development of the child. Lullabies and nursery rhymes are not only part of the cultural heritage but full of hidden images that sink deep into the young mind. Rich is the child that has music in its life as part of the everyday events. The selection of toys is all too often nowadays merely a question of buying the most expensive item or the one seen most on the television. It is a transient thing, played with for a few days, then left while a bored child looks for something else. Why? Because the toy is *too lifelike, too accurate*. It leaves nothing to the child's imagination, unlike the old-fashioned toys made of wood. An engine of rough blocklike appearance or a trolley full of odd-shaped blocks can be everything and anything a child desires.

Movement toys, such as swings and rocking horses, can provide endless adventures played on the inner screen of the mind's eye. Swinging is a return to the pre-birth state and gives a sense of security, while the upward swing provides a momentary feeling of weightlessness that seems almost as good as flying. Parents tend to think of bedtime as something rigid and unmoveable, but every once in a while a brilliant starry night with the Milky Way in full view is worth getting a child out of bed to look at and wonder, and wonder is every child's birthright. Forgive me if I go back once again to my own childhood, but apart from the fact that I like to share what was to me a time of pure magic, it is also the best way to illustrate much of what I wish to get across.

One winter in the late thirties my father came into my room and wrapped me up in a blanket. When I protested sleepily he told me that he wanted me to see something special, something that I might never see again. He carried me down on to the esplanade running the length of the wide beach of St Aubin and sat me on the sea wall there. All around us people were looking up into the sky with frightened expressions, some with awe, some with sheer disbelief. The sky was on fire with colour, reds, blues, greens, flashes of white, orange reds and yellows. I was totally amazed, shaken from sleep by something I could never have imagined on my own. My father explained; he always seemed to know what everything was about and had an inexhaustible fund of knowledge, but on this occasion he told me that what we were seeing was the phenomenon called the Northern Lights, and that this was the furthest south they had ever been seen . . . would probably not be seen in Jersey again for hundreds of years. That night has remained with me, a sight to look back on and still wonder about. Since then I have seen them again, much further north, but always that other, earlier experience overrides all others.

Experiencing the elements with the body as well as the mind is another way of storing data for future mental images in a child's mind. Mud may not be the best thing to have all over your floors, but to a child it is pure delight, and if provision is made for the prevention of ruined carpets, its value as an elemental experience is immense. Earth and water together are a captivating toy to a young child, just as bathtime is for the element of water alone, or a game with small waves if you live near the beach. A kite is the most magical of toys in a stiff breeze with the wind tugging it along and you caught on the end of the string, almost as if the kite is flying *you*, instead of the other way around. Bonfires are another excitement, though of course every child must learn quickly that fire must be treated with respect. But in the vigilant company of an adult, roasting chestnuts or baking potatoes and apples around a November bonfire can be a lovely memory to store away.

All such delights as these are part of a child's growing up, part of the memories that will be relived when they are old, precious things that we can give them if we only spare a little time. Time is the most precious thing we can give anyone, for it is a space, a part of our life itself. The ironing will still be there tomorrow, but a good kite-flying wind may not. Leave the washing-up, there are piles of autumn leaves to be waded into and kicked into the air, conkers to collect, acorns to plant. Such gifts of time and attention will give any child wealth beyond its adult dreams, and they will show the way through the gate of dreams and beyond space and time.

Comics and strip cartoons in the newspapers are also part of the inner life of children; the characters become real in their minds. Childish?

Not really when you think of the number of adults who regard characters in their favourite 'soap opera' as real human beings, even to the extent of sending them baby clothes or wedding presents. One man even phoned up the BBC and offered to pay for the wedding of one of these fictional characters, so convinced was he that they were real. Yet these are rational people in all other respects. Some comic characters go on for years – witness Mickey Mouse, Superman, Wonder Woman, the Fantastic Four, Flash Gordon, Buck Rogers. All such creations can, and do, provide ways in which both children and adults can escape, if only for a moment, from the pressures modern life places upon them.

For the child who is sick, or in hospital for a long time, perhaps having to lie very still after a serious operation, the pathworking can provide a way of enjoying activity without moving. A fairy-tale takes on twice the excitement if the child imagines itself in a part, and if he/she is allowed to extend the plot or change it as they will their character to do. Does Sleeping Beauty always have to marry the Prince? No, she can thank him politely and marry the young herdsman instead. And Jim Hawkins can go off with Long John Silver and become a pirate himself. Allow the child to bend the story to his or her own idea of how it should end.

A long enforced stillness can try the patience of a child even if it knows that movement will result in more injury, but the country of the mind provides freedom not available in real life. Water is just as wet, and there are gentle hills to roll down, caves to explore, trees to climb. If the pathworking is taken slowly and gently and the child is continually advised to 'feel and see, touch, smell, and taste' the whole adventure will soon become as real as if it were happening on the physical level. This can be even more so if the child has broken a limb, for the action of the mind in imagining movement produces a minute reaction in muscles and tendons, thus exercising the limb even while it is seemingly immobile.

School work too can be incorporated into the inner world. History becomes much more interesting if you take part in it via the time machine of the mind. Numbers make much more sense if you know them as funnily shaped friends in your dreamworld. Two is such a wriggly thing, always making itself into fours, or sixes, and nine is unbearably proud because he is the last number before ten. One can make a marvellous pathworking out of such material. Reading a map takes on a new perspective when you apply the power of the imagination to it. The single most important thing about the whole area of inner vision is that it has no limit.

Many years ago Enid Blyton wrote a series of stories about a brother and sister who met up with a pixie. Through him they discovered that the chair in their mother's study was a Wishing Chair, that each month it grew wings on its four legs and would take them anywhere they wanted to go. Enid Blyton is no longer fashionable; progressive schools say her books 'do not reflect reality'. No, they do not reflect reality, they reflect the inner ways, the dreams and secret wishes of a child who has to deal with reality soon enough. But those adventures of the wishing chair live on in the minds of my generation. What, I wonder, will live on, if anything, in the minds of our grandchildren. Precious little that is rich and strange, though to play fair, writers of the calibre of Susan Cooper, Ursula Le Guin, Margaret Mahy and Alan Garner still carry on the tradition of good writing for the younger generation.

Children love to 'dress up'; it is all part of the learning process, but at a deeper level they are making further inroads into the Land of Make Believe. My mother once had a wicker table on which she did much of her sewing. It was quite large but its most important feature to me was the ledge beneath it which had two closed sides, leaving two open. On this table there hung a dark green Spanish shawl with a long fringe that hung down over the ledge. That ledge kept me amused for hours. It was a sedan chair, a carriage, a sledge drawn by three black horses galloping over a snowy landscape (that was when I was being Gerda in The Snow Queen), and a flying carpet. No one ever had more fun than I had with that piece of furniture. My own hair was cut short but pieces of material plaited and fixed to a hair ribbon gave me the long plaits of Rapunzel. It was only when Mother refused to allow me to use the top of the wardrobe as a tower that I stopped playing *that* role. But with children's stories becoming more mundane and less stimulating, a book of pathworking for children is long overdue. Which is, as they say, a cue for a song, or in this case a pathworking to try out on your children.

Do you ever feel as if you would like to go adventuring to some place where no-one would ever find you? Well that can be very dangerous in the real world, but the world inside your head is just as real and has just as many wonderful places to explore as the world outside your head, and it is always safe there. If you would like to try, then wait until you are snuggled down in bed tonight and we will have a special adventure, just the two of us.

Make yourself nice and comfy and close your eyes. Don't screw them up, just close them gently. Now let all the things that I am going to tell you happen inside your head. First of all the bed will give a little hop, and then another, and now it begins to hop towards the window and when you are ready we are going to fly away all cosy and warm in your own bed to a special place.

Yes I know that the bed is too big to get through the window in the real world, but in the world inside your head everything and anything you have ever wanted can happen. So, the window gets bigger and bigger and the glass goes all misty, the bed lifts very gently and with a swoosh . . . it slides through the window and away up and up into the sky. By looking around with the special eyes you use in dreams you can see that you are flying over houses and churches and perhaps you can see your own school down there or a friend's house.

You can do this kind of thing in the daytime as well, just find a nice comfy armchair and curl up in it and close your eyes, or in the summer you can find a nice warm place in the long grass, you will soon find that the inside world can be a wonderful place in which to play.

Imagine that you are now sitting up in your flying bed and looking down over the edge at the lights and shadows below. The bed is going much faster now and heading towards the sea. There are ships down below and you can hear the chug chug of their engines. Right over the English Channel you fly and on over France. Now, because this is a dream land and you can have anything you want, you can make it daytime instead of nightime. So if you look straight ahead you will see the sun coming up over the mountains all pink and orange and gold. The birds wake up and start to fly around looking for breakfast and they are *very* surprised to see a bed flying along beside them.

Now just down below you can see the Mediterranean Sea and lots of little islands with warm beaches; just tell the bed to land and it will start to drop down very slowly until it plops onto a nice quiet, secret little beach that is just waiting for you to swim and paddle in its warm waters. You can get out of bed now and run along the beach to stretch your legs and feel how warm the sun is here in the lovely land of Greece. Explore all around you. Look there is an old olive tree, they always grow into strange shapes like that, all twisted up, with branches that hang right down, just right for climbing! How about a swim, just take off your pyjamas, or nightie, you won't need it, and run down into the water. Even if you can't swim in the outside world, you will be able to swim here, you can even swim under the water.

If you look out to sea you will just be able to spot some grey heads bobbing up and down, can you see them? They are dolphins, and dolphins love to play with people. Look they are coming closer. Reach out a hand and stroke them and they will take that as an invitation to play with them. If you hold on tightly to the fin on the back, they will take you for a ride round the little bay. Hold on, here we go . . .

Did you enjoy that? I did, let's think up a big coloured ball and see if the dolphins will play with us. A nice blue and yellow one. Look how clever they are at balancing it on their noses, but they always bring it back for you to throw. These dolphins will always be here if you want to come back and play another time, but we should be getting back home. So give them a pat and we will swim back to the beach.

Lying on the bed is a big fluffy towel so you can dry yourself and put your nightclothes back on, ready to climb into bed again. As soon as you are tucked up, off goes the bed straight up into the sky. You can see the dolphins below and wave them goodbye, at least for a while. The bed goes right up over the clouds and you are soon rushing over big mountains that have snowy tops and you can see right down into the valleys below them. These are the Alps. But now it is growing dark again and you snuggle down into the bedclothes as the bed flies over the Channel again and heads for home.

How you can see places that are familiar to you, and the streets and places of your own town. The bed drops lower and you can see your house just ahead, the window grows bigger and bigger and the bed flies right in to your bedroom and settles down in its usual place, just as if nothing had happened. The window is back to its right size and everything is just as it was before you went adventuring.

You can have another trip tomorrow night if you like. Why don't you look at a map of the world and find a place you would like to visit, then read about it in a book so you know what it will look like when you get there. This is because if you want to imagine a place inside your head you have to know what it will look like first. After a while, when you can think up things and places for yourself you need not do that, but for now it is better to have some idea of a place before you visit.

One more thing, keep your flying bed a secret. Secrets are always more magical if they belong to only you. Don't forget to go back and see the dolphins, and always say thank you to the bed for bringing you back safely, and if you really want to make it feel happy, always make it neat and tidy before you leave for school. Beds can get very upset if they are left unmade!

CHAPTER FIVE

The Wearers of the Silver Sandals

The psychopompoi of the ancient Mystery religions were those gods who acted as conductors of the dead, and as messengers to the elder gods. They were accredited with the special powers that allowed them to go where mortals, and even other gods, did not dare to set foot. They were the Walkers between the Worlds, and carried or wore the emblems of their function. All carried a staff or baton that gave them entrance to the Underworld. It was they who appeared when someone of note needed to be escorted either to the Realm of the Gods or the Afterworld of the Dead.

Mercury and Hermes were one and the same – the winged helmet and sandals and the Caduceus Staff are well-known from statues and paintings. Its wings symbolize the element of Air, the staff itself denotes both solar and axial power. The serpents are duality, polarizing opposites of male and female, life and death, sickness and health.

Anubis, son of Osiris and Nephthys, is the messenger in the Egyptian tradition. He, too, carries a staff and in his case it is sometimes the cross-bar of the Scales of Justice with which he weighs the hearts of the dead, or the rudder of the funeral barge which he, as helmsman, guides across the water to the land of Amenti in the west.

Because of their divinity as sons of the elder gods, they carried the *word* of those gods to mankind. In this they were the forerunners of the medieval heralds, an office which survives in England to this day. They had access to all levels of existence and were granted right of entry without question. Reading the legends associated with them will give anyone who plans to take the Path Between the Dimensions seriously a good grounding in how to behave. Remember that from the moment you set foot on the inner levels you are in the position of a herald representing this world of earth and form, and as such you take on a great deal of responsibility. All too frequently students or those who take up the art of pathworking seem to think they are superior in every way to those who have their existence on other planes of being. That is not so. You are there on sufferance in the beginning. From then on you will be watched and if you behave yourself and act with courtesy towards those with whom you will come into contact, then eventually you may well become one of a select and highly valued group of human beings. In ancient times they were called the Wearers of the Silver Sandals because such sandals were their symbol of office.

I have no doubt that having said this, within a month of this book being published there will be enough 'Wearers of the Silver Sandals' asserting their claims to such a title to fill the Albert Hall. However, they will need more than a pair of sandals sprayed silver to establish their claim since it also requires aspects of the old wisdom that few will possess, to say nothing of the signs, seals and symbols that will allow them to pass in and out of areas of the inner levels closed to others.

It takes a lot of specialized training to walk the two worlds. It is *not* merely a matter of being able to write pathworkings, you have to know *why* you are writing them, for what purpose. It is not just a case of writing a pretty story which you can then act out. There has to be an underlying reason for it. We have already established the role of the mid-brain in pathworking, but there is another area of the brain that needs to be mentioned, the *corpus callosum*, the thick bundle of nerve fibres that connects the right and left areas of the neo-cortex. We hear a great deal about using either the left or the right brain, but nothing about using the middle area, which also has a vital role to play.

The Rainbow Bridge does much more than carry messages between its two companions. It acts also as arbiter between them. You might almost call it a herald, a Hermes, a messenger of the gods, for it carries information backwards and forwards linking the logical with the intuitive. Situated in the middle it lies in the area most people think of as the Third Eye. This implies something extra, over and above the vision we get with two eyes, an inner vision that carries much more than a simple message; it carries the authority of that which uses the mind, the God Within.

Most people know that we use the left brain for everything that needs precise working out, and the right brain for the more abstract ideas and feelings we cannot put into words, but one can, with practice, learn to think 'straight down the middle', combining the best of both. It is in pathworking that one learns to use this Rainbow Bridge as a thinking area in its own right, just as Hermes, Mercury and Anubis were god-forms in their own right and not just messengers. Remember that they are also the carriers and protectors of the Saviour Gods. St Christopher, so lately demoted by the Vatican, was not the first to carry a child saviour across water. Hermes carried the young Dionysius, and Anubis carried the young Horus. Remember also that, in both cases, they were the *half brothers* of those they carried. All this makes them much more than divine errand boys. They are Cosmic Archetypes in their own right.

This central area of the brain is under the control of the messenger gods, and it is through them and the powers they can either grant or withhold, that we are able to cross the Rainbow Bridge between the worlds. As pathworkers, or more rarely, as Wearers of the Silver Sandals, we become priests of the messenger gods, heralds between the dimensions carrying information, teaching and comfort from the intuitive spiritual levels to the factual earthly levels. No, pathworking is *not* merely a pastime for day-dreamers – it is a means of communication with the God Within.

If you read the old legends and myths with care and understanding, if you learn to sift them for the minute pieces of information contained within, you will soon learn the first important secret . . . the way to get into these worlds. There is always a Door or a Gate or an entrance of some kind, a *key* that opens the way, just as the true name of Anubis opens the door to the Egyptian level, and the inner knowledge of the Caduceus of Hermes grants entry to the Graeco/Roman levels, so each type of working needs an entry point, and a *key* to open it. Of course, you can get onto the inner levels by simply visualizing any kind of Door, but you must understand that such levels are not the highest that can be attained. You must explore and map out those lower levels first, and then progress through the others at a later date when you have learned all you can on the lower reaches first. Every pathworking you can do can be worked in many ways, using different levels of your 'self' and learning very different things by doing so. Anybody can write a pathworking, literally anybody; writing them so that they can be worked on as many as seven different planes with correspondingly diverse effects is another matter entirely!

Human beings underestimate themselves and their capacity to learn, to experience, to understand, and to know in the fullest sense of the word. The ordinary person in the street thinks of himself as a body plus a brain; if he goes into it a little more deeply it adds up to a body, a mind and a spirit. But we have many, many levels where we exist *as a whole* on each one.

Let's look at this more closely. The physical body uses a physical brain; it has a physically recordable magnetic field. It also has a heat field. It is because of this that we now have instruments that can detect, through their body heat, people buried under snow or rubble. One level up we have the equivalent of a physical body, a lower astral body, we have an emotional overbrain concerned with finer feelings and the vague 'hunches' we sometimes get. The lower astral also has a series of 'fields' which correspond to the magnetic and the heat fields of the physical. In the higher astral we still have a body, though of much finer matter, a personality that can reach right down to the physical level and cause us problems if we allow it too much freedom without any restraints. It also has areas or fields of influence that surround it and through which it works and learns on its own level.

From here we reach up to the mental level where the body becomes so tenuous that it is totally without shape as we would understand it, but now resembles a pattern of energy-charged particles to the same number of atoms in the physical body. These particles are aware of themselves as a wholeness, and of the *mind* as an individual part of themselves to which they owe allegiance. They move in certain well-defined patterns, and so quickly that they create about themselves similar fields of influence to the kind that surround the planets of our solar system.

Higher still we move into the intangible levels of pure spirit, where the particles of the level below are refined still further, but now each particle is fully aware of itself as an individual, and at the same time of itself as part of a united whole. The Spiritual Self is now conscious on all levels, from its own right down to the physical. On extremely rare occasions the physical reciprocates and for the smallest fraction of time there is a total awareness of being between the highest spiritual level and the lowest physical. The resulting lightning flash of absolute Knowledge of Self and the Divinity of that Self is so overwhelming that certain things may happen. If the physical is totally unprepared the earthly body may be consumed by its own inner heat. Or there occurs a spiritual transmutation, the kind of which we read in the Bible: 'And Enoch walked with God and was not.'

It is these multi-layered facets of ourselves that are stimulated when we begin to use pathworking as it was used centuries ago, and this is the main reason why pathworking has been kept from the 'outer courts' for so long. It is rare indeed for those using the art to touch such levels, but when a serious student begins to work on the higher levels this is the kind of thing that must be impressed upon them by their teachers. There is as you can see a world of difference between the simple pathworking and their higher counterparts, but you cannot use one without being touched, be it ever so lightly, by the other.

There are many kinds of Doors, Gates and Keys with which you may open the levels between the worlds. Simple visualization of a Door is the beginner's way. This progresses to using a Door of a special type, aligned with the age, tradition or god-form being used. Symbols on the Door, or specially shaped keys for the locks, or mantras that open the door by sound (similar to the opening of the Doors of Moria by Gandalf in the Lord of the Rings), are typical of elemental keys. These keys are embellished with the signs of the elements and one can see the landscapes behind them that are associated with each quarter. Pillars with a veil or mist between them are another favoured entrance and this is particularly effective when using a cabbalistically inspired pathworking.

Cave mouths can be used for paths of a descendant nature, those pertaining to the Underworld, or the thirty-second path on the Tree of Life. Walls of stone that pivot or slide up or sink down revealing a flight of steps usually mean a going down into the depths of one's inner self. In such cases, tradition says, always carry a light of some kind with you so that you 'go with the light' into the depths. Very often, as in the *Inner Guide Meditation*, a book that should be read by anyone aiming at specialization in pathworking, a guide either human or animal will appear and take you down into the inner parts of yourself. These are more usual when the working is a passive one, however. Certain kinds of workings can be entered through the elements; for instance, one can take a small boat out on to a river or out to sea, then dive from it into the depths and into the inner world. Taking a winding road up a mountain and simply walking off onto and through a bank of clouds when the path comes to an end is another very effective entrance. When I was young I found one of the easiest ways to project astrally was to catch the moment just before sleep and imagine myself entering a lift on the ground floor of a very high building. The lift went right up to the top floor and opened onto a corridor that had no wall, just space at the end. I would walk down the corridor and 'out'.

Fire dreaming is something both children and adults love to do. Gazing into a fire and seeing shapes in the flames and embers can be an unusual and effective way of making an entrance, and stairways hidden in hollow trees can provide the ideal way into an earth-type working. I have been asked many times if a stone circle or a burial mound, barrow or dolmen can be used and my advice is *no*. By all means use a stone circle or whatever that you have made up, but *never* use an image of a real one or, heaven forbid, do a pathworking actually sitting inside one. You simply do not know what that particular place was used for, or what has gone on inside it after it was built, and such things hold power for centuries. You could end up going 'under the hill', not a nice way to make an entrance I assure you; some strange and alien things live under such hills! Having said that, there are hills such as Glastonbury Tor that open up and provide entrance to very special places.

Walking into the inner world is another way and can be effected simply by imagining a path with which you are familiar, a footpath or country lane for instance. You walk along for a while and then allow it to change and move back in time, growing greener and thicker underfoot, houses and telephone poles vanishing until you are in a quiet green world. A five-bar gate will then give access to your working.

Entry through a symbol is commonplace. Choose your symbol to work in with the subject chosen and project it onto the wall in the mind's eye. Allow it to grow to a size where you can step through and place an intention on it to stay open until your return, something people often forget to do. The gaping mouth of an animal or fish can be used if you are within sight of an initiation in your work. This can be highly effective and give somewhat startling results, but such a thing has very ancient precedents: remember Jonah! Equally unusual results can be had by using Hebrew letters as entry points. It can also be done with Greek letters, but the Hebrew are more effective, to say the least. However, you should be familiar with the letters and the number they represent, along with any other information you can get. I would advise a series of meditations on the letters before using them as entry points, just to be on the safe side.

A good entry for children's pathworkings can be through the medium of a carnival park. Set them to climb the steps of a helter-skelter and then slide down and straight into the working. A ferris wheel or a carousel is another very effective doorway. So is a train ride, going into a tunnel and coming out into a different world where rabbits are station-masters, and badgers drive ancient taxis. A maze for children or a labyrinth for adults can comprise a working in itself, leading to a discovery in the centre, the Mad Hatter's Tea-Party for the children and something more heart-stopping for yourself.

A shaman's drum can be a whole new experience when used as a means of entry to the inner levels. I have only recently tried this for myself in the company of some Swedish friends who belong to a shamanistic group in Stockholm. I can say with perfect truth that it is stunningly effective. When the drum beats start it seems to rock your whole body with every beat. Soon it gets too loud for comfort and then progresses to a point where you want to scream and break away from the sound, then just as suddenly you break through a barrier into a silence within the sound itself. From then on the images build up and carry you along as if you were in a fast-flowing river. Colours seemed brighter than any I have seen before, but that I am sure is due to the effect of the drum's vibrations working their way into the mid-brain and causing the images to pulse to the same beat. I have experienced something similar during a lecture given some years ago by Mr Donald Campbell, a fine musician and world-renowned choir-trainer in America. He used a triangle and a board with geometric designs. When the metal was struck the lines changed and altered the symbol. Of course, in reality they did nothing of the sort, but the sound altered something in the mind that, in turn, impinged on the optic nerve and caused an illusion to take place.

The Tarot Trumps are the Doors most often used and one of the best and safest of all. However, it goes without saying that they will inevitably impose something of themselves on the pathworking. The Trumps are, after all, Cosmic Archetypes in their own right. They act like mirrors showing you possible causes of potential events that have their beginnings inside you. You should have a good working knowledge of the Trumps and their inner, as well as their outer, meanings before you use them.

Don't forget that you can also use the Minor Arcana as well. This is not so well known but, believe me, they can make very effective Doors. But again, I must emphasize that you should have a working knowledge of what they stand for before using them. In fact, that goes for any symbol of any kind. If you use it make sure you know what it stands for and how it may affect the working. It is not that, on the level most people do their pathworking, you will come to much harm, but you can end up with migraine, upset stomachs and even things like physical bruises. You must get it into your head that every level can and does affect all the levels to a greater or lesser degree. If you come a cropper on the lower astral where 99 per cent of pathworkings take place, the physical suffers most, but it will also carry on up to the highest level getting weaker as it does so. That intangible workings can have extremely tangible results is a fact of occult life and one to ponder on in your quieter moments.

There are two main ways in which you can use the Major Arcana to the best advantage. You can simply make them a painted curtain that can be pushed aside; this is best where your working is not fully concerned with the Trump but has a loose connection that makes the Trump a good choice for a Doorway. Or you can make the Trump a living thing, fully three-dimensional, and walk into the actual landscape and either continue passively allowing the card's influence to raise images and actions in your mind or, if the working is active and already has a scenario worked out, you can simply walk through and take up the action beyond the immediate picture. You may sometimes encounter figures from the Trump intruding on your working when there is no provision for them to do so. Then you have a choice, to allow the figures to enter and see what they have to contribute or *gently* put them to one side and not allow them to intrude. The choice must be yours, and of course you could make the wrong one . . . but you must learn to listen to the inner voice and follow it or not, as the case may be.

With the Trumps you can work on higher levels with a certain degree of safety, using them deliberately on the higher astral and mental levels. Where the court cards are concerned you must exercise a little more caution. Many people divide the Tarot into the Major and the Minor Arcanas but, to my mind, there are three divisions and not two, for the court cards appear to have a balancing influence that comes between the other two groups. I personally have found that using the court cards as Doorways brought me up against personal inner problems with a less than gentle touch. In fact, I had to stop using them for a while until I had worked through the effects. It is worth noting that they are often used as significators and so would seem to have a very personal effect when used as Doorways. The Minor Arcana must be looked at thoroughly and fully understood in both correct and reverse positions. No matter how well-disciplined your mind, it sometimes happens that a card will materialize the wrong way up. In fact, the Tarot seems to have a mind of its own at certain times and will often affect the working according to its own inner meaning. It also has a disconcerting habit of facing you when you are both entering and leaving a working. It can also follow you like a shadow as you go through the scenario, sometimes copying your movements, which can be unnerving. All this goes to emphasize the fact that there are levels, obstacles and unexpected effects that can be encountered within pathworkings of which the average student knows nothing, simply because he never uses them on anything but the lowest levels. But sooner or later those levels will shift and it is as well to be warned that these things can happen.

If you really want to push your luck, trying throwing a spread of Tarot cards, then building those cards into a pathworking and making your way through them as they come up in the spread. Instead of reading a spread try pathworking it for a change. It can be interesting. I can think of other ways to describe it but that seems the most innocuous. It is not to be recommended for the faint-hearted, only for the foolhardy! The cards can also be used as milestones within a working and in this position they can give a lot of support to both an active and a passive path. We will discuss this at greater length in another chapter.

Another way of effecting entry into the inner world is through the use of runes. Like the Tarot cards they can be used by themselves, or as symbols on curtains or doors. You can go into *their* world and follow the experience or you can impose your working on them simply by using them as a point of entry. *But*, like the Tarot, they will eventually cause an effect somewhere along the line. Runes are extremely ancient, perhaps as ancient as pathworkings themselves. It may be that some of the strange, almost geometric, symbols found on some of the painted cave walls were the forerunners of what today we know as runes. Be that as it may, there is no doubt that if used as entry points in their own right, they can be very powerful, sometimes unpleasantly so. For this reason alone, be sure you fully understand just what the particular rune you are using stands for on all its levels.

Celtic designs are not only decorative but make good starting points for any working along the lines of the British Group Soul. Some of the convoluted interlacings make a good maze pattern to follow and you could do worse than use some of the beautiful imagery shown in the illustrations of James Fitzpatrick, an Irish artist with an amazing ability to bring the legends of the Tuatha De Daanan to life.

We must not neglect what modern science can offer us either. Some of the pictures sent back by Voyager of Saturn, Jupiter and Uranus would make superb Doorways for certain types of pathworkings. You must search out for yourselves anything and everything you can find, get into the habit of doing your own research and not relying upon the work of others.

All myths and legends have a kernel of truth at their centre. Because of this they can be applied to situations in any era. By reading slowly and carefully you can soon learn to see in any legend the basis of something you have experienced in your own life. The ancients were a very practical people, and they envisaged their gods to be like themselves only more powerful. They figured it was quite all right to leave your wife at home and go off with another woman because after all, Zeus did it any number of times. Aphrodite was more often found with Ares than she was with her husband Hephasteus, and if Hermes could steal fifty head of cattle at the age of six months, then it was all right for a man to do the same. A very simplistic view of things; however it means that most of their legends present a very human outlook on life. That, in turn, means that anyone can use them as a base on which to build a pathworking that will help them to look at certain situations in their lives and, hopefully, come up with an answer.

As an example one might look at the very natural grief felt by a woman who has lost a much-loved husband. A pathworking based on the Sorrows of Isis would provide an outlet for her grief, but within its context she might also find the same strength that Isis drew upon when she went into exile determined to find her husband's body and give him the honour due to him. A lack of willpower might well be helped by working through the legend of Orpheus and Eurydice. The story of Eros and Psyche will provide an example of devotion, of determination and endurance, of the unswerving love needed to erase a past misdemeanour. All myth is close to the condition of humanity. It explains it and dissects it, but it also shows how it can be solved and healed. The very human errors, hopes, fears, falls from grace and eventual transmutation shown in the Arthurian cycle make a good example. These are not just legendary figures, they are shown to have very human faults, tempers, and a capacity for the seven deadly sins! Here is a saga of love, betrayal and separation of lovers, adultery, and children (both Arthur and Galahad) conceived by trickery and born out of wedlock. It has all the ingredients for a modern soap opera, but it is hundreds of years old. Things do not change, but they can be endured and if we strive hard enough they can be transmuted into something higher and finer than we have ever hoped for.

By living through such legends and taking on the personae of those characters nearest to our own condition, we can get a bird's-eye view of ourselves and how we are appearing to others at that moment. By following the story through, as it is told, and then as it should have been to obviate the pain and hurt, we may be able to lessen the impact of a similar situation in our own lives. Indeed, it can be done without recourse to the legends, simply by building a pathworking out of a situation and going through it, following it to its implied ending. Then go back and change certain actions or words and see how they work out. Keep doing this until you find a set of circumstances, words and actions that cause the least damage. In this way you can change some situations very much for the better, and what is more, do it without having to hurt others, or at the very least, not hurt them as much as you might have done. This use of pathworking can be used in many ways and for many purposes. It can be used, for example, for going through job interviews before you actually go into them. You should sit down and go through the interview in your mind several times, imagining the type of interviewer you might get, and the kind of questions you might be asked. By giving different answers and observing their effects on the person in front of you, you can change them around to suit yourself. Then you can start again using a quite different type of interviewer. In this way you are gradually rehearsing every situation that may arise and preparing your response to it. When you get to the real interview you will be able to deal with anything that comes up because you have already foreseen and rehearsed it.

Taking up the word 'rehearsal', if you can get permission from a local theatre company, professional or amateur, watch one of their rehearsals. It is a good example of the type of working explained above, where the actors are preparing for the real performance. Theatrical productions border on pathworkings for they stimulate the imagination of the audience and induce a reciprocal emotion between them and the actors up on the stage. In the old music-hall days the very popular 'monologue' acts did the same thing. They could sway their audiences either to laughter or tears, with the recitations of such things as 'Gunga Dhin', 'The Green Eye of the Little Yellow God', and 'The Death of Nelson'. In a sense such artists were the natural successors to the ancient bards and story-tellers of earlier days.

In the Mystery religions the term pathworking was not used; more often it was called spirit travelling, scrying, walking with the gods, or the hidden roads. This last has come down to us in song and myth as the Low Road, the Faerie Road, or sometimes the Second Road. For the ancients such methods were the foundation of their priestly training and every effort was made to make the mind more supple and more expert in the creating of such inner images. Dreams of both the night and daytime variety were used to receive messages from the gods, to obtain answers to questions asked by kings, travellers and dignitaries that came to the temple requiring help in one form or another. They were also used in healing by the priests of Aesculapius and their clients, in Greece, and by the Therapeutoi of Egypt. The famed temple at Epidauros offered small private sleeping cells where patients could spend the night having been given a poppy-based drink to send them into a deep sleep. Their dreams were analysed the next day and the cause of their illness or its treatment was based on the interpretation.

Workings were used to train neophytes in every aspect of temple life and gradually they became so at home in the inner world that it seemed totally real to them. It was here that they were encouraged to meet with their deities, walk and talk with them and seek to know them as deeply as possible. Here they were united with the gods in the exercises we call the Assumption of God Forms. For them it was nothing out of the ordinary and the pressure that accompanied such high-level work was easily dealt with because of the frequency of practice. For us in the modern world such a thing can be hard to cope with and can cause a sudden drop in blood pressure, migraines, palpitations, and a general feeling of malaise. Only when it has become an integral part of one's inner life can it be dealt with easily and without harm. The work must progress slowly so that, little by little, the inner self grows accustomed to the strain and finally is able to cope with it whenever necessary and for considerable lengths of time.

All young children entering the service of the temple were required to keep a record of their dreams and were taught to control them until they were able to dream at will on whatever subject their teacher gave them. Creative dreaming we call it, and it is still taught and practised in some Mystery schools. From then on they were shown how to accomplish the same thing by the use of the creative imagination. First they would have been told stories such as children down the ages have enjoyed. Then they would have tried to recreate the same stories inside their heads, looking as if in a dream and watching the stories unfold before their inner eye. When they grew proficient at this they would move on and weave their own 'stories' and actually take parts in them. They were encouraged to look on this as a genuine visit to the world of the gods.

In time such workings would grow longer and the neophytes would encounter strange forms and terrors as well as the benign gods and be shown how to control their fears and dispel the shapes to which their minds gave birth. In this way they gradually built up over many years an incredible mind-control. One of the many powers that manifested was that of being able to enter into another's working, or even influence it from a considerable distance away.

Even today an adept in the art of pathworking sitting alongside one who is new to the work can influence and strengthen the mental images of the neophyte simply by aligning his more clearly defined images to theirs. However, the newcomer should realize that the marvellous pictures entering his inner vision are being boosted by the strength of the teacher. He must work hard to achieve the same clarity and definition without any external help.

The discovery of oneself on all levels, the exploration of the personal inner world and its subjugation to the will was an important part of these inner journeys for the young temple aspirant. With the help of teachers on both the physical and the higher levels the young men and women were taught to *Know Themselves* in every sense of the word. Their life was hard and every hour was full of some form of teaching even if it was simply decorating the temple with flowers; the underlying discipline of learning to understand *why* it was done, and *why* this flower instead of that one was used and, even more important at that time, to obey their teachers without questioning. There was a time and place for questions, a time when they were actively encouraged, but in the day-to-day work of the temple one obeyed the teachers, and at once, with no hanging about.

Within a few years the youngsters would have been divided into their categories – healers, seers, counsellors, chanters, dancers and scribes, all of whom would be in the priesthood to a greater or lesser degree. Those who showed promise would be gently led into the more difficult disciplines that awaited those destined for the higher grades of the priesthood. There was also the question of which god-form would command their allegiance. We have already discussed the work of the priests of Anubis and, although most would want to follow one of the main gods or goddesses of the city, some would wish to enter the service of a different deity. Most cities in ancient Egypt honoured a triumvirate consisting of a male god, his goddess consort and a third who was either their divine offspring or a god-form connected to them in some way through legend or correspondence of symbols and attributes. Choosing to enter the service of a different god-form might mean travelling to another city to enter the temple there. But the work, the training, and the discipline went on and the varied uses of the mental journeys were extended still further.

One of the most exacting tasks was simply remembering all that was taught. There were extremely long invocations and prayers to memorize. Astrology and its attendant discipline of mathematics, the genealogy of the gods and the Royal Family, the Law both spiritual and temporal and the knowledge of the innner worlds they had already collected – all had to be remembered and passed on, for by now they would be in their late teens and already teaching the young ones coming into the temple for the first time.

Using an inner journey as an aid to memory is a very ancient method. Both the Egyptians and the Greeks used what is known as the *locus.** The word actually means *place*, and the idea is to choose a *locus* in which to store whatever it is you have to remember; a sort of mental filing cabinet. This 'place' can be either an imaginary one or a large local building such as a college, university, museum or public library. You can use different buildings for different categories of memory, for example, the library or college for long-term memory items, and the museum for things like telephone numbers and shopping lists. The whole thing is ridiculously easy, and simply by using it you are linking yourself way

* See J. H. Brennan, *Getting What You Want* (Thorsons, 1985), and F. A. Yeats, *The Art of Memory* (Ark, 1984).

back to the temple priest of the ancient world, but it depends on your ability to visualize and take an inner journey in your mind. It is one of the most practical earth-level uses for pathworkings there are.

Start with something small and simple, your own home or flat and your weekly shopping list. First of all practise walking around the house or flat in your mind's eye. Take note of every shelf, table, ledge, stair or any place where some article can be set down. When you are satisfied that you have the complete pattern fixed in your head you can move to the next step. Write out a fairly comprehensive list of groceries. (It doesn't matter whether or not you actually intend to buy them.) Make it about twenty items long and let it contain a mixture of the ordinary and the uncommon, marmalade and escargot, margarine and curry powder, eggs and some Chinese gooseberries, that sort of thing.

With the list in your hand walk around the house or flat and mentally place each article on a shelf, table, chair, ledge, or stair. A bag of potatoes on the first stair, eggs on the hall table, butter next to the telephone, the escargot on the window seat in the front room – keep going until you have placed every item somewhere in the house. Then go back and do it again seeing each item as clearly as you can in your mind's eye. Now go and sit down, close your eyes and go round again but this time only in your imagination, as if you were doing a pathworking. Stop at each point as before and name the item placed in that position. You will find that you are able to remember a remarkably long list with little or no difficulty. You are associating place and article together; one will call the other to mind. Now go and do something else and forget about the list. After lunch go and sit down and mentally go through the list again; it should be just as easy to remember it exactly. Now leave it until the next morning and try again. I think you will be very surprised at the result.

The same method can be used with anything you wish to remember. It *does* take a little practice to get it exact but then so does anything worthwhile. You may have to go over your list several times. If your *locus* is near, you could try actually going round it and mentally depositing the items or phrases to be remembered in various places. Walk around a few times, and don't worry if the next-door neighbour sees you muttering to yourself by a couple of Assyrian pillars in the museum, or staring with a fixed expression at the head librarian's desk. The British have a reputation of eccentricity and you will be in good company. Besides you will be able to remember things and they won't!

The very same method was used by Roman orators to commit their speeches to memory. Bards used something similar as they struggled to memorize the stupefying amount of material that was a [part] of their training. Egyptian priests used it to remember th[e] complicated invocations and prayers and the complex laws p[ertaining] to the Two Lands. If you make it a part of your training you will become another link in a chain that is centuries long. Teach it to your children at secondary school, and those preparing for exams or university entrance. Like all the best things it is simple and easy to use and, above all, it *works*.

Pathworkings were also used as an integral part of initiatory tests. The build-up of the first part of the ceremony would be made into a mental journey which the candidate would undertake again and again until it became second nature. The latter parts of the tests would, of course, be withheld until the actual moment, thus making it the supreme test. But the movements, invocations and preparatory rituals would have been undertaken in pathworking form so that the timing was perfect and the whole thing memorized down to the last detail. The difference between the known part of the ceremony and that part still veiled in mystery would have added to the feeling of tension building up to the climax of the whole thing.

Later on, when it was all over, the same techniques would have been used to recall the entire proceeding so that nothing, down to the smallest detail, would have been lost. It would all be gone over and interpreted and analysed and, finally, would have sunk deep into the mind at all levels of consciousness to become part of a lifetime of experience, and the basis of what that priest would eventually teach to his own students as they gathered around him in the late afternoon sun to listen and learn.

We can visualize the teacher, now grown to full adepthood, teaching wisdom gathered over a lifetime of experience, and guiding the new generation into the ancient ways by example, by talking and by the use of parables, descriptive stories that conjured up images in the mind, just as that teacher himself had been taught many years before. Such stories were always built to accommodate three levels of understanding.

The first level would be for the youngest listeners, stories that explained the ways of the temple/god-form/religious faith. It was a level of emotion and the youngsters would equate them with the world around them and the everyday things they knew and saw each day of their lives.

The next age-group up would hear the same story, but they would listen with more knowledge of what it was all about. They would be well into their training by now and could comprehend that such stories carried a seed of wisdom hidden in the words. At night before sleeping they would recall the story in the form of a pathworking and search out the pearl secreted in its depths. It was very much a mental level and concerned with teaching the mind to understand the different levels in the story, each level holding a different facet of the single truth.

Finally, sometimes before initiation, and sometimes after it, the same stories would be told, but this time they were seen for what they really were, spiritual revelations of a very high order revealing the inner core of the temple's teaching. Sometimes it was the final underlining of the initiation and set the seal on it, sometimes it pointed the way towards initiation and a sudden insight into the hidden meaning of such a story discussed with the teacher would indicate the readiness of that student for the higher grades of the priesthood.

Jesus of Nazareth was well-versed in such ways of teaching and we can see in the parables he used the three levels of understanding such as had been taught to him during his own training. He made it different by teaching to mixed groups, to children, the uneducated, the merchants and more well-to-do classes and to those who followed Him. He gathered them all around and spoke, knowing that those who had the ears to hear would sift through the words and find the hidden meaning. Later in the day perhaps He and His disciples would talk over what had been said and each would offer the meaning as he or she had interpreted the story.

Let's look at the parable of the Wheatsower, from Matthew 13: 3-9:

And He spake many things unto them in parables, saying, 'Behold a sower went forth to sow; and when he sowed, some seeds fell by the wayside, and the fowls came and devoured them up. Some fell upon stoney places, where they had not much earth; and forthwith they sprung up because they had no deepness of earth. And when the sun was up they were scorched; and because they had no root they withered away. And some fell among thorns, and the thorns sprung up and choked them. But others fell onto good ground, and brought forth fruit, some an hundredfold, some sixtyfold, some thirtyfold. Who hath ears to hear, let him hear.'

The Nazarene was telling the same story to everyone gathered around Him but it was saying very different things to different sections of the crowd. To the children and the uneducated He was talking about things they knew and understood. They nearly all had small fields that they sowed with wheat, and, listening to Jesus, they understood that He was saying, 'Be careful how you sow. Don't throw it just anywhere. Choose the best places, control the swing of your arm so that the seeds fall as far as possible only on the good ground. Be a careful man and your fields will yield twice as much.'

To wiser men and women He was saying, 'Look at your deeds and actions in your life, those things that you do without thinking or in a hurry and without due care. They will come to nothing. Such actions will yield only lost time and extra work, but if you watch what you are doing and place your work and plans where they will do most good, you will benefit from your labours.'

To teachers He said, 'No matter how hard you try there will always be some that you cannot teach. They will not listen, but will look out of the window, or fall asleep in the sun. Some will try to understand and will make some progress but do not expect too much from them. But some will delight your heart and learn well. Such as these will be your harvest of wise men.'

To the disciples He was saying, 'Many wise men have come before the multitudes and spoken words of wisdom, and they have not been heard. Some have not even stopped to listen when they spoke but passed by and the words of wisdom were lost to them. Some stopped for a little while and even listened and tried to understand, but when they saw that they had to give up the things they valued in order to become wise men they too departed. But some listened and listening understood and they followed the wise men and became like them.'

Jesus made it even clearer that He was speaking on different levels for different people. 'Let those who have ears to hear, let them hear.' You could do worse than go through the parables and look for the many levels, writing each one down as you find it. But do not stop at the New Testament. Look too at such vastly different things as Mother Goose Nursery Rhymes and the Vedic scripts, fairy-tales and the Meditations of Marcus Aurelius. For instance if you read carefully the fairy-tale of the Twelve Dancing Princesses, you will find something that can be used as a pathworking for the Thirty-Second Path on the Tree of Life.

'Seek and ye shall find', says the Bible, 'Knock and the door shall be opened', 'Ask and ye shall receive'. These are not just ancient proverbs, they are very wise sayings that pertain to the Mystery teachings. They tell us that sometimes the simplest way is best, go out and try it. If you have read Ursula Le Guin's book, *The Wizard of Earthsea*, re-read the part where Ged tries to get past the Doorkeeper; it holds a salutary lesson.

There are two exercises that will be of benefit when you finish this lesson:

1. The building-up of the image of the Boat of Anubis with the Jackal-Headed God at the helm. Look along the boat and see people that you knew and who have already taken the road to Amenti. Do not get into the boat but look at it closely and take in as much detail as you can. Watch as the new arrivals take their places, smile and wave to them. When Anubis tells you to cast off the rope that holds

the boat to the river bank, lift it off the wooden peg and cast it into the water. Now you will see the boat glide gently down the river towards the setting sun, and onwards to the Halls of Osiris.

2. Build up a scene with a quiet house of biblical times. There is a small fire burning in the hearth and the smell of woodsmoke is thick and pungent. There are some eight to ten people with you. Suddenly one of the men sitting near the back of the room starts to speak. His voice is low and gentle and he speaks about a householder who built a vineyard and let it out to tenants.* Follow the story intently and see what inner meaning it has for you. Then return to your own time and place.

* Matthew 22: 33-42.

CHAPTER SIX

The Bards

In a book dealing with the power of the creative imagination there must always be a place of honour for the ancient bards, harpists, skalds and troubadours of the past. It is to them we owe much of our knowledge of the ways, manners and rituals of the ancient world, as well as the feats of their heroes and great rulers. Their songs and poetry have been handed down, often mixed and incomplete, but always conveying with vivid insight the time and the people of which they sang.

Theirs was a long, hard training involving prodigious feats of memory and it was by no means unknown for a young boy to spend twenty years or even more learning, memorizing and following his teacher around the countryside before being recognized as a bard in his own right. There were many levels to which a bard could aspire. A court bard was attached to the demesne of a local chief or prince. He was held in high honour and given his own quarters, servants, horses, etc. He took on pupils, who would come from miles away to learn from the best of such men. Such masters of the art were the professionals of their kind and not to be confused with the wandering minstrels who acted as news carriers as well as entertainers, singing and playing and telling tales of high deeds for their board and keep for a few days. But even though they were not of the same calibre as the master bards, yet their coming was eagerly awaited and they were made welcome, given the best food and wine available and questioned for their news and gossip down to the last detail by folk hungry for news from the outside world.

There were differences in both style and delivery between the Welsh bards and those of Ireland but both had an entire body of poems, sagas and tales, many of which could take an entire evening to render. All these would have to be committed to memory, and woe betide the bard whose memory played him false. It was a disgrace from which it was not always possible to recover.

A famous bard was worth his weight in gold to a prince and brought both honour and, it was believed, good fortune to the family, and there were many bards who were not above playing one patron off against another in order to secure the best position possible. In Ireland a master poet was expected to evolve his own original style of poetry and poems. Any important event was always 'put down' at once in the form of a poem and chanted to the music of the harp. If it went well it was added to the repertoire and passed down to those who came to learn.

But the wandering bards or minstrels were not to be despised for, if anyone kept alive the old ways, songs, practices and beliefs, it was these men. Some of their mythic retellings were of an age that links them with the Stone Age of Britain. Robert Graves in his book *The White Goddess* quotes a Triad from the Red Book of Hergest:

> Three things that enrich the poet:
> Myths, poetic power, a store of *ancient verse.*

The italics are mine. On such frail links rests our knowledge of the ancient world; the wonder is that they have survived even in such a fragmentary form. The burden is now upon us to preserve them further.

When Christianity reached Wales and some of the bards, though by no means all, converted, their poems and songs were put under a new restraint. The ecclesiastical laws required them to record only what was defined (by the Church) as truth. They had to keep to the letter, and any intrusion of the 'creative imagination', or 'poetic licence' was not allowed. Gradually their greatness declined, the vividness of their art form, so long the lifeblood of the people, congealed and came to a halt, and left only the ancient lays as a mark of what had been. The poems produced in this era show a stultification of the natural talent of the Welsh as it ground to a halt under the hand of the Church.

But though the court bards bowed to the bishops, the wandering minstrels did no such thing. They for the most part went blithely on their way as they had always done. They preserved the old sagas and romances and handed them on as best they could.

The bards were not the only makers of inward dreams. The troubadour, the minnesingers, the skalds of the northern countries, all held the same power of enchantment over their listeners. All could mesmerize a crowded hall with their voice and personal charisma. Imagine a smoke-filled wooden hall filled with men, women and children, dogs asleep by the fire and very probably hens and pigeons roosting in the rafters. Everyone is full-fed, perhaps slightly drunk with an unaccustomed amount of ale. The master of the hall calls for silence and asks the bard to begin. All lean forward not to miss one word of a tale they probably know by heart, but which will be rendered new by the different style of a new 'teller of tales'. For them the dim smoky light of the hall would give way to a battlefield where mighty heroes refought ancient battles out of time, or they might see an enchanted castle surrounded by a magical forest littered with the bodies of knights who had tried to find their way through to the treasure lying in wait for the victor. Perhaps it was a tale of gods and men and the beautiful women coveted by both. Whatever the tale, it would have enraptured them for a while and they could forget the harsh winter, the lack of fuel and food and their hungry bellies as the wandering bard wove his magical web of words and music about them.

It is the same today. Someone with a knowledge of how to weave words and match them to human emotions can weave a story, a pathworking or a book and use it to call the heart of the listener to do their bidding, to laugh or to cry, to suffer or to triumph, to love or to despair. Such is the power of the bard for it flows still in the mixed blood of the British and will continue to flow until time's end. We find the names changing from era to era, from bard to skald, to minstrel, and on to troubadour and gleeman. The Irish Seanachai still exists in Ireland though now diminished to just a few souls but, so long as there is one to whom the tales of olden times are more than just folklore - the word spoken with disdain - then will the ancient bardic tradition still live, albeit by a thread.

In Ireland the master poet, or *ollave*, was given higher honour than even his Welsh counterpart. His place in the hierarchy was second only to that of the Queen. His mark of office was a many-coloured cloak that immediately set him apart from all others. He would have seemed like a living rainbow of colour, sound and movement to those who were conditioned by birth, race and heritage to look upon the poets as something more than human, men who walked with the gods and spoke with heroes. Most if not all of them laid claim to some mastery of the magical arts, for sound and colour have always been an integral part of magic. How else, the common men reasoned, could he have conjured up the castles and fairy raths and peopled them out of thin air with the Hosts of the Sidhe and the mighty figures of Midir, Angus Oge, Cuchulain, Diannecht, Bodh and the dreaded Morrigan. That it was all raised in and coloured by their own imagination roused by the word-art of the bard was beyond their understanding.

The usefulness of a court bard or ollave went beyond the telling of tales. They were also the repository of historical events and the geneaology of the great families of the time. Thus, in a single man one had a library, a magician, a story-teller and a historian-cum-record-keeper. It is no

wonder they were held in such awe; and the source of their mental power
was that of the creative imagination, the same power that can enable
a man or woman of our time to achieve almost anything upon which
they have set their hearts.

At the seasonal fairs many itinerant minstrels would be found willing
to sing or tell stories, carry a letter (and write it for an extra fee) or simply
to spread the news he had gathered in his travels since the last time the
fair was held. One such fair was immortalized in a poem that one can
still read in the Book of Ballymote. It is called The Fair of Carman
and just reading it to oneself can recall something of what it must have
been like in its heyday. It is described as:

> Carman, the field of a splendid fair,
> with a widespread unobstructed green.
> The hosts who came to celebrate it,
> On it they contested their noble races.

At the Fair of Carman could be found:

> Steeds, swords, beautiful chariots,
> Spears, shields, human faces.
> Dew, fruits, blossoms and foliage,
> Day and night, a heavy flooded shore.

Certain things are forbidden:

> To sue, levy, to contravert debts,
> The abuse of steeds in their career,
> is not allowed to contending racers,
> Elopements, arrests, distraints.

A very law-abiding lot indeed. There was even some segregation of the
sexes for we read:

> That no man goes into the women's Airecht,
> That no women go into the Airecht of clean fair men.

On top of all this we are told we can be regaled with:

Proverbs, Maxims, Royal precepts,
And the truthful instructions of Fithal.
Occult poetry, topographical etymologies,
The precepts of Cabiri and of Carman.

Could any Fair offer more than this?

Even those who would become warriors, part of the Fian, the army
of the High King of Ireland, were required to know by heart the twelve
books of poetry. Can we wonder that in the heart of the Celt the art
of the poem and the creative imagination that gives it birth have been
held in such high esteem down the ages. Amergin, Taliesin, Aneurin
and many others, their names stand for ever as men who knew the power
of the inner world and its messenger, the mercurial 'word'.

In later times the Courts of Love and the troubadours, and the
minnesingers, would take on the mantle of the bards and enrich it with
the language of Romance and Languedoc but always, behind the words,
lie the hidden countries of the inner worlds to which their poet's mind
gave them the key. Their wanderings, too, made them the ideal gatherers
of information and they became the eyes and ears of Europe. And if
that information was coloured by their love of words and music, surely
they can be forgiven a little poetic licence for it made that information
live in the minds of those who received it.

The passing of information in the teaching sense via the use of the
imagination was surely in the mind of T. H. White when he wrote *The
Once and Future King*. In this story of the youthful King Arthur
(nicknamed The Wart), Merlin arrives on the scene determined that
the future king shall have as wide a knowledge as possible of the art
of being self-sufficient. In order to accomplish this task he turns him
into a succession of animals, birds and fishes, each shape-shift teaching
the youngster a valuable lesson. The book does have its darker moments
and is not altogether suitable for younger children. In this it mirrors
White's mental state at that time, and shows the discerning reader some
of the author's own fears and self-doubts. Still, it offers two things, the
value of shape-shifting as a means of teaching (not exactly what the
education authorities or the National Union of Teachers would have
in mind but it would go down well with the children!), and these glimpses
of the workings of someone else's imaginative world.

Into this category of teaching by the use of creative imagination we
must place all the great epic poems, sagas and narratives of the old world
and some of early medieval times. All of them were constructed to be
read aloud by a gifted teller of tales, and all of them offered something

to be learned. The sagas and epic poetry taught the illiterate people of that time about their own land, laws and law-givers, history and customs, and boosted the patriotic feelings with tales of their heroes. They taught them about the beginnings of their world as the writers saw it and the great events that had helped to shape them into a race. All this was repeated by the bards or skalds over and over again at every feast, fair and gathering until it became part of the people's way of thinking and so passed into the genetic make-up, enabling that race to see itself as a whole, as a powerful group mind with its own symbol(s) and its own magical guardians.

Into this category come the Poetic Edda and the Prose Edda, the Kalevala and the Volsunga sagas. From Denmark comes the Vilkina and from Southern Germany the better known Nibelungenlied. All of these will repay slow and careful reading *especially* if read aloud even if only to oneself. Better still record them and then listen to the playback. Add to this the tale of Beowulf and the monster, Grendel, which incidentally was the very first legend I read unaided and I was inconsolable for days over the loss of Grendel's arm and regarded Beowulf as a big bully. In my own defence I must add I was only 7 at the time!

Joseph Campbell, in his book *Creative Mythology*, states that 'The amalgamation of local, spontaneously generated folklore and saga with the larger heritage of Aryan myth, must be attributed to a traditionally trained, highly appreciated generation of consciously creative poets.' He goes on to say that the more sophisticated poetry of the skalds occurred in about the eighth and ninth centuries and continued up to and including the fourteenth century. So we know that the great oral tradition of creatively inspired poetry was still maintained up to that time, but from then on the tradition began a long, slow decline.

In approximately 1345 Geoffrey Chaucer was born in London and, while still a young boy, became a page in the household of the Duke of Clarence. But it is not until 1369 that we become aware of him as a poet and a writer. All in all, his output was not large but there is no doubt that he was the first purely English poet. His *Troilus and Cressida* is held up as the best of his work, but it is for his *Canterbury Tales* that we know him best of all. Unlike the more solemn epics of the bards, his collection of individual tales told by an ill-matched group of pilgrims travelling to Canterbury has a high humour that falls on the side of bawdiness, changes to pathos and continues with a series of beautifully descriptive vignettes of the travellers. This was quite different to anything that had gone before. And although Chaucer followed the bardic pattern of reading his tales aloud to the King (there is a delightful little painting of him doing just that), the ordinary people soon heard them in the market place and, because they were a series of tales strung together, they were probably the very first serials. Such stories tend to stimulate the imagination of those who hear them. They start to think about ways to change them, especially the endings. It becomes a case of, 'If I'd been her I would have done so and so . . .', or 'Fancy letting him get away with that, what he should have done was . . .' and we are back in the old tradition of the imagination being stimulated to take over and draw the person away from the everyday world into that of the inner levels. Chaucer seems to have led a rather unlucky life plagued by debts and lack of money but his name will never be forgotten while the Canterbury Tales live on. He was the first poet to be buried in what is now known as Poets' Corner in Westminster Abbey. I recommend his Tales to you for they show the best in descriptive writing which is to say they will provide something for your creative imagination to chew on. They would, in point of fact, make a delightful series of pathworkings on their own account.

Now came the Renaissance and though it started the thought processes that were to free mankind from ignorance it also began the decline of interest in poetry as something to be read aloud for the benefit of others.

Yet there were pockets where the free flight of the imagination was still to be experienced but *now* in the art of the story rather than in the poem. *The Adventures of Don Quixote* holds a special place in literature for it marked a meeting point of what had been the saga and what was to become the modern novel. A new creative force was entering the world: the story that the ordinary man and woman could read for themselves, without the mediation of the story-teller bard. For the first time the creative imagination of mankind was being catered for by the medium of the written, and printed, word. The very story itself invokes images in the mind of even the most unimaginative, for the theme is that of a man driven by the twin furies of despair and old age to . . . 'lay down the burden of sanity'. Cervantes was writing from inside himself, from the other side of the mind. He was putting himself in the mind of Don Quixote and, like an inside, hidden reporter, relaying the emotions, the agonies and the despair of the old man to an unknown audience. The invention of the printing press had put the world of books within the grasp of every man but it was the writers who now picked up the many-coloured mantle of the bards and handed mankind the key to open or close his inner world at his own discretion; all it needed was the opening of a book.

Around this time there was also an upsurge of interest in alchemy and all things magical and it was quickly realized that the imagination and the various ways in which it could be used were of immense value. This, in turn, brought about a new wave of poetic genius and we entered the age of Marlowe and Shakespeare. To take in the ramifications of their genius and its application to both the art of magic and to the way of creative imagination, would fill a book by itself. Suffice it to say that anyone interested even slightly in magic will be aware of its influence running through Shakespeare's works. Marlowe's *Dr Faustus* stands alone. A leap of such imaginative genius it goes far beyond my ability to write about it, except to say that I agree with Lessing (1729–1781), who claimed that the end of Faust should have been salvation and not damnation, and also with Goethe, who saw him as a 'striving creative spirit' and Mephistopheles as the 'principle of negation'.

But what of later poetry, say from the mid-1700s? Does that offer anything to the pathworker? Yes indeed, it offers a great deal both as possible workings and as insights into the imaginative world of the poet himself. Samuel Taylor Coleridge and William Wordsworth have, over the years, provided many writers and critics with enough material to fill a library on the one subject. Coleridge, in particular, is of himself a crossroads in the history of English verse. With his works we move into an entirely new phase of poetry. His command of the tremendous faculty of his creative imagination, his insight into the images and symbols with which it presented him, marks him as one touched by the finger of genius. The trouble with genius is that it fluctuates and can sometimes desert its host for long periods, or it flourishes for a certain time, then drops away. But there is no doubt that Coleridge represents a peak in the history of poetry.

It is accepted in the practice of magic that the strongest of all formations for the bringing down of power is that of two priests and a priestess. The inner plane power of the woman flows down into the temple and then outwards to her two male counterparts. In effect, she is the Well of Knowledge we sometimes call Daath and, from this feminine matrix, the power wells out, connects with, and stimulates the spheres of Justice and Mercy (Geburah and Chesed). This may have been what happened, all unknowingly (?) to Wordsworth and Coleridge and Wordsworth's sister, Dorothy. There can be little doubt that this unusual woman acted as a muse, an encourager and a source for both men.

The depth of feeling in their poems, the rich imagery and finely drawn detail, the observation of *all* levels, seems to have stemmed from her in the beginning. Her diaries should be read to give the full idea of the rather strange relationship between the three people. Dorothy had an amazing ability to 'see', and more than that, to communicate to others the essence of what she had seen. This, to the two men, was a gift they could not ignore. If she went out for a walk alone, on her return she was able to convey exactly what had passed before her eyes and through her mind with such clarity that it seemed as if they had accompanied her.

For a short while the three shared a house in the Lake District and spent long and, at first, happy hours discussing, walking, arguing and writing. Above all, writing, but it was not to last. There is a fund of literature concerning both men and I recommend that at least one or two books be read, if only because Coleridge offers an insight into the use of the creative imagination that is both lucid and inspiring to anyone who is interested in the use of guided imagery.

Wordsworth suffered a personal depression at the time of the French Revolution and it was due to the efforts of his sister and those of Coleridge that he found a way through this mental miasma and, from then on, became almost 'renewed'. Much of what he went through during this time can be read in 'The Prelude', a poem dealing with his thoughts and feelings during his breakdown. Out of this 'Dark Night of the Soul' came a flood of the most sublime poetry, most of it pure pathworking, mental images of such clarity that we can, after two hundred years, take the same path in our mind's eye and feel what he felt, see what he saw. There is no space to look at more than a few of his poems and discuss their potential as pathways into the mind, but search them out for yourself and use them to build the images that he built and you will get as near to the mind of another person as it is possible to get.

Imagine that you stand upon Westminster Bridge just before sunrise looking down the river. Everything is waiting, breathlessly, for the dawn and as you wait you hear these words:

Upon Westminster Bridge

Earth has not anything to show more fair:
Dull would he be of soul who could pass by
A sight so touching in its majesty:
This city now doth like a garment wear
The beauty of the morning; silent, bare.
Ships, towers, domes, theatre, and temples lie
Open unto the fields and to the sky;
All bright and glittering in the smokeless air.
Never did sun more beautifully steep
In his first splendour valley, rock or hill;

Ne'er saw I, never felt, a calm so deep!
The river glideth at his own sweet will;
Dear God! The very houses seem asleep;
And all that mighty heart is lying still.

Now go through the whole thing again but translating those words
into pictures. You stand upon the bridge, everywhere is silent and hushed.
The light is pale gold and luminous. Look around you, turning on your
own axis, see the buildings, the wharves and moored barges, the massive
Dome of St Paul's, and the high buildings that line the banks of the
ancient river. That river itself is silent, dark and deep in its running
to the sea, the rhythm of its wavelets gently lifting the moored boats
up and down. Nothing moves or causes sound. Now, the sun lifts over
the trees and roofs and casts a golden net of light over it all. The windows,
water, gilded figures and the bridge itself all catch fire by that light and
throw it backwards and forwards across the Thames. Far off a clock sounds
the early hour. There is within you a feeling of utter calm, a feeling
of being close to the sleeping heart of a great city, just before it wakes.
In a few hours all this will be a vast cacophony of sound, colour and
moving masses of people but now, here, this moment is yours alone.
Look at the windows of the buildings, see them as eyes that are fast
shut as the promise of a new day draws closer. Listen, listen hard, can
you hear a faint throb, a stirring, a steady beat? That, my friend, is the
heart of London.

An exercise such as this, using the carefully chosen words and images
of a poet of Wordsworth's calibre, can teach you to see with other eyes
and understand that seeing just as he understood what his sister, Dorothy,
had seen when she came back from her walks along the banks of
Ullswater. For a contrast, let us now take one of his best-known poems,
'Daffodils'. For Wordsworth the symbol of a flower was to hold a great
deal of meaning all through his life. This particular poem holds a lot
of interest for our purpose since the incident that gave rise to its birth
has been recorded for us by the ever-vigilant Dorothy. The following
is an extract from her journals.

When we were in the woods beyond Gowbarrow Park we saw a few daffodils
close to the water-side. We fancied that the lake had floated the seed ashore,
and that the little colony had so sprung up. But as we went along there
were more and yet more; and, at last, under the boughs of the trees, we
saw that there was a long belt of them along the shore, about a breadth
of a country turnpike road. I never saw daffodils so beautiful. They grew
among the mossy stones about them, some rested their heads upon these

stones as on a pillow for weariness; and the rest tossed and reeled and danced, and seemed as if they verily laughed with the wind . . . they looked so gay.

Her brother saw exactly the same thing, but took what he saw apart bit by bit and recreated it in his imagination. It was, to use a cabbalistic phrase, almost a Geburic act, this tearing down of an image and its regeneration into something far more potent for those who would never see what they had seen except through his genius with words. This incident was a turning point for the poet for it brought him out of the long depression into which he had fallen some time before. Now once again he could see an underlying harmony between man and nature. From our point of view it also shows how deeply the healing properties of the pathworking can reach into the distressed psyche.

As we read the poem we can share and feel with the poet his new-found exhilaration with life, but careful reading can also show us how he was feeling immediately before the sight of that golden carpet. We know he was walking with his sister, yet he tells us:

> I wander'd lonely as a cloud
>   That floats on high o'er vales and hills,
> When all at once I saw a crowd,
>   A host of golden daffodils;
> Beside the lake, beneath the trees,
> Fluttering and dancing in the breeze.

Although he was with someone physically he felt alone inside himself. The near-breakdown he had gone through was still heavy on his mind. Then, without any warning, he is accosted by a blaze of colour, and not just any colour, but golden yellow, the warm Apollonian sun colour that heals and soothes. This colour corresponds also to Mercury the Messenger, and the shock unlocks his ability to paint with words once more. All at once he can see, and feel and experience the world around him as he used to do. In the third verse he confesses:

> A poet could not but be gay,
>   In such a jocund company:
> I gazed — and gazed — but little thought
> What wealth the show to me had brought.

The healing goes on and on, it does not stop when the flowers are no longer in sight for the memory acts in the same therapeutic manner when the poet is alone and a little low in spirits:

For oft, when on my couch I lie
  In vacant or in pensive mood,
They flash upon that inward eye
  Which is the bliss of solitude;
And then my heart with pleasure fills.
And dances with the daffodils.

Those words are telling in their aptness. The poet knew well enough the power of 'that inward eye, which is the bliss of solitude'. He is very familiar with the fact that he can recall the scene, indeed any scene, in the mind's eye and recreate the sight, sound, scent and, above all, the emotion of gladness and at-one-ness locked within the momentous experience. Such is the power of the creative imagination, of which the part of pathworking is the outward sign. Do go over the poem for yourself and write it into a pathworking to suit yourself. Don't be afraid to do this. You are not destroying the masterpiece of a genius, all poets write to cause something to happen within the heart and mind of the reader. You are merely making that happen in your own way. Wordsworth's poem is beautiful, but it is the *experience* hidden within the words that holds the key. Get at that experience in any way you can.

When you have written it out, record it if possible, then sit back and try to put yourself in the position of the poet when he says, 'For oft, when on my couch I lie in vacant or in pensive mood . . .' Try to feel your way into the mind of Wordsworth himself for a short time and don't pathwork, *remember* the scene and experience it to the utmost.

The last poem of Wordsworth's that I particularly want you to read is called 'The Solitary Reaper'. Go through it in the same way as the others and build a pathworking from the images it gives you. If you have the skill you can over-record suitable music to this kind of work and the Eriskay Love Lilts fit well with this last poem. For 'Westminster Bridge' try 'Morning' from the Peer Gynt suite. For 'Daffodils' I think Delius' 'A Walk to the Paradise Garden' would be a good choice.

It is almost impossible to separate Coleridge from Wordsworth when speaking of poets, but they were very different in temperament and in their approach to writing. Both were greatly concerned with the value of 'perception' both in its physical and superphysical sense but Coleridge's more intuitive approach was, for a short time at least, to take him higher and deeper into the region of the mind and its ability to fashion, and use, images, than any other poet before him or, in my personal opinion, since then. For a deeper insight into the personalities involved read

Stephen Prickett's book *Coleridge and Wordsworth, the Growth of Poetry* (Cambridge University Press).

Although these two men were so close to begin with, eventually Coleridge's addiction to opium led to a bitter split. This was made much worse by Coleridge's over-sensitivity, and Wordsworth's rather holier-than-thou attitude and, although in time they were reconciled, there was never to be the same affection and closeness that had been before. Thus came to an end a rare and valuable closeness between two remarkable men.

An experience that made an enormous impact on Coleridge and which was to 'haunt' him for years was his vision of the Brocken-spectre. This is a phenomenon sometimes seen in the area called the Brocken in the Hartz Mountains of Germany. It happens when a human shadow is cast by the rays of the rising or setting sun on to a bank of low cloud or mist. The image is giant-sized and the head is surrounded by rings of coloured light called coronae. It seemed to him to be the perfect Doppelganger, his other, perhaps his creative self, from which the fountain of his genius flowed. It became a recurring theme, usually disguised, in many of his poems. Coleridge's idea of the Creative Imagination is far too complex to go into here but for anyone who works with, or intends to work with, the creative mind in all its phases, a knowledge of this brilliant man is essential. He writes of his beliefs in the *Biographica Literaria* and comes closer than almost anyone to defining the words 'creative imagination'.

Time to turn to his poetry and allow it to speak for itself, which it does most adequately. There are three that I particularly recommend to anyone interested in using poetry as a ready-made pathworking. The first is the famous 'Kubla Khan'. Its comparative shortness belies its ability to create images in the mind and especially for those who wish to use the 'descent' myth, for the words can be used to create the image of Xanadu as a 'lost' city approached through an underground journey. The mind picture invoked by the words

> Where Alph the sacred river ran,
> Through caverns measureless to man,
> Down to a sunless sea . . .

can bring a shiver of apprehension as the mind follows the twists and turns of a subterranean river through seemingly endless tunnels full of rushing darkness, only to come out onto a sea where no sun shines. And yet in almost the next breath the poet writes of 'Forests ancient as the hills enfolding sunny spots of greenery'. Later on we hear of a 'lifeless sea'. All in all, this poem offers a richness of imagery enough for several pathworkings and, because of this, I would suggest you make it into two separate workings, the first being the journey itself, used as an approach to the underworld; then, later, using the actual description of Xanadu for the second working. You will be able to fill in the poet's images with side trips of your own, building up to a greatly enhanced pathworking.

The second poem, 'Christabel', is rather long and needs careful reading but, for all that, its narrative is so clear and precise that it will build into a working with little trouble. Its theme is the classical 'battle between good and evil', the prize being the soul of Christabel herself.

'The Rime of the Ancient Mariner' is probably the best-known of Coleridge's poems, one of the most often quoted, and usually wrongly quoted at that. Running to seven parts, it is a very long poem indeed and certainly too long for most people to try as a pathworking although, having said that, it has been done and done successfully, but it did take almost two hours! The main reason for its inclusion here is that whether Coleridge was aware of it or not it recounts the story of Initiation through the Levels.

An oft-repeated saying is that 'When the student is ready the teacher will come.' That is exactly what happens in the poem. Three young men arrive for a wedding but one, just one, is stopped by an old man purporting to be a mariner; but are the oceans he sails those of earth, or is it the Great Sea of Binah that washes the shores of the inner worlds? At first the wedding guest tries to get past (tries to refuse the offer of wisdom), but the mariner has chosen well and he sits down to listen. The old man starts his tale of the long sea-voyage (often a euphemism for a single lifetime).

> The Sun came up upon the left,
> Out of the sea came he!
> And he shone bright and on the right
> Went down into the sea.

This means they were sailing towards the south of the Great Sea (Binah, who is often called the Black Isis). Strangely enough, the black miracle-working Madonna is often referred to in medieval scripts as the Queen of the South who calls men to her and endows them with the gift of understanding. This female power is confirmed almost at once for:

> The Bride hath paced into the hall,
> Red as a Rose is she.

The guest would like to leave the old man and join her but is held in the grip of his tale. Besides, the Bride, i.e. the favour of the Great Mother, is not easily won. The mariner goes on with his tale. The ship now hits a fearful storm and is driven before it into a region of ice and snow where everything seems frozen and dead. (The would-be initiate undergoes the trials and tribulations of the world which are sent to refine his psyche and strengthen it.)

Out of the seeming frozen waste comes a bird, beautiful, white, graceful, and friendly. It takes food from the hands of the seamen and perches on the mast for nine days (nine, the triple three, is the number of Binah, the Great Mother). But the mariner, unknowing and uncaring, shoots the bird (the symbol of the watchful Mother), and so he fails the first and very important test. This is given by way of a warning to the young guest. The ship sails on and soon,

> The Sun now rose upon the right:
> Out of the sea came he.
> Still hid in mist, and on the left
> Went down into the sea.

They have now turned north again and, still shrouded in fog, sail on, but now the seamen have turned against the mariner. (Those companions met and made in daily life often turn against the one who seems to be out of step, but then within the space of a few lines they are taking the opposite view and praising him for his action. This is typical of the see-saw treatment a really serious student of the Ancient Arts can expect from those around him.) Then disaster strikes: they are becalmed in an unknown sea. The mariner's description indicates the horrors they now face:

> All in a hot and copper sky,
> The bloody Sun, at noon
> Right up above the mast did stand
> No bigger than the Moon.

The symbols of both the Male and Female deities are here displayed, and the means and the power of their displeasure.

Day after day, day after day,
We stuck, nor breath nor motion;
As idle as a painted ship
Upon a painted ocean.

The power of Coleridge's imagination grips that of the reader and forces upon our inner vision the horrors that beset the ship and its crew. He tells us with mounting tension,

The very deep did rot: Oh Christ!
That ever this should be . . .

The lack of water plus the effects of the blazing sun bring on a series of hallucinations . . . or are they hallucinations? Creatures of slime rise up from the ocean and St Elmo's Fire dances in the rigging. But, amid all this horror, they become aware that a benign spirit has been following their progress from the time they left the land of ice and snow. In the commentary set in italics at the side of the poem Coleridge states that it was 'One of the invisible inhabitants of this planet neither a departed soul nor an angel. They are very numerous and there is no climate nor element without one or more.'

His shipmates have once again decided that all this is the fault of the mariner and was caused by his shooting of the albatross and they hang the decaying corpse of the bird about his neck. His Dark Night of the Soul is beginning now. There comes into sight a ship, but a Ship of Death, for she sails straight with no wind and no tide to guide her. Her crew consists only of Death himself, and the Nightmare called Life in Death. They are playing dice for the souls of the terrified crew. Life in Death wins the soul of the mariner, and Death, the loser, claims the rest of the crew in lieu. In terms of the initiatory drama, this is the moment when it seems that every last thing is taken from you, that you have nothing more to lose. The head bows and the soul learns the bitter truth, that it cannot go on alone, that it must turn and ask for help from whatever deity is worshipped, acknowledging that it is the Divine Will of that deity alone that has full power over life and death.

The souls of the ship's crew are claimed by Death. Alone of all of them the mariner survives. The guest is terrified at this and tries once more to leave but the mariner reassures him that he is not a ghost and continues with his tale.

> The many men, so beautiful!
> And they all dead did lie:
> And a thousand thousand slimy things
> Lived on: and so did I.

Now he enters a dreamlike state in which he begins to feel his way towards at-one-ness. For seven days and seven nights he endures this hell surrounded by the bodies of his fellow crewmen and weighed down by the rotting corpse of the albatross about his neck. He looks to the Moon, the symbol of the Great Mother, who loves all life, human and other. He sees the creatures of the deep and begins to understand their happiness in their natural environment and the perfection with which they have been created. Their beauty touches him and he blesses them with a full heart and, at that moment, the albatross falls from his neck and he falls into a gentle sleep from which he wakes to find it raining. But his troubles are not over yet. A storm rises and drives the ship onwards and, to the great fear of the mariner, the dead crew come to life and begin to man the ship as before.

The mariner tells the overwrought guest that the bodies were inhabited by a troop of angels invoked by the ever-present Spirit that had followed the ship since the slaying of the seabird. With its blessed crew the ship sails on to the sound of angelic voices, then it stops suddenly and, just as suddenly, bounds forwards again, causing the mariner to fall unconscious and, while he is in this state, he hears two voices speaking about him, one asking if this is the man who shot the sacred albatross for,

> The Spirit who bideth by himself
> In the land of mist and snow,
> He loved the bird that loved the man
> Who shot him with his bow.

We are beginning to see that the Albatross itself is a symbol, but of what? It can only be the soul of the mariner himself, disdained and profaned, shot by the arrow of the ego.

> The other was a softer voice,
> As soft as honey-dew:
> Quoth he, 'The man hath penance done,
> *And penance more will do*'

Clearly, although he is being helped to make amends, the scales of justice have not yet been completely balanced. The ship moves on at a speed that the mariner's physical body could not endure were it not in trance. When he wakes the dead crew have assembled and are looking at him accusingly, but then finally the curse is lifted and he is free. The ship sails on and comes at last to its own harbour with the lighthouse and the church on the hill. He turns to find that where the crew had stood there now stands a band of seraphs who salute him ere they depart.

The pilot boat with the pilot and his apprentice now appear to see the ship safely into harbour. They bring with them the hermit who lives in the wood, and who immediately perceives that this is no ordinary ship and no ordinary man. Suddenly and without warning, the boat spins round and sinks and the angelic host departs, which occurrence causes the pilot to 'fall down in a fit', and the apprentice to go mad. The hermit alone, although awed, stands firm and finally, when they reach the shore, he shrives the mariner of his sins. But the mariner is changed beyond all knowing and passes from place to place compelled to tell his tale to those who stand out in the crowd. This is how it must be for all initiates. They must find those who are ready for such an experience and pass on all their knowledge. Students too must take that perilous inner journey of the soul and survive, if they can. A teacher can only help a student cope with the experiences; he cannot show exactly how to deal with them for that must come from within. No teacher, however high his grade, may say, 'You are what I have made you', for that is folly. Only the student can 'make' himself, the teacher can only advise. The student, i.e. the Wedding Guest, rises stunned and, forgetting the wedding feast, walks away, perhaps to begin his own inner journey of the soul.

And what of the mariner, and the hermit? Are they one and the same? Has it all been the inner experience of the latter as he meditated in his cell? We must each put upon it a personal interpretation, but there is no doubt that this poem holds layers like an onion: as each layer is peeled away, another presents itself. But it stands in the history of English verse as a high example of an inner journey and, as such, deserves its place in occult teaching.

Coleridge, although outstanding, is not the only poet you can turn to for mystical poetry that can be used as a pathworking. There is Francis Thompson's poem 'The Hound of Heaven', most of Walt Whitman's poetry, and a great deal of Longfellow's. Try his 'The Belfry of Bruges', 'Endymion', and those much-slighted narrative poems so loved by the Victorians, 'The Village Blacksmith' and 'Excelsior'. Laugh if you will, but read them and then tell me they do not make good pathworkings.

Maybe the sentiments they express seem old-fashioned to modern ideas, but they represent values we are fast losing in this era. Nor should you neglect Longfellow's magnificent poem 'Hiawatha'. You will find, if you care to look, a wealth of ready-made pathworkings and inner journeys to take either alone or with a group of students or friends.

The last poet I recommend to you is Alfred, Lord Tennyson, the Victorian 'Bard'. His verse lends itself particularly well to the inner journey and indeed, Tennyson himself was well aware of such practices and made use of them in solitude. His beautiful Arthurian poems, and 'Locksley Hall' illustrate this and you will find in 'Godiva' a wealth of descriptive imagery that begins with the poet waiting for the train at Coventry and, as he waits, goes back in time to the famous 'Ride'.

Too little, by far, is made of poetry nowadays, especially in schools. It is part of our heritage and should be given its rightful place. Our folk music too in relation to the mystical and the occult is in danger of vanishing, although it has a stout-hearted champion in Bob Stewart and, if anyone can save it, it will be he. See particularly his *The Under-World Initiation* (Aquarian Press, 1985).

CHAPTER SEVEN

Capturing the Bird of the Mind

We have all had the experience of buying a book because we were attracted by the title, the cover, the publicity blurb on the back or the first few pages of text, and then finding when we get it back home that it fails to hold our attention. On the other hand, there is the book we buy almost casually and which becomes a favourite, getting more and more tattered and dog-eared as the years go by. Such books do not come to us by accident. They come because something inside us calls to them, because we need what they, or rather the author, has to tell us. Often we keep them for years unable to let them go, they have become a symbol of a certain time in our lives when we, or life around us, changed.

Pictures have the same effect. If you go to one of the big exhibitions, more often than not you will find people buying pictures they do not really like, or which they will pretend to like because, like Hans Anderson's Emperor, they do not wish to be thought lacking in appreciation of 'true art'! You should buy a painting or a picture for one reason and one reason only: because you like it, because you feel comfortable in its presence or because it says something to your inner self.

Again we all have favourite authors, favourite poets, favourite artists. We feel there is something in the nature of that person or the way they look at life that makes them understandable to us. Their view of the inner world approximates to our own, and we are in sympathy with them.

There is no doubt that certain people have a power of description that puts them on a par with the ancient bards. They exercise a fascination over us and compel our attention, whether it be by words or images on canvas. They 'stir' the imagination of others by using their own. You must always remember that the creative imagination is not a special talent reserved for poets, painters and writers; it is something we all have within us to a greater or lesser degree. I like to paint with words; I could not plan the interior of a house with wallpaper and furniture, etc. to save my life. I love to design costumes for theatre and make them, but

don't expect me to be enthusiastic over planning a garden. We all have
different ways in which we use the imagination but we all use it, and
every day of our lives. It is not too strong to say that we rise or fall in
a chosen profession or in our lives because of the way we 'imagine' our
inner scenarios.

Quite often a writer or a painter will suddenly stray from their usual
pattern and break new ground. Just as often it is a one-off and they go
back to the usual routine but that one example shows where something
happened to them on an inner level, something so big that it broke
through into the everyday world. It is like that when we find just the
book or the picture for a certain moment in our lives.

At the beginning of the last war I was just 10. As the German Army
prepared to land at the Jersey airport my parents and I were escaping
on a little Norwegian coal boat from the harbour. We were full of inner
turmoil. Our home had just been left as it stood. We had one case between
us, very little money and even less hope. After a nightmare journey to
Weymouth we took the train for the north and on a warm June day we
stood in a forlorn little group in Lime Street Station. While the adults
talked and planned, I wandered off and, as usual, ended up at the station
bookstall. There I found it, a book that was meant for me. The book
and I looked at each other and knew that nothing could keep us apart.
It was six shillings, a great deal of money in those days especially for
a book.

It was months later that I had enough money to buy that book, and
I had to play truant from school to collect it. The original woman at
the bookstall had been replaced by another, but the book was still there.

It was late when I got to bed that night and I had to read under the
covers with the aid of a torch. It was then the wonder seized me. In
the story a boy bought a wondrous boat in an antique shop from an
old man with a patch over one eye. It was a magical boat called *Skibladneir*.
For it, he paid all the money he had in the world, and a bit over. It
was exactly what I had paid for the book. For me it was real magic.
I still have the book, *The Ship that Flew* by Hilda Lewis. My children
have read it and I hope one day to read it to my grandchildren for it
is surely one of the classic books that stretches beyond age and changes
in taste. It is one of those rare books that catch 'the bird of the mind'
and hold it fast for a short while before releasing it again. The kind
of book that draws you back to its covers again and again. You may indeed
forget it for years, then suddenly you come across it when cleaning out
the attic or a bedroom seldom used. There is something about cleaning
those kind of places - you always end up sitting on the steps or stairs

and reading. Taking up carpets and lino incurs the same risk – the old newspapers underneath seem so much more interesting the second time around!

Every now and then a writer appears with more than the usual ability to reach the inner world of ordinary people. Writers whose talents open up the inner levels of people who didn't know they had any inner worlds. Even I, who teach about such things every day of my life, am continually amazed at what goes on behind the eyes of the nine-to-five brigade, and not only the quiet, studious ones, but the hell-raisers, the seeming dropouts, policemen and traffic wardens, lollipop ladies and doctors. Not all the inner fantasies I get to hear about are dreams of 'lotus eating' in the sun. A surprising amount are, to say the least, if not illegal, somewhat anti-social! I was surprised to find for instance how many people fantasize about being cat burglars! A gentleman well over retirement age dreams of leading a band of mercenaries on daring exploits and avidly reads anything on arms, explosives and like subjects.

It seems there is a very different personality in all of us trying to get out and, because the world in which we live does not always provide the right circumstances, the human race has called into being an inner world where all things are possible, where age can be reversed, and talents we do not possess in the real world are on tap. In some cases this can save our sanity.

There are times when a human being is forced into the inner world through physical or mental torture. Odette, the heroine of the French Resistance, was for a long time placed in solitary confinement. Kept in darkness and with no way of knowing how time was passing, she used her imagination to create an inner world where she could retain her sanity. Safe within this world she cut out and sewed dresses for her daughters and knitted jumpers for them, all of it in the mind. Many prisoners kept in these conditions used similar methods; some would fix their eyes on a minute spot on the wall and allow it to grow into a picture, others would 'dissolve' the wall and take long country walks or run along far-off beaches in their own country.

Since the beginning of the space age it has been necessary to find the breaking-point of an astronaut when subjected to the kind of loneliness found only in space. To this end isolation tanks were and still are used to determine how much isolation the human mind can stand. Deprived of all senses, floating naked in a tank of warm water, using a small breathing apparatus, with no light, no sound, in fact no contact of any kind, the volunteer is totally alone. There is, however, a panic button near at hand and the subject's physiological responses are monitored continuously.

Under these conditions it is not surprising that many do indeed panic. The time varies considerably from a few minutes to several hours, but women always seem to come out better. Why? Because they are more used to living in or experiencing an inner world, their psychic senses are closer to the surface and so more readily available in times of need. But men also, when pushed beyond endurance, can reach down inside themselves and through their anima draw on exceptional power. Such a man was Ed Morrell, author of *The Twenty-Fifth Man*. Morrell was gifted with an above-average psychic ability and it saved his life and his sanity. Some fifty years ago he was given a gaol sentence in Arizona, USA. That particular prison had more than its share of sadistically minded guards. Their favourite 'game' was to strap Morrell into a straitjacket and then soak him in water. The effect was to shrink the jacket causing near suffocation to the victim.

One night when he was close to the edge of death and insanity, Morrell suddenly felt free of the constraint put upon him. He found himself in an astral body and was able to pass through the walls and experience a full and conscious freedom. When he returned he no longer felt pain, anger, and frustration, but instead a feeling of being revitalized. Not surprisingly this infuriated the guards who redoubled their torture and once left him tied up for five days. But to no avail. Morrell had discovered not only how to travel astrally, but how to live in his inner world. This amazing talent only left him when he was freed and the desperation that enabled him to use his mental powers was removed.

His story was a true one and shows how the mind can offer help and even an 'escape' when it is needed. But there are many writers of fiction who can offer a similar escape, but this time for pure pleasure, and not because circumstances make it a matter of survival.

Some authors seem to be able to plug into this world and to offer us glimpses of things we had not thought of for ourselves. Many of them have produced books that have become cult symbols and given birth to a whole industry of spin-offs. This is no bad thing, for mankind must have its dreams, or it will die inwardly.

Tolkien springs immediately to mind of course and his books are now classics. Leather-clad bikers read them and dream of being Aragorn or Eowyn; bank managers keep them in their desks and snatch a few minutes to be one with Gandalf (or should that be Smaug with his pile of gold?). Old and young alike have been captivated by the world Tolkien created out of bits and pieces of ancient myth and history over a period of many years. The characters he drew from his own inner world of imagination will never die, and like his own Race of Elves, they are immortal.

This longing for a race that is older, wiser, and more beautiful than our own, and which moreover is blessed with immortality, is a continuous theme in our dreams and it surfaces in much of our literature; a harking back to an age of comparative innocence that we have lost aeons ago. Is it any wonder that the sales of fantasy fiction have more than trebled in the last five years?

Ursula Le Guin is a writer of considerable note and the winner of many awards in America and elsewhere. Her science fiction novels are masterpieces of their genre and few can match her ability to present themes of startling complexity and descriptive beauty. Then, somewhere along the line, she came up with *The Wizard of Earthsea*. When I first saw it, it was published by Puffin and intended for children of 9 to 12. That age-group rapidly expanded and now encompasses the 7 to 70s and possibly well over that.

The one book became a trilogy that has been enchanting people for years and will continue to do so into the foreseeable future. The series interests me as an occultist because it accurately describes the ideas behind occult teaching and, as the series goes on, digs deeply into the ethical side of the occult which many of our critics will claim does not exist! But the story of the young boy who rises in rank to become the Master Mage grabs our imagination from the start and leads it through as many twists and turns as has the labyrinth which is the setting for the second book of the three. It totally entranced me, and especially the last book of all, for it shows that there comes a time in the lives of all who practise the art of magic when they must lay down the wand and the sword, bury the pentacle in the sweet, clean earth, and drink for the last time from the chalice. The power *must* be given back at some point and the erstwhile magician must prepare for a transmutation into another level. That is the law and that is shown in full in *The Wizard of Earthsea*.

Susan Cooper was born in England and gained a degree in English at Oxford and had the distinction of becoming the first woman to edit the university magazine. Later on she was to become the senior feature writer and deputy news editor of *The Sunday Times*. Then she married and went to live in America where she started to write. Like Ursula Le Guin, she suddenly came up with a children's book which was published first by Jonathan Cape in 1965 and then by Puffin in 1968. *Over Sea and Under Stone* was publicized as being for readers of 10 and over; considerably over as we shall see. This first of what was to become five books was a child's story pure and simple, and yet there was an indefinable something that made one pause and wonder . . . but what about you didn't exactly know.

In 1973 we found out what we had been waiting for when Chatto & Windus published *The Dark is Rising*, Puffin following with an edition in 1976. Again it was for 'readers of 10 and over', but some of the material in this and in the three other books subsequently published, contained occult lore that, had the critics of the occult movement realized it, would have had the books off the shelves of junior libraries within days. But adults began to buy them, seeing in their pages hints of the dreams they were looking for to fill their inner worlds. Although, as I have said, the first book of the five is just a child's book, it has to be read in order to get the sense of continuation that flows through the entire series. Not all the books have the same power of holding the mind in thrall but who will quibble when there is a whole world of dreams to use in our secret dreams and fantasies.

Some very similar books were published about the same time, written by Alan Garner. These included *The Weirdstone of Brisingamen* and *The Moon of Gomrath*, quickly followed by *The Owl Service*. Garner's approach was different. He seemed to be aiming at a market that was at the time only just being explored, the age-group of 12 to 17. The first two were similar in many respects to the Susan Cooper books, but there was an underlying current of menace that, for me personally, was to mar all Garner's writings. *The Owl Service* was televized quite successfully and many people have enjoyed the book; certainly it must be included here for it holds back the veil between the real and the mental worlds and affords us a glimpse of what is normally hidden. But I must confess that Garner is not a favourite author of mine. I concede that he is a brilliant writer, but I still do not like the undertone I feel runs through his work.

From the mid-seventies there was an increasing interest in fantasy fiction but now writers were exploring the adult market. André Norton, Tanith Lee and Lin Carter in America were to become a prolific trio. Norton in particular brought out a series called *The Witchworld*, and although they were all mind-grabbing in their way, there was one that stood out. *The Year of the Unicorn* was a quite brilliant mix and match of modern fantasy and ancient myth for it took the story of Eros and Psyche as a broad base and built on this a story that more than any of the others in the series held the attention and reached the inner world of the reader. Besides the obvious fantasy there was the underlying story of a love that not even the power of the Underworld could break. The determination and courage of one person tested to its limits on the physical and the spiritual was very well presented and, although I have since given away the others in the series, I still keep that one book and reread it.

Michael Moorcock is a name well-known to readers of fantasy but I personally find his earlier works more to my taste than the later. My favourite is called *The Blood Red Game* which in the beginning was a sequel to an earlier novelette published in a science fiction magazine. However, no one can doubt Moorcock's ability to use his creative imagination with telling effect, though he has tended to repeat himself somewhat.

A classic in this kind of book is Arthur Clarke's *Childhood's End*, and though it does not have what might be termed a happy ending, it still stands out as a masterpiece of imagination.

Anne Macaffrey's world of Dragons and Dragonriders has an enormous following and I have enjoyed most of them, but it was the first two that had the most impact from an inner journey point of view and they were *To Ride Pegasus* and *The Ship who Sang*, both of which can be used for pathworkings/fantasies with stunning effect.

No book that deals with the use of imagination can help but mention Katherine Kurtz. This writer has an uncanny power to present the unusual as the completely acceptable and her *Deryni* and *Camber* novels have a deservedly wide following in America and are now available in England as well. Her novel *Lammas Night* is arguably the best truly occult novel in the last twenty years. Besides being a writer she holds a B.Sc. in Chemistry and an MA in Medieval History. She is also a professionally trained hypnotist and a practising occultist, which is one in the eye for some people who hold the firm belief that all occultists are either cretins or schizophrenics! Besides these things Katherine Kurtz is a writer with a richly endowed creative imagination and her books will repay reading with a treasure trove of images, and data with which to embellish your own inner journeys.

What is the point of presenting to you this list of authors? It is to remind you yet again that, unless you have a source of pictures, images, knowledge and information, you cannot build a pathworking with 'punch'. These people and this type of writer offer from the richness of their own mind all that you need and more for your own use. There are many others and you will more than likely have your own favourite authors which may range from Ray Bradbury to Barbara Cartland! But the value of their writing is in their intimacy with the inner world and its potential, for they can act as lamplighters to others and guide them into a world of healing and fulfilling dreams that it would otherwise take them much longer to find.

Painters too can be our heralds to the Land of the Ever Young and, if we choose carefully those pictures with which we surround ourselves, then we can use them as pathways into the mental realms. Use the art galleries and the exhibition halls to search for pictures to open the gates of the mind. Invest in a couple of plain wooden frames and buy prints that can be changed to suit your mood. Secondhand shops often have pictures. Look specially for Victorian ones. They often depict scenes that have a natural invitation to 'go inside'. Auction sales, jumble sales and local fundraising bazaars are other hunting grounds you can try, but be sure the picture is something you can use or live with. Don't buy it because you feel you have to do so.

Magazines often have pictures that can be carefully taken out and used and, although I have mentioned frames, don't feel that you have to frame them. A piece of card and some clingfilm will give it enough body to hang on the wall for the time you feel you want to use it. Nature and geographical magazines yield some really beautiful pictures and some travel agents will part with large posters if you ask them. In short, you don't have to have a lot of money to enjoy pictures that offer ideas for pathworkings.

Brush, pen, and voice are very powerful agents in this kind of work. Use them to the full. The New Age Cassettes range offers some beautiful music that can be used either as background or pathworkings in their own right. Sulis Tapes offer a good range of recorded pathworkings, lectures and music and produce several new titles each year. It is well worth sending for their list, and it includes some of Bob Stewart's own music and recordings he has made of folk music.

If you have ever seen a master of mime you will have seen what might be termed a silent pathworking; the story told by gesture and movement will differ considerably as interpreted by different people. To one it may be a simple acting out of, say, a visit to the seaside. To another member of the same audience it may suggest a man joining his ship in the harbour. For some he may be a bachelor, to others someone who has stolen an afternoon away from his irritating family. The mime artist will become all things to all people by the medium of his art. He does the same act for us all, but we give it flavour in our minds.

We do the same with the lyrics of songs, and the story behind the great traditional ballets and operas. It is because we add our own emotions to these things that we end up liking or disliking them. I love *Swan Lake* and *Aurora* and *Giselle* but would not bother to go and see *Coppelia* or *Les Sylphides*. They 'say' nothing to me. I enjoy *Turandot* and *Lucia de Lammamoor*, but dislike *Il Trovatore*.

Everyone colours what they see and hear with their own feelings. Pathworkings are no exception. I may write one and give it to a group of say ten people to experience and ask for a report from each of them. I will get ten very different experiences back because they are individuals and are colouring the working with their own 'in store' data. If the working is about a journey through an underground maze of caves and one person suffers from claustrophobia it will not be the pleasant experience that it might be for someone else. All this has to be taken into consideration when writing them. The main thing is to provide enough mental 'hooks' on which they can hang their emotions and feelings, and enough description to give them a fair chance to build an accurate landscape.

There is one more place that can provide Gateways into the inner world of the mind, and that is tapestry. We are blessed with many beautiful castles and great houses in England and most of them are open to the public. They abound in richly designed tapestries depicting scenes from the past, or from the pastimes of the area such as hunting, hawking, or simply riding through the countryside as it was then, perhaps anything up to three or four hundred years ago. They were made by people who lived at that time and who have depicted with great accuracy just how the world looked to them. Such things can offer an amazing experience if used as a starting-point for a working.

I can still relive the awe I felt when I saw the Bayeux tapestry. Here was a reconstruction of life in the Norman era as seen by the women of that time. One could walk slowly around and see the whole thing coming to life in the mind's eye. If they had had cameras in those days it could not have offered a better 'album' of memories. All such things provide the all-important data banks with which you can enrich your inner life. Learn to look and to remember, and then store away.

CHAPTER EIGHT

The Mystical Experience

Because we are looking at the entire range of pathworkings, from the guided imagery employed by psychologists, through the fever- and drug-induced nightmares of illness and drug abuse, to the highly complicated inner journeys of the trained magician, we must also look at the mystical and ecstatic experiences of the saints and visionaries. That a few of them were induced by fasting, self-inflicted pain, and a somewhat warped idea of what was asked of them by God, does not invalidate the fact that some of them were genuine, and truly mystical inner journeys. As such they have a special place in this book.

The narrow confined life of the convent and monastery in the Middle Ages was very conducive to the use of mental imagery. The habitual practice of meditation and contemplation in quiet and often solitary surroundings made for an introspective viewpoint. When that viewpoint was aligned to a deeply held religious fervour and either a certain degree of natural psychism (which opened the door to the true vision) or a tendency to self-induced hysteria (such as occurred at Loudun), the outcome was inevitable.

With the modern trend away from church dogma and towards a more open and questioning outlook it is not surprising that many people today look with a sceptical eye upon the visions of the saints. In doing so they make the same mistake as those who take all such things literally and without question. To use one of W. E. Butler's favourite idioms, 'they throw the baby out with the bathwater.'

We must look upon the true religious vision in the same way that we look upon the inspired hunch of the bio-chemist that results in a medical breakthrough. Or the intuitive leap made by an investigator who, when faced with several alternatives, unerringly picks the right one, or the inspiration of a writer, artist, or poet that strikes to the very core of the psyche. It is at such moments that the spirit, mind, and heart of a human being are fully and completely aligned with a creative force of immense power, and not just aligned but, far more importantly, the human channel is clear of the usual debris that blocks the way. This was the way we were intended to think all the time but against which we are continually erecting barriers, denying our inherent divinity and making ourselves slaves to centuries of wrong thinking.

The inmates of the medieval cloister were there for a variety of reasons: they had been 'promised' to the Church by their parents from birth; they had a genuine and true vocation to the religious life; they had experienced some kind of mental of physical trauma and had withdrawn from contact with the mass of humanity; they simply wanted a quiet life in which to study and work; or, like Bernadette of Lourdes, it seemed the best place to put someone you didn't quite know how to deal with in terms of belief. The stillness, the feeling of being apart from the rest of the world, the ordered way of life which although harsh and demanding in those times nevertheless offered security, all this often brought the mind to a point of introspection where the inner sight opened and the images, emotions and experiences that flooded through were coloured by the continually recurring symbols of the Church and its teachings. When this happened the human being caught up in the ecstasy of the moment became either a true visionary or a fanatic with 'a message'.

On rare occasions it was contagious and spread through the tightly enclosed community like wildfire causing everything from mass hysteria to outbreaks of self-inflicted pain, i.e. flagellation, starvation, and acts of penance that sometimes brought the penitent to the point of death, and on some occasions actually caused it. This usually brought about a visit from the bishop or the cardinal who diagnosed the cause – almost always a demonic possession of some kind – exorcized it and things calmed down again once the inmates felt themselves 'cleansed' of all those disturbing thoughts. Often such times became an opportunity to get even with a superior or cause harm in retaliation for imagined slights. One must remember that in such small and rigidly enclosed conditions every action, word, or gesture became important and was sometimes seen as constituting either dislike or favouritism. In such fertile soil enmity grows fast.

In 1633 the Ursuline convent in the French town of Loudun became the focus of such an outbreak resulting in the torture and death of a priest. Urbain Grandier was the confessor and priest to the convent and it seems fairly certain that he had taken one if not more of the nuns as his mistress(es). This was by no means an unusual occurrence; there are many instances of both convents and monasteries giving little more than lip-service to the law of celibacy as demanded by the Church. The full story has been set out in the book *The Devils of Loudun*, from which a film of the same name was made some years ago. Suffice to say that in what amounted to a fit of pique Sister Jeanne, the Mother Superior, together with several of her nuns accused Father Grandier of bewitching them. They exhibited all the usual signs of hysterical behaviour – convulsions, uncontrollable laughter, fits of breathlessness that left them gasping, screaming obscenities at all and sundry and what is coyly described as 'exaggerated erotic behaviour'. On top of this they described events in which they claimed that Grandier had seduced them and which were quite plainly sexual fantasies.

Although Grandier himself denied all this plus the claims that he was in league with the demon Asmodeus, Cardinal Richelieu commissioned a Church enquiry and as a result of its findings Grandier stood trial for the practice of witchcraft. There can be little doubt that the documents produced by the accusers were forgeries, and after many weeks of the most appalling torture, Grandier was burnt alive, having been carried to the stake because his legs and feet had been reduced to a mass of broken flesh and bone in an effort to make him 'confess'. The nuns were given penances and some were sent to other convents in the area, but the event remains as a classic case of mass hysteria caused in all probability by a surplus of sexual emotion in a group of women with little or no hope of releasing it except through fantasy and hysteria.

But not all religious fervour and emotion ends so tragically; in some cases the power so generated is channelled into works of insight that become shining paths guiding those that follow into the miraculous world of the visionary. One definition of ecstasy reads, 'A state of exaltation; excessive emotion, or rapture, a prophetic or poetic frenzy; a trancelike state of the nervous system in which the mind is completely absorbed by one idea, a state of mind often used to describe the experiences of medieval saints.'

On 28 March 1515 in the town of Avila in Castile there was born a baby girl who was to become one of the greatest mystics of the religious world. Though born of noble and wealthy parents the little girl grew up with an overwhelming vocation for the life of the cloister. In 1533 she entered the Carmelite convent of Avila and there as Teresa of Jesus she started her life as a nun. The burning fervour of her faith and the continued practice of asceticism soon brought about certain well-documented changes of consciousness, altered states we would now call them. During these ecstasies she saw and experienced a world within a world, or perhaps one should say a world outside a world.

It was during one of her visions that she beheld an angel who pierced her heart with a golden arrow bringing about a pain so sweet in its intensity, a conviction of 'belonging to Christ' so overwhelming that it was to carry her through the long difficult years ahead. It provided the strength and endurance needed to bring about the reforms that would divide the Calced and Discalced Carmelites and cause for a time her brush with the Inquisition and the imprisonment of her beloved friend and contemporary, St John of the Cross.

Teresa was not your average mystic, withdrawn and sour-faced. She had a lively wit and a caustic tongue that spared no one . . . even the Almighty. The story goes that she fell from her horse while trying to ford a flood-swollen river. Arriving on the bank soaking wet and cross she heard the voice of God saying, 'Thus do I test all those who would follow me', to which the sodden saint replied, 'Maybe that is why so many of them give up!' She loved life with a passion and lived it for her faith and for others. Almost single-handed she brought about the reform of the Carmelite rule and taught those who followed her with love as well as strictness.

In her autobiography she wrote of God as a person, not as some unattainable and totally unknowable spirit. In reading it one feels that this tiny woman was a valued friend of the Creator and knew Him well. She speaks in intimate terms of her visionary experiences, describing them and the physical sensations they brought about in terms one would more often come across in romantic literature than in the life-story of a saint. Her book *The Interior Castle*, called in Spanish *Las Moradas* or *The Mansions*, takes us into the realm of her inner world and describes what she sees and feels with such clarity that it seems one is with her all the time.

The book had its origin in one of her visions in which God showed her a crystal globe in the shape of a castle containing seven mansions or rooms, each one being enclosed by another. The seventh and innermost holds the place of the King of Glory where He sits enthroned. The nearer one got to the centre and the Godhead, the brighter the light grew. From this inner experience comes the description of a journey taken through each of the mansions, clues written for her sisters in the Carmelite Order for their instruction and guidance in prayer. The saint writes of her vision in simple terms such as would have been within the grasp of the least educated novice:

I began to think of the soul as if it were a castle made of a single diamond . . . in which there are many rooms, just as in Heaven there are many mansions. Now if we think carefully over this, sisters, the soul of the righteous man is nothing but a paradise in which, as God tells us, He takes

His delight. . . . What do you think a room will be like which is the delight of a King so mighty and so wise.

Such is the start of *The Interior Castle*. She goes on:

Let us now imagine that this castle, as I have said, contains many mansions, some above, others below, some at each side, and in the centre . . . is the chiefest . . . where the most secret things pass between God and the soul.

These are the words of someone who is fully conversant with the art of pathworking, in experiencing them and in building them for others. At one point in the narrative she apologizes, saying:

Now let us return to our beautiful castle and see how we may enter it. I seem to be talking nonsense for, if this castle is the soul there can clearly be no question of entering it, for we ourselves are the castle . . . You must understand there are many ways of 'being' in a place.

And so the reader is taken by the hand and gently led from mansion to mansion, all the time with the explanation and description going on in our ears. If these parts are extracted from the surrounding text and recorded or set down they can be made into one of the most beautiful pathworkings ever devised, and one that will take you, especially if you are a practising Christian, into a whole new dimension of your faith. It is impossible to give more than a passing glimpse of the richness of Teresa's work and the clearness of her visionary powers, but *The Interior Castle* should be read even if the Christian way is not yours for it contains a true visionary experience and one that transcends faith, tradition and creed and goes far beyond mere doctrine.

Her other major work, *The Way of Perfection*, is equally readable and enjoyable. In Chapter 16 she exclaims, 'Lord help us, that we should be hurt about some small point of honour. . . . I used to laugh at the things I heard in the world, and sometimes for my sins, in the religious Orders . . . we cry out . . . "Well I'm no saint" . . . I used to say that myself!' One can hear the self-deprecating chuckle down the centuries between the reader and the writer.

Where did this wealth of inner sight come from? Teresa was from a family not given to psychic visions and holding firm ideas about such things. This, remember, was Spain and an accusation of heresy could bring the rack and the stake even to those in a Religious Order. We must look back into her family history to see the answer. For much of the following I am indebted to Dr Deirdre Green of St David's University College.

The paternal side of the saint's family originated in Toledo. A city that had a large Jewish population, many of whom had converted to Christianity, and were known as *judeoconversos*. Her grandfather Juan Sanchez de Toledo had renounced his Jewish faith in 1485 and there is a record of this declaration made at the time. It is also possible that Teresa's mother was of Jewish descent and as the family structure of a Jewish home is something that persists even after conversion, her early life may have held some lingering fragments of Judaic teachings, perhaps in stories and little family habits that would have remained in the memory of the child years afterwards.

It was understandable given the religious and political climate that the family would strive to conceal its Jewish origins in any way it could. Quite literally it was a dangerous time for such *conversos*. In fact Teofanes Egido in his *The Historical Setting of St Teresa's Life* suggests that she had to fight hard to convince the Inquisition that the religious reforms she instituted in the Carmelite Order were not part of, or due to, her Jewish antecedents.

However, her ancestry becomes a crucial point when one goes more deeply into her writings. As Dr Green points out in her pamphlet *St Teresa of Avila and the Hekalot Mysticism*, her father 'carried over into his new religion certain instincts and practices acquired in a different . . . religious environment and . . . in turn would have created a domestic situation that affected his sons and daughters.' Gareth Davies in *St Teresa and the Jewish Question* (Trinity and All Saints, 1981) says of her that she shows a Judaic sense of the division of objects into 'clean' and 'unclean', and later adds the fact that the order to which she belonged through its direct connection with the Holy Land and Mount Carmel 'epitomized the Judaic element that had gone into the making of the Christian tradition'.

Given all this, it is hardly surprising that the account of her vision is described in terms very close to those of the Hekalot mysticism of the older Jewish culture. That she was a visionary and an ecstatic confirms it even more for there was a strong tradition of such gifted women in the Old Testament. The working, and the whole vision of the Interior Castle, show that deeply embedded within her subconscious mind Teresa must have had racial memories, memories that welled up in the ecstatic moments of her visions causing her to revert momentarily to the older and far more powerful symbolism - symbolism moreover that Jesus would have understood and known well. We will look further into the mysteries of the Hekalot later in the chapter but now we must pass to another visionary, the dear friend and contemporary of Teresa, the gentle, diminutive St John of the Cross.

In a quiet square in the walled city of Avila there stands a simple, unadorned statue of a man who could well be called God's Poet Laureate. Anyone, no matter which tradition they follow, should read at least some of the poems of this gifted man who spent a great part of his life imprisoned by his own kind for the 'sin' of disagreeing with them. When reading his poems you will find an almost pagan joyousness in them, a feeling, a longing, for the ultimate union with the Creative Force that engendered all life. Like Teresa, he was a true mystic, one whose inner self was genuinely transmuted as it rose through the levels of being, experiencing things we can only guess at, but always striving to bring back a faint echo of what had been revealed so that others might share it with him.

There are some people who transcend faiths, traditions and ways of belief, whose gift of inner sight is so strong and so pure that it speaks to all, even though it may be couched in the terminology of one particular faith. Such a one was the man born as Juan de Yepes, later to become Juan de la Cruz, St John of the Cross. His birthplace, Castile, is still called by its people, *Tierra de cantos y santos*, the land of song and saints, a name well deserved.

At 25 he met Teresa of Avila; it was the beginning of a deep and lasting friendship. The two had much in common, a love of God, a love of people, and a love of words. In later times St Teresa was to overshadow the little Carmelite friar, and even today in Avila there is more attention given to her, but very little to be seen of St John. A diligent search revealed only the one statue outside of those in the churches, and when Avila is mentioned it is still Teresa who comes to mind, yet in the end his was the purer voice, with the greater power to move the hearts of men. If Teresa wrote as a teacher, John wrote because he could not contain the power and the passion of the inward glories he had seen and heard. They poured out of him with the same golden fluidity that had marked the great bards centuries before. His life was one of hardship, imprisonment and interrogation, but through it all the secret world he held within offered peace, solace, and an escape.

Those new to his poems will find them strangely erotic coming from a man who had given his whole life to the Church. But in them there is the same power to transport others that typified the early Greek poets. If one can conceive of a Catholic Orpheus charming man, beast an ' bird with the power of song, then this is he. 'In order to arrive at that which thou knowest not', said John, 'thou must go by a way that thou knowest not.' He himself described a mystic as an *alma enamorada*, a soul totally in love with its Creator, and it is in such terms that he describes his own, mystical pathworkings which were to lead him to the highest spiritual levels and sustain him throughout his life.

Unless one has enough fluency to read his works in the original Spanish it is sometimes difficult to catch the finer feeling of the poems, but I recommend the Harvill Press edition, *Poems of St John of the Cross* translated by Roy Campbell (1972). This has the Spanish text on one side and the English translation on the other. It is only a selection and not a complete collection* of his works but it contains the best of them.

'The Dark Night of the Soul' is the best known of his works, and 'The Ascent of Mount Carmel', but in all of them you will find inner journeys of great power glowingly described and easily made into a pathworking for your own use. For those who follow a purely Christian path they offer an insight into the spiritual world of a remarkable man. In Chapter 2 I spoke of the theory of Dr Eugene D'Aquili that as the result of a neural 'lightning flash' striking through the mid-brain area, a transformation in a person can occur, usually in a spiritual context. Might it not be that in such mystics as Teresa of Avila, St John of the Cross, and Bernadette of Lourdes the sudden 'flash' clears the channels between the subconscious, the conscious, and the higher conscious selves so completely that they stay open on a permanent basis.

It could well be, though I do not expect everyone to agree with me, that the 'Lady' seen by Bernadette of Lourdes was an image of her own higher self projected from within during a state of high spiritual exaltation brought on by ill health, fever, and simple religious fervour; after all, the saint herself never claimed that the Lady was the Virgin Mary – everyone else assumed it to be so. The Divine Spark, or higher spiritual self, having never fully descended to the earth level could be classed as being without sin and therefore immaculate – though I can understand that such a statement might set a sleek black cat among many snowy-breasted pigeons!

St Ignatius of Loyola was born in or about 1491 in the small Spanish town from which he took his name. When he grew up he became a soldier and fought bravely in many battles. At the siege of Pamplona a cannonball ended his military career, breaking his leg so badly that it caused a permanent limp. During a long convalescence he read his way through *The Life of Christ* and many biographies of the saints. With a suddenness that took family and friends by surprise he renounced army life and went on a pilgrimage to the shrine of the Black Madonna at Monserrat. It is there that people still go to pray for a child, or for those

---

* For this, see *The Collected Works of St John of the Cross*, trans. by K. Kavanagh and D. Rodrigues (Nelson, 1966).

who have died during the year. She is in fact the Binah image of birth and death. Here in the mountains, far from the sound and fury of his former life, the soldier found peace of mind and heart, and here the Black Madonna came to him in visionary dreams as a result of which he entered the Church. During the years of study he put together the basis for a new system of religious training, and in 1528 in Paris he gathered around himself six companions of like mind. When they were ordained three years later the little group decided to raise a new Order, and in 1540 the Society of Jesus was formed. The leadership qualities of Loyola made him the obvious choice for Superior General as the head of the order was and still is called, a term which recalled his army life.

The Jesuits as they are most commonly known have a reputation even within the Church itself. That reputation has often brought them into conflict with other orders and even popes. In 1773 the order was suppressed by Clement XVI and not restored completely until 1814. They were and are a teaching and missionary order and are extremely good at what they do. Why then were they so disliked and why even today are they looked at askance by both laymen and priests?

The training of a Jesuit is peculiar to them; they are different in the way they dress and in the way they teach. A child taught by Jesuits will retain much of their way of thinking for the rest of his life. They are noted for their intelligence, scholarship, and wide scope of study. They are the most efficient of exorcists, and one of the finest minds of this century, Teilhard de Chardin, was a Jesuit. 'Minds like razors and tongues like hornets' tails', said W. E. Butler of them. Even in the last few years they have caused rumblings in the Vatican with their independence of thought and speech. Although they remain solidly Catholic in outlook and practice, many Jesuits are, as a result of their studies, well aware of such things as the Cabbala and the Mystery teachings of ancients. But it is their method of mind-training that places them above other orders, a method pioneered by the founder.

The Spiritual Exercises of St Ignatius de Loyola can be found in most large bookshops with a religious section. It is a slim booklet that belies its power. At first glance, dipping here and there, it is easy to be disappointed in the contents. You must remember that the exercises described are almost 400 years old and were meant only for the use of ordained priests or students in the seminary. But as a guide for Christian pathworkings they are excellent. However, a word of warning: the 'pictures' suggested are distinctly medieval and need a little judicious alteration. The suggestion that one should look upon the foulness and ugliness of one's body or regard it as an ulcerous and running sore is likely to horrify modern minds taught to care for and enjoy the strength and beauty of their bodies. But if you take the time to go through and change the obviously outmoded pieces you will also see that these little pathworkings must have been far ahead of their time, and if you know anything about the power of pathworkings you will also see that such practices must have greatly enhanced their powers of concentration. Here is the 'Composition of Place' clearly set out, not in a book on the occult but in a book used by priests in training for the Church. It seems there is little new under the sun!

While the study of the Cabbala is widespread among occultists, and much use is made of its mandala, The Tree of Life, very little is known of the much deeper and far more magically centred system of the Hekalot. But within its teachings one may find rituals, magical invocations, pathworkings and many other techniques that would be very familiar to the modern occultist. In the *Hermetic Journal* for Spring 1986 an article by Dr Deirdre Green explained the finer details as well as the far-reaching ramifications of this system.

In the space available I can give but a brief idea of the Hekalot, but it has a very definite place in both the book and in this particular chapter. The system was carefully guarded and dire warnings given about its use by the unprepared and the unworthy. One story concerned four rabbis who attempted the work but only one of whom survived. There are two main streams of this tradition, the Hekalot, which deals mainly with the visions and illuminations experienced within the Seven Palaces of Hekalot, and the Mysteries of the Merkavah, which in turn deal with those experiences of a like nature but do not necessarily refer to the said Palaces.

Time after time in the art and practice of pathworking we come across the use of seven levels, areas, palaces, towers, rooms, castles and even in the case of the Creation, seven Days. The Vision of Ezekiel seems to have been the foundation for much of the Hekalot system although in later times the idea of the seven palaces or chambers was added. Dr Green quotes in her article,

Many sages maintain that one who possesses all the necessary qualifications has methods through which he can gaze at the Merkavah and peek into the chambers on high. One first fasts for a certain number of days. He then places his head between his knees, and whispers into the ground many songs and praises known from tradition. From his innermost being and its chambers he will then perceive the Seven Chambers of the Hekalot. In his vision it will be as if he is entering one chamber after another, gazing at what is in each one.*

Here it is plainly suggested that there are chambers within the sage, that are quite separate from the Heavenly Chambers to which he desires entrance. The seven rooms within the body appear to be equated with those on the higher levels. 'As above, so below' in fact. Those who have read my earlier book *The Ritual Magic Workbook* will also note the body position in which the sage is said to sit - namely with his 'head between his knees', a position often favoured by Jewish prophets and for the reasons set out in the book.

Dr Green goes on to say, 'The Hekalot initiate does not see the Seven Palaces as something exterior to the self but rather with the power of inner vision.' We are speaking here of pathworking pure and simple and what is more, pathworkings very far back in time. Another example of antiquity, and the high regard in which such practices were held.

When the spiritual ascent begins, the traveller encounters a Gate at the entrance to each Palace that is guarded by angels and before entry is granted certain seals, signs and passwords are required. Modern ritual magic has an ascent that is very similar, rising through the levels and making oneself known to their Guardians before proceeding further.

Each Palace would have triggered off specific mental and spiritual changes in the one attempting the journey until the sixth Palace was reached, and this would appear to have been the most difficult to enter. In her important and absorbing article Dr Green quotes from the 'Hekalot Rabbi' (Great Book of Palaces) in detail explaining the Inner Journey and some of the instructions.

The whole pathworking is vivid, full of beautifully descriptive passages and well worth reading in its entirety. For those following the Cabbala it will give a new dimension to their work, offering new information of which they may have been unaware.

It is not surprising with her Jewish ancestry that St Teresa would have chosen to describe the Interior Castle in almost the exact terms of the Hekalot Palaces. Besides drawing on her own subconscious family memories, the mental and spiritual link of the Carmelite Order itself, stemming as it did from Judaic sources, would have welled up in her at the moment of her ecstatic vision. Nothing is ever really lost, but is held safely within the world memory and can be recalled through meditation and through pathworkings.

* Hai Gadn (938–1038), quoted in A. Kaplan, *Meditation and Kabbalah* (Weiser, 1982).

The Mysteries of the Merkavah or Chariot also pertain in the first instance to the Vision of Ezekiel, and it is curious that many rabbis speak of 'descending' into the Merkavah rather than 'ascending'. Kaplan says of this: 'One who gazes on the Merkavah must first ascend to the highest level which is the place of Light. It is here that he receives the influx of insight. Only then can he descend and look into the Merkavah.' The Chariot is often referred to as a Throne, and we may theorize that this may well have a connection with the mysterious 'Mercy Seat or Throne' that surmounts the Ark of the Lord in the Old Testament.

Students working in my own school of the Servants of the Light will recognize the idea of working through the chambers of a castle as being part of their own course work, and indeed the SOL is far from being the only school that uses such a method. I recommend Aryeh Kaplan's book for it offers a detailed and very clear insight into this area of Jewish mysticism and a chance to work on a *modified* ascent to the Seven Palaces themselves. You will also find traces of the Merkavah wisdom in the Revelation of St John and in the Acts of John in the Apocrypha.

Where else in the biblical tradition can we find evidence of the mental journey or pathworking? You will find them everywhere, in the visions of the Prophets, in the calling of the child Samuel in the middle of the night. In the stories of Elijah and Elisha, and above all in the Psalms of David and the mysterious Song of Solomon which has yet to be fully understood but which almost certainly contains a visionary pathworking and perhaps a full ritual.

But it is to the Psalms that we turn next. For the young David with his harp is surely the biblical equivalent of the Celtic bard, singing his songs of praise and joy and transporting those who listened to him including Saul the King. Though not all of them can be modified into pathworkings, there are others that lend themselves well to the building of guided imagery. Psalm 43 is a short one but one that can be built into a working quite easily. On reading it through we understand that the singer is asking for strength in the face of adversity. From this we can build a working using the imagery of the words.

PSALM 43

You stand upon a green meadow looking up at a temple of white stone set upon a hill. Behind you stormclouds are gathering and the wind blows cold. Before the storm ride a host of chariots and fighting men. They are your enemies, but you are weary and have no strength left in you.

Standing with your arms raised you call out to your God saying 'What have I done wrong that these people come against me? Thou alone art the judge of my actions and my words. Thou alone art my strength and my safety. Send me thy help and thy light of truth that I may be saved, if this be thy will.'

From the temple on the hill come two beings of light. They descend and you see that they hold swords of flame in their hands. Taking you by the hand they lead you up the steep path to the top of the hill and there you see the hill is surrounded by those that judge you unfairly, yet now there rises within you a new strength and a joy that your prayer has been answered. No longer do you fear those below, or even hate them, you can see with the eyes of the spirit and know that they fear you and that this is why they seek you out to destroy you.

You enter the temple and stand before the altar with its burning light, and there on the altar steps is a harp of gold, decorated with precious stones. You pick it up and try the strings; they respond with a sweetness of tone you have never heard before. You sit before the altar and sing in praise of the One who has delivered you: 'Be not cast down my soul, be joyful and of good heart, have hope in God for it is He who gives health and strength to thee.'

Still singing you go from the temple and accompanied by the angels of light you descend the hill. The chariots give way before you, and the men bow down before the brightness that goes with you. You pass through the serried ranks and on towards the distant city. No longer are there clouds and wind, the sun shines down as you stride forward. Gradually the angels fade and return to their vigil on the hill, but you go forward and behind you come those who would have slain you but who now follow you, won over by the strength and light that emanates from you. Leading them you pass over the plain and enter the city in triumph.

It is essential that you read the psalm many times and understand what the singer is trying to express, then write the working to encompass the meaning using as much of the original words as possible. The 23rd Psalm can be made into a beautiful pathworking that will act as a psychic protection when sleeping in a strange place.

Those who work and study in the alchemical area of the occult will find a ready-made pathworking in the description of the Chymical Marriage of Christian Rosencreutz. Again you will find seven levels of ascent, learning and wisdom, each of which offers a specific symbolism that in turn will result in images presenting themselves to you in a spontaneous manner. Take careful note of them and research them afterwards for the pathworking is far from being just a pretty walk through the inner levels, it is a method of reaching down through your conscious mind into the subconscious and releasing the hidden and forgotten wisdom of your many lives until now, and up through the spiritual levels to your higher consciousness, riding the Chariot of Thought to the Crystal Palaces of the Spirit.

CHAPTER NINE

Sex, Healing and the Public

We all need to fantasize at times and anyone who says they never do anything of the kind is simply not facing up to the fact. There are some who feel that such behaviour is a waste of time, time that could and should be spent more profitably. But there is deep within all of us a need to dream and without our dreams we become depressed and morose. We need to build our inner landscapes according to the need of the moment, and to experience within those landscapes the kind of relationships that we lack in real life. The danger comes when we elect to stay in the inner world and forget the outer world of our birth. We tend to make black jokes about the number of men who think they are Napoleon or Julius Caesar, or the women who imagine they are Cleopatra but we forget that, for them, this is an escape into an environment that gives them something they cannot have in this world.

There is nothing wrong in indulging in fantasy when we feel a need to be loved, respected, looked up to, admired or envied. Why else is there such a following for Dallas and Dynasty and similar 'soaps' if not to provide a scenario for the millions who use the characters as alter egos for their day-dreams. For the fans each episode provides grist for the mill of their inner fantasies, acted out in the secret depths of the mind. I defy anyone to say they have never imagined what it would like to be James T. Kirk of the Starship *Enterprise*, or to walk down the curving staircase of the Carrington house of the Dynasty series dressed in a one-off designer dress, wrapped in sables (or not as your conscience dictates) and wearing half a million in diamonds and emeralds on your person. Very few of us will ever be in a position where we are the envy of others; even fewer will live in the world of the rich and the beautiful and, although it has been rightly said that money, power, beauty and position are not everything, there is nothing wrong with slipping back into the inner world and indulging in the game of 'What if . . .'

A drink in the ubiquitous English pub, Greek taverna, Spanish cantina or New York bar will soon reveal one of the favourite dreams especially of the male sex. You could call it the 'How I would run the country if I were in power' day-dream. We all feel we could set the entire world to rights if given a free hand. Thank God few of us are given that power, for the average person is thinking of what he/she would like the ideal world to be like, and not what others, who might hold an opposite view, would want to see. Bias is in all of us. I once knew a young girl who stated with frightening intensity that in her opinion the entire world should turn Catholic. When I asked her about those who had no wish to give up their own faith, her reply was a conversation stopper: 'Then they should be whipped until they do', and she meant it. We cannot have exactly what we want, except in that solipsistic universe we hold within ourselves, the source of all our day-dreams and fantasies.

We all find pleasure in anticipating certain events – birthdays, parties, holidays to a new and potentially exciting location or the return to an old and favourite one, a wedding, an anniversary, our first date, seeing a loved one after a period of separation. All these things we go over again and again in our minds, unconsciously visualizing them and constantly changing the imagined conversation or action of the coming experience. Is it any wonder then that we also take great pleasure in imagining experiences that have no basis in reality, and in all probability never will have? Mankind is a creature who has learned to create within himself the ability to dream not only when he is asleep but also when he is awake, thereby doubling the value of his dreamworld. As he progressed in intelligence and knowledge he learned to put his dreams to profitable use in the art of healing, precognition, and in the training of the mind. Then, when science overcame the intuitive processes the old ways were partly forgotten, but never entirely; the old knowledge persisted and surfaced in those children who grew into the poets, artists and writers, and men and women of power and far-seeing abilities. Such people have changed the course of history and their childhood dreams played a great part in the way their adult lives were lived.

Day-dreaming gives us a chance to look at every side of a situation and to make a choice of action. You may call it looking ahead, if that sounds better to you than day-dreaming, but it means exactly the same thing. If you can train yourself to use the untapped power of your imagination you can change your working life. If you can expand it to include your leisure time you can increase your ability to relax and avoid stress. If you learn to train it, curb it and make it a tool to be used to its fullest extent, some of those day-dreams may well come true, for thought is of itself creative.

We have seen that the daydream and the more sophisticated pathworking have much in common and, once the basic differences between them are grasped, they can be used in conjunction for many different purposes. The daydream can be taken and enlarged, more finely tuned and aimed at certain areas of our lives for a variety of uses. One of its greatest uses is that of the alleviation of loneliness, although in this area there is also the greatest danger of it becoming an obsession. The feeling of being alone can come in many forms. It happens to people who live their lives in the very middle of a large, noisy and loving family. There can be the odd one out, the one who doesn't seem to fit, the quiet one, the studious one, the one who never seems to make friends at school.

This type learns early the value of the inner world. I know from experience the feeling of standing alone in a playground, feeling totally apart from what was going on all around me. I suppose one could say it was in the family. My father, one of three brothers, was and still is completely different to his siblings. He too learned to be alone in his head. My mother, the middle child of five, learned the same hard lesson, and used the same escape. As an only child and one whose clairvoyant faculties opened up at a very early age and never closed down even during adolescence, I too found the Gateway to the Land of the Mind and learned to open it wide. But there was a difference. It evoked in me a surge of recognition, memories of times and friends long past. From that moment I knew I would never be alone again, that I could use this Key to rejoin old friends and revisit old haunts. But for those who do not learn of the Gateway until later in life, growing up can be a hard time. Parents and teachers alike can help such a child to adjust by encouraging them to use their creative talents, thus using the inner eye and the mind in conjunction. This will inevitably lead them to the Gateway of their inner world.

Pathworking can also be used as a means of profitably passing time on long journeys. I travel several thousands of miles each year and on long journeys I use pathworkings as a means of passing the time and also of preparing the kind of atmosphere I wish to build up when I begin the workshop, seminar or whatever kind of teaching work I am going to offer. This means I arrive with a programme that is flexible and can adapt to any type of audience or group of people. I seldom get more than the odd flutter of nerves because I have already given the lecture or taken the worshop many times and coped with as many different and unforeseeable happenings as I could think of, within the pathworking. This done I then settle back and enjoy more leisurely day-dreams for the rest of the flight. Delays at airports offer another opportunity and I often use them to search out 'storylines' for future pathworkings for students, jotting down themes and making notes of any points that might need special care when writing them out.

Visiting new places and areas of interest can often stimulate the mind to adapt the surroundings and any local legends or beliefs into workings that can tune the subconscious more finely towards certain god-forms or traditions. I said earlier in this book that observation was vital to the deeper understanding and use of pathworkings and this means cultivating an alert state of mind at all times so that anything that can be used is seized upon and stored away.

But there are other more secret, less known and understood areas of our lives where these inner journeys and experiences can help to keep loneliness and depression at bay. It is only in the last few years that we have begun to understand the complexity of human sexuality, to admit, even to ourselves, that sex is a great deal more than simply going to bed with someone. Out of this new awareness has come the realization that almost everyone, including those most happily married and secure in the love they share with their partner, has sexual fantasies in which they indulge even in the most intimate moments with their lovers, husbands, and wives.

Those who are young, attractive, or who have partners with whom they enjoy a full and rewarding sex-life cannot possibly know the despair, loneliness, and sexual frustration of those not so fortunate. The newly widowed man or woman has to cope with not just the loss of a companion, a friend and dear helpmate, but the loss also of their sexual activity. A woman still young suddenly left without her partner will have many friends, relatives and other sources of help and comfort with regard to insurance, mortgages, coping with the grief of the children as well as her own. But when the grief has died down a little, when the interrupted patterns of life are slowly rebuilding themselves, then comes the loneliness and the realization that the closeness and the wonder of making love has also been taken from them. It is not just younger people that suffer in this way. All too often it is taken for granted that because someone is in their sixties or even older, sexual desire is already dead or dying and they will not miss making love. Think again, people are sexually active for a great deal longer than is generally thought. Both men and women can and do enjoy sex up to and even beyond their seventies and well into their eighties. Consider the remarks made by one gentleman of 82: 'I can still look and enjoy the looking even if I can't always do anything about it', and, 'I still have a few ambitions left . . . one of which

is to die in the arms of a young woman.' You have to admire the cheek
of it if nothing else!

What about the man or woman who for any number of reasons finds
it difficult to make the kind of friendship that can lead to the enjoyment
of making love? They may have less than pleasing features effectively
disguising the loving nature beneath. They may not have the slim figure
demanded by today's ideal of beauty, yet they too have love to give. They
may be painfully shy, or handicapped in some way; that does not mean
they are also devoid of the usual male and female urges that rise up and
demand to be fulfilled.

Every summer there come to Jersey several groups of handicapped
men and women. The visits are regular and because it is a small island
one gets to recognize some of them as they appear year after year. I have
watched one young man in particular. He is now probably somewhere
in his late twenties, a thalidomide baby, he has neither arms nor legs,
just small travesties of hands and feet growing directly from the body.
Every summer he is pushed along the esplanade in his chair by those
who give him a lot of care and attention, and he is passed on every side
by young girls in minute bikinis and young men with graceful athletic
bodies. Those who devote their lives to looking after him and those like
him, do they never stop to think of the cruelty such trips inflict? I have
seen him cry tears he could not wipe away when a young girl offered
him an ice-cream, patiently holding it to his lips, a young girl in a swimsuit
who, but for the accident of birth, he might have chatted up and taken
out, started up a holiday romance with, maybe fallen in love with and
married. The young girl was startled and embarrassed when her kindly
gesture, along with her revealing swimsuit, brought about the inevitable
male erection that he could do nothing to hide. But he was only human,
his body though cruelly deformed was reacting in a typically male fashion.
This man and others like him have to rely on the sexual fantasy for their
relief and perhaps, if they are lucky, on the help of an understanding
nurse. Does that shock you? Why? Did you think such people have no
sexual feelings, that it was not in them to be sexually aroused?

There are those who would have you believe that the sexual fantasy
is something perverted and abnormal, whereas the truth is that it is as
normal as breathing in and out, and just as vital to life. Of course, like
anything else, it can be perverted by human beings, but of itself it is
normal and healthy and, if there is complete trust between lovers, it
can be used as an extension of their love-making. Neither is it a new
invention; it has its roots in the ancient world as does much of occult
teaching and training. In the old Mystery religions sex was considered

a vital part of the worship of the Divine. It was God-given and therefore respected both for the creation of new life that it afforded and the pleasure it gave. When the world was younger, taking pleasure in making love was not considered to be a sin, or dirty, nor were its gifts either of children or pleasure denied to the priesthood. Certain times and certain rituals demanded celibacy for a time, but not permanently. Apart from a normal family life there were some rituals that required the enacting of the act of love as part of the ritual itself. This might seem shocking to some people now but then it was as normal as a celebration of Harvest Festival is to us. Nor was it undertaken for personal pleasure but was exactly what it implied, the union of two god-forms, one male and one female, according to the ancient texts. Such a ritual required that the couple taking part would spend many hours meditating upon the god or goddess they would represent and thinking, or pathworking, themselves into the role.

When they came together all thought of pleasure between them was quite secondary to the bringing in of power, the particular form of power accorded to the deities being represented. Though, as one ancient papyrus states in rather quaint fashion, 'When the gods have departed [the sexual climax being the portion of the rite offered to the gods], they that remain may take the remainder of the feast.' Rather neatly and delicately put.

For those without a partner, combining the sexual fantasy with a pathworking offers some comfort at least. Of course, it is not as satisfying as actually having someone to hold close, but it is a lot better than tossing and turning and being unable to sleep because you are so full of pent-up sexual energy that you will not, or feel you cannot, let out. By now some people will be getting ready to throw this book into the wastepaper basket. Why? Because we are actually talking about – let us lower our voices – masturbation! A few pages ago I said that anyone who says they have never had a sexual fantasy needs to face up to the facts of life. I'm saying exactly the same thing about masturbation. Tell me you have never done it and produce a sworn statement signed by the bishop of the diocese to that effect and I might, I just might, believe you. There may, indeed, be the odd one or two who never have.

The old tales of 'going blind, going mad, and growing hair on the palms of your hands' have been given the thumbs down. If they were true the human race would by now be nine-tenths myopic, suffering from a variety of mental ailments and much given to the use of razors! As a practice it was, is and always will be, prevalent in the most unlikely places as well as the most likely. Any psychologist will tell you that it is both normal and healthy to use this form of sexual relief when and if the occasion needs it. Even those with a seemingly full emotional life will need this kind of stimulation at times, but it is always tied into the sexual fantasy, for one will strengthen the other. Sexual imagery is a very private imagery and one that can only be shared with a partner one fully trusts. Nancy Friday is an American journalist who stood the world of sexual therapy on its head in 1975 with a book called *My Secret Garden*. She placed adverts in both American and English papers asking to hear from women of all ages and social groups about their secret erotic fantasies. The result, thousands upon thousands of letters from which she interviewed the authors of four hundred. The book that came out of those interviews has been described as a pioneering study of female sexuality. Until then few men had known or even cared that their wives and lovers were indulging in a mental fantasy before, during and even after making love. Not surprisingly, few of them took it as a compliment for it began to show up their shortcomings as lovers and providers of women's sexual pleasure.

In her preface to the book Nancy Friday writes, 'For the first time in our history women are trying to discover what it is they have to share with other women.' She goes on to say that the most often reiterated phrase is, 'I thought I must be some sort of freak for having such sexually *wrong* ideas [my italics]. Now I feel I can accept myself, thank God I am not alone.' With the publication of this book and those that followed, *My Mother, My Self,* and *Men in Love,* Ms Friday began to open up the realms of the sexual fantasy and proved to a stunned society that they were all doing the same thing, and they had all been thinking that they were indulging in some terrible perversion. If ever a Tarot card came to life, here is the Devil of the Major Arcana: illusion and the chains of self inflicted shame where there was nothing of which to be ashamed. There are bound to be those who will be put off by her revelations, who will denounce them as crude and obscene, but what is the definition of obscene? 'Offensive to delicate feelings', says one dictionary. Well, if your feelings are that delicate no doubt you will go on being offended even by the sight of a couple of sparrows happily celebrating spring in the time-honoured fashion. However, you have no right to object to what other people see as something that is both natural and beautiful. We still have a long way to go before we can finally shake off the medieval view of sex and woman as the twin evils, a viewpoint forced on mankind by the churchmen of the time, though it did not stop several eminent popes from indulging in both.

Some people, of either sex, find no trouble at all in producing their own mental fantasy for sexual relief, others need an outside stimulation,

either pictures or books. Men tend to go for the girlie magazines that
so infuriate the militant women's-libbers. Women go for the written word,
the so-called romantic novel which is used as the basis for the
fantasy/daydream/pathworking. Strange as it may seem in this age of
the newly Liberated Woman, sales of the romantic novel have increased
tremendously. It is a strange fact that the advent of Women's Lib has
coincided with what has been called the Mills & Boon Phenomenon.
This publishing firm has been churning out the romantic novel at a
steady pace for many years but, in the last three or four, their sales have
virtually gone through the roof. They have one of the most up-to-date
printing plants in the UK where the raw product goes in at one end
and the packaged books emerge at the other. They have almost cornered
the market in this type of book and I have seen them in airport bookshops
and supermarket stores all over the world and in an amazing variety
of languages. Apart from their modern novels they also publish a series
called Masquerade which caters for those with a taste for the historical
romantic novel. Some time ago a third imprint called Temptations was
introduced to combat two newcomers to the market, Silhouette Desire
and Silhouette Special Edition. These last are imports and most of their
settings are American, and their introductory advertisements offered a
'newer more enticingly sensual storyline'. In short, they were offering
what amounted to a neatly wrapped ready-made female fantasy-cum-
pathworking.

In the early days there were strict rules laid down for M & B writers:
no explicit detail, no sex before marriage, no adultery unless by the 'scarlet
woman' of the plot, and no outlining of the hero's physical charms beyond
the bounds of what then constituted decency. The storylines of today
are very different. They offer a far more detailed description of both
the hero and heroine in the physical sense and, even more so, in the
sexual sense. Every month the three major imprints publish some sixteen
new titles between them and the shops sell out within days and are asking
for new deliveries.

What makes them so popular at a time when women are being urged
to seek their freedom, to spread their wings outside the traditional duties
of home and family? Quite simply, they provide an escape into the inner
world of the mind for those women who, deep down, do not want to
be free from that traditional image. When I became aware of this other
side of the coin, I looked around, asked questions, made enquiries and
came face to face with the fact that not every woman wants to be liberated,
that a great many of them simply want to be wives and mothers and
no amount of banner-waving and rallies will change them. We come

back to something I said earlier in this chapter: 'We all feel we could set the world to rights if given a free hand.' I also said there is bias in all of us and what is right for some is not right for all. There is also the fact that the M & B's are strangely popular even among the banner-waving sorority.

It so happens that the SOL school of which I am the Director of Studies had, and still has, some authors of romantic novels working through its curriculum. Two years ago, when this book was taking a vague shape in my mind, I queried my theories with them and asked them bluntly why their books sold – and remember, some M & B authors are making something in the region of £25/30,000 a year and some a good deal more. At that time I was inclined to look on such books with a jaundiced eye and not a little contempt until one author in particular, a lady well-trained in the occult arts and fully aware of the use and importance of pathworking, put me in my place.

She explained how she saw the romantic novel and how she used her own occult training to weave pathworkings for women. Inner journeys that offered a Gateway to another world where, for a little while at least, they could forget the drabness of everyday life and, like Cinderella, experience a very different environment. Just like the fairy-tale character, they too had to return to reality but they returned refreshed and ready to take up the chores of home and family again.

Consider the wife who has little time for herself and whose husband has perhaps slid into the dullness of routine, or perhaps he drinks, or is indifferent to her after many years of marriage. She may be past her youth, her prettiness and her figure lost over the years. She may look back and long to be young again, and may even indulge in the day-dream of . . . what it would have been like if I had married James instead of Richard . . . The repetitive routine of housework and cooking can wear one down. But the odd hour or so can be snatched to sit with one's feet up and a cup of tea, and the newest M & B paperback. For a few hours she is no longer a size twenty with middle-aged spread and greying hair. She is 22, a slender size ten, a tender young virgin playing out the written drama, experiencing every kiss and caress with the heroine and, for a while, the outside world ceases to exist. It gives her back her youth and beauty, for they are still within her, deep inside that inner world of the mind and ready to come alive again at her call.

When I came to write this book I looked at the women who bought this kind of book and began to see that I was making a judgment I had no right to make, that such books filled a need in them, even if it bored me to tears. In short, I was biased and had fallen into the trap of thinking I knew what was best for people other than myself. The final rap on the knuckles came when, on a flight to Sweden, I sat beside an elderly couple. He spent most of the time dozing and reading his paper, she had a half-read M & B novel. She was totally wrapped up in it, occasionally smiling to herself or biting her lip, once even clenching her fist as if wanting to hit the infuriating hero. At last she finished and with a deep sigh closed the book and lay back, turning her head to her husband who smiled at her indulgently and asked if she had enjoyed her book. 'Oh yes,' she said, 'it took me back to when we were just married. He was *so* like you!' Her husband roared with laughter and they spent the last half hour of the flight remembering the early days of their marriage.

That woman had lived for a short while between the pages and, far from committing mental adultery (one of the accusations hurled against the romantic novel), she had seen her own husband in the role of the hero. Together they had been young again in her mind. The books may not be your taste, or mine, but allow others to know what they need and enjoy. You may have the ability to weave your own romantic fantasies, others need help.

What other areas can use the pathworking/day-dream in a positive way? Self-healing for one. We all take our bodies for granted and rarely, if ever, accord them our full attention, yet they serve us faithfully for many years and take the full brunt of the wear and tear of simply living from day to day.

There are many ways in which we can use the power of inner journeys to help our bodies as well as our minds. They can help us to start out each morning feeling ready to cope with the day. They can heal cuts and bruises very quickly. They can relieve aches and pains and even overcome travel sickness. The first thing is to allow your body to have its own existence, that is to say, think of it as something that you and your mind use every day and and which has its own little ways and likes and dislikes. The first lesson to learn is this: *you are not your body*. You are something quite different, your body is the 'car' you use to get around in, experience life with, and generally live in, through, and with. It is something you 'put on' in the morning when you wake up, and 'take off' at night when you sleep, always keeping in mind there is a resident caretaker looking after it when you are elsewhere.

Given a brand new car fitted with the ultimate in computers, that can run more or less efficiently for three score years and ten without too much trouble, and you would take great care of it. A body has all that and more and we fling it around with no thought for its welfare.

We overfeed it, tank it up with alcohol, tan it in the sun, take it up mountains and freeze it, hurl it around in jet planes and confuse its mechanisms, push it to its limits in every possible way and then complain when it wears out!

Make a friend of your body by pathworking your way through it once in a while. Once a day just before you leap out of bed is ideal. If not then, how about Sunday morning during the extra lay in time you always allow yourself. Imagine that your body is a large and very busy factory, which it is, and wander through it. See each organ as a different department rather than as it is physically. See the foreman in charge and ask if everything is going as it should and if there are any complaints. If there are, look into it because you are tapping into your subconscious mind and it will certainly know if anything is not going as it should. If there appears to be a 'complaint' keep a look-out for physical symptoms for the next few days. Once your subconscious mind realizes it can get through to you via your walkabout it will start to rely on that to pass you information that may well help you to prevent trouble later on.

With a deep cut or wound of any kind you can use the same inner journey. Imagine yourself in the brain control room and send out the Red Alert signal requiring antibodies and rebuilding cells to report to the scene of the accident. Children, in particular, will play this game with great willingness and it will also help to keep their minds off any pain there may be until the natural painkillers, provided by the brain chemicals, can start to work. We are often told, usually by somebody who isn't in pain themselves, that 'it is all in the mind.' Well, the pain is real enough, but the cure for it may well be in the mind if you have a well-trained imagination.

It has been proven that if you can distract your attention from whatever part of your body is giving trouble, you can overcome quite a considerable amount of pain and bypass other things like travel sickness. A story often told describes how a traveller laid low by a violent attack of seasickness was distracted by the conversation of two stewards outside his cabin door. Their gossip was so interesting that he forgot how bad he felt; the only trouble was that as soon as they finished their talk and moved away, the seasickness returned, but the mind had been fooled very effectively by the distraction.

When taking your stroll around the body, make certain that it is done along what might be called Disney lines. See each department being busy and effective, and chat to the head of that department, then move on. In this way make a quick tour of your physical self at least once a week. This in itself will start to make you more aware of your body on the inside rather than the outside. It will also make you aware of each organ and its locality, so that if you have to make a visit to the doctor you can say to him, 'The pain is just here, about one and a half inches in and an inch to the right.' Pinpointing pain is very difficult because pain refers from one place to another: a painful foot can mean a displaced vertebra, and so on.

Relaxation is something people can find difficult but I was taught a simple trick that works for me every time. I lie down and after a few minutes I imagine my tension to be in the form of a dirty brown liquid filling up my entire body. It feels horrid and downright uncomfortable, but at the end of each thumb and big toe I imagine a large cork and when these are removed the liquid tension spills out and drains away. I can feel it leaving my body nicely limp and relaxed and I am able to rest awhile before getting up again (remembering to replace the corks!). The more vividly you can imagine it, the easier the relaxation will be.

You can learn to cope with each new day in a similar manner. Just before you get up, lie quietly with your eyes closed. Quickly run through your day imagining what you have to do and who you have to meet, etc. Decide what is the most important asset you will need. Is it alertness or maybe cheerfulness, patience, astuteness at a board meeting? Maybe you feel you need extra energy or, if it is a cold day, simply some inner warmth. Once you have decided to start this simple inner journey, imagine there is on the inside of your wardrobe another door leading into a secret room. In this room there is another wardrobe, but this one contains some very special clothes. When you open the door a multi-coloured light streams out from it. Inside you can see a selection of things that look like all-in-one body stockings. They are in every possible shade and colour and each one shines and ripples with the power of that colour. If you need courage or energy, choose a bright scarlet; business acumen, what about blue or perhaps a clear yellow. Calmness: go for green; harmony, a warm amber or deep rose. If you have many decisions to make, go for a deep indigo or violet. Make a list of colours and write beside each one the emotion, feeling, attribute or energy you think it represents. Remember, colours mean different things to different people so *your* feelings on the matter are the only ones that will work.

When you have selected a colour, take out the matching garment and put it on, looking in the mirror to see how it glows, then return to your room. Now you can get up, but keep thinking about the colour you are wearing beneath your everyday clothes and let it percolate through into your body, your work and your whole day. Keep referring back in your mind at odd moments and make yourself conscious of the living colour you are wearing beneath the business suit or the neat office dress or uniform. There is a lot you can find out for yourself about pathworkings simply by doing them and, later on, I will tell you how to write them, but, when you are new to the whole idea, you should rely in the first instance on workings that have been written by others. What kind of people write and use pathworkings? In Chapters 6 and 7 we spoke of the ancient bards and their power to create images in the minds of others, and of the modern writers who do much the same thing, but do we have today the equivalent of the bards? Yes we do, although they no longer wear the many-coloured cloak and travel with a harpist from hall to hall but, yes, there are still the Tellers of Tales.

Around the peat fires of the Irish hearths, if you are lucky you may still hear the Seanachai telling his tales of the Sidhe and the Tuatha de Danaan, wringing your heart as he speaks of Deirdre of the Sorrows and her love for Diarmuid. True, there is only a handful left but they manage to keep alive the ancient traditions. In the Western Isles of Scotland they keep up the tradition of story-telling and the old tales are told in the long winter nights to regale the young people. They are stories of Kelpies and Silkies and the hearth Brownies. The mother who tells her child a bedtime story, the teacher recounting the Battle of the Nile in a history lesson, the whispered ghost stories shared around the fire at Hallowe'en, all are descendants of the bard, the troubadour and the jongleur.

The pathworking has a part to play in the new Age of Aquarius for it keeps alive the old ways in new forms. It still takes hold of the mind of those who listen and spins them into another world full of impossible delights. In many ways the television has become, for us, the modern-day Seanachai with its children's programmes that aim at mixing stories and games and, if that is the only way the telling of tales is going to survive, we had better make sure that those tales include some of the oldest and the best-known, and that they include some of the special ones that turn the mind inwards to the Land of Dreams and lead it along strange and wonderful paths.

It would be wrong to think that pathworking consists merely of one person telling a story and the rest listening. To tell a tale well requires great skill and so does the writing of special kinds of pathworking, one that teaches as it entertains, one that touches the heart and makes the tears flow, for when the emotions are touched the mind and heart are lifted up towards the spirit and the three become one as they were meant to be from the beginning. To write you must feel, to speak you must have seen, but to understand you must listen to what the teller is *not* saying out loud. Today we read and listen to ancient tales still, but in a thousand years who will listen to our tales and wonder at their power? We must learn to spin the silver word with as much magic as did the bards of old and enclose within them the truths we have sought out and found for ourselves. Then and only then can we match the skill and power of the Old Ones.

For centuries the power of the pathworking has been known and kept a secret from all but the most promising of students. There was a genuine concern that if given out to all and sundry it would either lose its ancient power or the power would be recognized for what it was and used for gain. That will always be a possibility because there is an innate power locked away in every single pathworking that could cause trouble if it were unleashed but, despite all I have written about them both in this book and elsewhere, there remains untold the innermost secret of the pathworking. It cannot be passed on because there is no way to tell it, no words to describe it or ways to enable it to be understood by another person. It comes of its own accord to the person who is ready for it. Its realization is tantamount to a lightning bolt, but once hit with that realization you *know* the secret of the pathworking powers. But of course whether you can use them is another matter.

Since the technique has become more widely known, pathworking has tended to become in unskilled hands merely a gentle stimulation of the senses, a quiet walk in the meadows of the mind, or by contrast an indulgence in glamour that will lead one in circles. Used and taught in the correct way it can stimulate the mind and help it make the link between the subconscious, conscious and superconscious minds of the student and bring about an intuitive understanding of the hidden kernel of wisdom. The pathworking by its very nature can protect itself, for if by chance someone hits the right button, they will either recognize it for what it is or they will never do another pathworking in their lives. Always remember there is a subtle difference between a pathworking, a day-dream and a fantasy.

In the last seven or eight years pathworking has come into its own; that is to say it has been made public in so much as it is now talked about and written about, and public pathworkings are fairly commonplace. If there is any blame in this it will probably be laid at my door.

In 1980 I decided to do a public pathworking and got some surprised – and a few horrified – looks. All those people, and a good part of them not knowing a thing about the occult, said it would be dangerous. All this went into one ear and out the other for I was determined to do it.

But even I was not prepared for the enthusiasm with which it was received. I did more of them and they began to be a feature of the SOL conferences and I received requests to conduct them at other meetings and Festivals. In 1983 I went one better and devised a dramatized pathworking called The Journey of the Fool.* This was performed at Caxton Hall to around 250 people as the culmination of the SOL Conference that year. It had a number of advantages, not the least of which was the fact that I was not required to speak the whole thing. From something a little over twenty minutes it now took up about an hour and its impact was quite incredible. The following year when the Conference moved to Manning Hall the idea of the dramatized pathworking was firmly embedded in the pattern of conference events.

Other teachers in the occult world had almost simultaneously come to the same conclusion, that it was time the art of pathworking was given to those in the 'outer court'. Gareth Knight used pathworkings with telling effect in the series of lecture weekends conducted at Hawkwood College in Gloucestershire. At times the effect was almost too much to take but out of them came a whole new approach to teaching in the occult. In addition to this, people were beginning to respond to them on much higher levels and bring through some amazing link-ups to the inner worlds.

Bob Stewart, the author and musician on whose shoulders the mantle of the Bard of Britain has surely fallen, now began to combine specially written music with pathworkings and opened up the dimensions even further. His hauntingly beautiful 'Journey to the Underworld'* gave even the most experienced of us a glimpse of just how much the pathworking could offer both student and teacher. With Dick Swetenham he set up Sulis Music to provide professionally recorded pathworkings, with specially written music to enhance them still further.

Marian Green, the editor of *Quest* and the author of *Magic for the Aquarian Age*, had been successfully using pathworking as a teaching aid for many years and now began to put them before the public in print describing their usefulness in magical training and including specially written workings in her books.

At the other end of the world in Australia, an SOL student, Moses Aaron, latched onto the idea of pathworking in a big way. It seemed to awaken within him far memories of bardic training and he set himself to study them and their effects. Together with author Neville Drury, he experimented for several years with many different types of path-

* Obtainable from Sulis Music, BCM-SCL, Quest, London, WC1V 3XX.

working and finally decided to give up his work with autistic children and 'take to the road' as a modern bard.

Both he and Neville worked with a group of SOL and non-SOL students in Sydney, exploring the deeper reaches of pathworking and, in Neville's case, extending it well beyond the mythic traditions of his own racial group to embrace any and all archetypes that presented themselves. Neville then introduced another dimension to the whole thing by double-tracing the spoken word over selected pieces of music chosen for their 'atmospheric' content, and he found, as did Bob Stewart, that this enhanced the workings far more. There is no doubt in my mind that Moses and Neville between them have taken the traditional pathworking and opened up levels that have been long forgotten.

From there Moses prepared to take it all a step further and set up a service to schools, colleges, lecture halls, groups, television and radio. He used pathworking as a means of communication with people, and more importantly as a means of getting them to communicate with their own inner worlds and those who live within those worlds. He has travelled extensively in Australia and the United States with great success demonstrating just how much the pathworking has to offer.

In America itself Edwin Steinbrecher, head of DOME with its headquarters in Los Angeles, had written a highly successful book called *The Inner Guide Meditation*. This was enthusiastically received not only by students but by their teachers as well for it extended the idea and practice of pathworking a little further, aligning it to astrology and to the natal chart of the individual. This opened up some quite amazing insights, and it is my own theory that in this book Edwin had psychically brought through an aspect of the work that had been lost in ancient times, and restored it to its place in the scheme of occult teaching.

Simon Court and Ann Smith, both of them SOL students and supervisors in Australia, had, in the early eighties, set up a series of group workings in Sydney, Canberra and Melbourne, and had written many excellent pathworkings that are still being used and are available in the SOL Knowledge Papers. At this moment there are many young writers coming up from the ranks of various occult schools who are well-versed in the art of pathworking, and with fresh approaches to the whole area of working that can only be of benefit to occultism as a whole.

My own involvement with them, as I explained at the beginning of this book, stems from my childhood, albeit unknowingly at the time, and has persisted throughout my life both as an individual and as a teacher. It led to my writing *The Shining Paths*, a series of pathworkings concerning the twenty-two paths on the Tree of Life, and extended into ritual and *The Ritual Magic Workbook*. But I still get asked many questions concerning this part of magical training and it was to answer those questions that the present book was first projected. It is my aim here to describe, explain, and hopefully to demonstrate that the pathworking happens both deliberately as a carefully prepared scenario for oneself or for a group of people sharing the same experience, or spontaneously as a day-dream or fantasy that fulfils a need at that time; also that the creative imagination is not just the prerogative of artists, poets and writers, although they may have a greater, more fluid access to it, but that it is a valid part of the daily life of all of us, crossing the barriers of race, religion, sex, colour and class.

Once you have been through the experience of a pathworking you never really forget it, and it is only a matter of time before you are anxious to try your hand at writing your own. However, until that time you may need the help of one already written and containing all the ingredients needed to stimulate the inner eye and open the Gateway of the Inner World. It was to supply this need that the SOL Knowledge Papers were brought into being. They come in three different sections:

1. Lectures and articles of interest and which in themselves can offer seed ideas for your own future pathworkings.
2. Pathworkings dealing with a variety of themes, archetypes, and traditions.
3. Rituals ready prepared and carefully put together to ensure no inopportune kick-back for the newcomer.

A list of these Knowledge Papers can be obtained from:

> Director of Studies (Knowledge Papers)
> PO Box 215
> St Helier
> Jersey, C.I.

CHAPTER TEN

Putting It Together

There comes a time when all theories have to give way to practical experience, and we have reached such a point. So far we have turned over everything that might possibly be connected with the art of pathworking; now we must learn the methods of construction and pay attention to the rules and regulations that govern them. It is sink or swim time, but you should manage a respectable doggy paddle if not a racing crawl.

No matter how carefully I have written this book you will always find the one pitfall I have missed. This is not a bad thing, for such pitfalls are part and parcel of occult training. W. E. Butler used to tell his students, 'You will learn more from a handful of burnt fingers than any lesson or lecture I could give you.' This is quite true and over the years I have found that mistakes are the most valuable of lessons because they teach you to *get it right*!

Take everything you have learned in the book so far and use it as a basis, a foundation for your own experiments. You will then have the glory of your own realizations when things go right, and the wisdom that comes of climbing out of your own pitfalls! But let me recap on a few things before we start the construction work.

You will be working with the creative imagination. Clear visualization and attention to detail is of the greatest importance. *Learn to look and observe things around you*. Gather data in the form of pictures, descriptive passages from books both old and new. Make visits to places associated with your racial archetypes, and the assimilation of the myth and legends of the Western Tradition.

Remember also that your pathworkings will be of use in a wide range of situations - learning, training the mind, easing stress, producing more confidence by pre-experiencing potentially painful, irritating, or vitally important meetings or interviews. All this is on the physical level. On the higher levels they will allow you to experience the subtle realms of mind and spirit and, at the same time, open up an inner realization of the world within that will sustain you throughout your future life.

There are some points you must hold in mind when you start using the information I have given you in this book. You can learn a lot from a book but you have to take the information and mould it to your own requirements. That is something I cannot do for you. In occult training much emphasis is placed on the students learning to rely on themselves after a certain time; otherwise there is a danger of becoming an 'eternal student, but never a master'. Seeking out and assimilating knowledge is a passive occupation but using that information and experiencing it on all levels is active. You must learn from now on to balance one with the other. How you do it is up to you. I have given you information that has been locked away in the adytum of Mystery schools for far too long. Like other teachers before me this state of affairs has exasperated me beyond measure, for the seekers of this world *need* such information now. They are ready for it and can use it if it is properly explained. Again, like others before me, I have chosen to let several cats out of centuries old bags of secrecy and, no doubt, will be castigated for it, which worries me not in the least!

A pathworking will give you experiences you can get in no other way. It can give you pleasure and the thrill of doing something you cannot do on the physical level and, as I have explained in Chapter 9 (which will certainly not put me on the Christmas card list of Mary Whitehouse), it can help people who find themselves in situations where the inner world is the only one that can offer help and consolation.

If you build a working correctly and tailor it to your needs you will open a whole new world for yourself. More importantly you will start to build a new image of yourself. People vary wildly in how they see themselves. Some overdo it and become boring egotists, not a few of whom are in the occult! But by far the biggest category holds those who are unable to see themselves as successful, worthy, beautiful, clever or popular. Pathworking can change your self-image but it does take time. It will not all happen overnight, or in a week, or even a month, although you *will* begin to see improvements within three to four weeks as the new *you* begins to show through, but the consolation is that you will find the method enjoyable, because in the inner world of the pathworking, you can be what you want to be.

One of the most important occult truths is this: all things stem from the inner places. If you want to change yourself, start by changing the inner you through the medium of pathworking, then, slowly, the change will seep through into the everyday world. It will not necessarily make you look like Robert Redford or Raquel Welch on the physical level, although you could do that as well if you strengthen your will to the extent of physically training, exercising and shaping your body, but the way in which you *see yourself* will change. You will like what you are and see the good things about yourself that you overlooked before. It has been said that it takes about twenty-one days for the beginnings of change to be seen on the physical level. Three weeks appears to have some significance about the 'acceptance of change'. It usually takes someone who has lost a limb about three weeks to adjust to the loss; until then there is a feeling of still having the lost arm or leg attached to the body. When you move house you need three weeks to a month for it to begin to feel like home when you return from work. So give yourself the same amount of time before you begin to look for the emergence of the new you.

How do you build a new self-image? Sit down and make a list of your good points, physical and mental, and another of your bad points. (Ask a good friend to do it if you feel you can't.) Then build a pathworking that will give you an opportunity to use those good points, and which will emphasize your best physical attributes. Use the same working again and again but altering it slightly to allow your inner self to acquire the new image you wish to build. Learn to see yourself in clear detail on the inner levels and alternate the observant and participant modes during the pathworkings. You will remember in an earlier chapter I said that the mind cannot tell the difference between a real and an imagined experience, for example if you blindfold a man and threaten to burn him with a red hot iron, then touch him with an ice cube, he will jerk his hand away convinced that it was red hot, and might even blister. By the same token in a pathworking, providing it is built correctly and worked with emotional force behind it, the inner self will see and accept the image you have given it. Write the following sentence out in large letters and hang it up where you can see it all the time.

> *We are what we imagine ourselves to be.*

Your inner self needs an image to work towards, so work out such an image and 'think' yourself into it and remember you must want to be that image with as much passion and intensity of desire as you can muster. Also the environment of any working you create for whatever purpose *must* be as detailed as you can get it simply because you are aiming to create a *practical experience* within an *imaginary* world. You are not alone in doing this. Many famous people rose above physical defects and lack of wealth and even education to achieve greatness. Success is only a thought away; Napoleon did it, so can you.

You will find at the back of this book some titles that I highly recommend for your reading; with them your future work will be greatly enhanced. I have used them and the methods they describe over many years, both for myself and to teach others. Get them as soon as possible.

There will always be some who think they can take a short cut, by which I mean the use of drugs. *Don't*. It may enhance things for a while but, in the long run, it will take bigger and heavier doses to obtain the same effect, then you are on a road with no turn-offs. Let me put it on the line: no drugs, no excess of alcohol. You can do it all without them and do it better. The ancients knew of certain 'herbs' that caused visions. They also knew the cost in health, both mental and physical. No Mystery school with any contact behind it will advocate the use of such things and, if you are wise, you will never undertake any occult work if your system is riddled with them because that work will never be right. It takes three years to clear the system and seven years altogether for the body to renew itself completely; that is the amount of time you will lose. I don't give a damn what Timothy Leary and Carlos Casteneda said; if you want to study any form of occult work you stay off hallucinogenic drugs.

To enter the inner world when your mental processes are not fully under your control is like jumping out of a plane with no parachute – suicidal. You are going to ask why? Simple, when the control goes, old fears, phobias, nightmares from childhood, from the racial memory and in bad cases from the world memory, arise and enter the working. Ninety-nine per cent of the nasties you encounter on the inner levels are from your own mind, which is why any teacher will warn you against slashing about you with a 'magical sword' when on the astral, killing everything that stands in your way: you may just cut your own head off. This is why alcoholics get delirium tremens, the drink lowers the natural guard we all have against the invasion of our own lower nature and lets everything through onto a level where it can be seen and experienced in a most unpleasant manner.

People often come up to me at seminars and conferences and say things like, 'How wonderful, it must be to have the gift of clairvoyance, I do wish I could see things.' Yes, it can be wonderful and sometimes it can be terrifying. People simply do not understand that, if you can see the nice things, you can also see things that are, to say the least, not nice at all. With time and training you get used to it and learn to ignore it, or put on the clairvoyant equivalent of dark glasses, but they are there and you have to learn to cope with it. As a child and even as a young girl, driving past old churchyards late at night was not something I enjoyed. It takes a long time for some people to tear themselves away from their mortal remains; for the same reason I do not linger in museums after sunset, and the rooms reserved for certain exhibits in the British Museum are taboo as far as I am concerned.

Fever is something else that can erase the guard between the lower self and the higher. If you have ever had to listen to the ravings of someone in the throes of delirium you will know exactly what I mean. But, in such cases, control is re-established once the fever has gone and few people remember anything of their wanderings between the worlds at such times. But when the patient has undergone occult training the fever can produce some strange reactions; sometimes there is a kind of oversoul that protects the mind as it wanders, or even guides it into a higher level where healing contacts can get to work.

Some people have to take medicinal drugs for things like asthma or antibiotics after an operation or during a bout of illness. This kind of drug is fairly safe in connection with occult work and only very rarely does it have any ill effects. However, if you catch something like bronchitis and have to have drugs to combat the infection, try to do as little magical work as possible until you no longer need to take them.

In the past there has been recourse to certain 'potions, herbs and ointments', the most notable being the Flying Ointment. If you are offered any do not accept it; it can have some strange effects and you could injure yourself. Nor should you use peyote even if you are following the Path of the Shaman. The American Indians know just how to use the drug and in what quantities. For them it is regarded as part of their religious ceremonies and, after many generations, they have a tolerance towards it that few white men and women can hope to acquire. You can 'Follow the Drum' without using anything like that.

Your physical brain can and does produce substances that are natural painkillers, can wake you up or put you to sleep. The hormones and chemicals your body manufactures every day of your life are just as powerful as any you can chew, inject, sniff or smoke, and they will not ruin you mentally, physically or financially. Any yogi can stimulate his brain and body processes to boost his body heat, cool it down, slow the heartbeat, lower blood pressure, and induce something close to a coma. Why should you want to fill such a marvellous instrument with something potentially lethal? Leave well alone.

Some of the most important building bricks in the construction of a pathworking are the milestones. These are the entry points, the half-

way marks, and the furthest point before you return. The entry points
we have already dealt with, now we come to the half-way marks. These
milestones can be of various kinds. In the cabbalistic paths they are usually
simple stones bearing the Hebrew letter associated with that path. In
the Hermetic tradition they may be a geometric figure, or an alchemical
symbol, or even something like a Kamea whose basic number equates
with the meaning or goal of the path being worked. In workings
concerned with or based upon mythic images they can take the form
of a person, a god-form or even a statue, something that causes an effect
within the context of the working, for example Saturn with his scythe
and/or sandclock on the 32nd path. When you are building the working
yourself you should choose your half-way mark with care; if you are
working passively then be sure to look for the mark for it will certainly
be there.

Such marks have several purposes. They can simply indicate a place
where a newcomer can halt to think things out, or even turn back if
the pressure is too much – something that can happen with a novice.
Or it can be placed there to remind you of something that lies ahead
on the path, perhaps something you would have to prepare to meet.
The path may demand that at a certain point you give a password, but
which is not given to you before you leave. If you stop here at the milestone
and look around you it is more than likely that the password will present
itself. It may even be found actually on the milestone. Always look closely
at any symbols for they may offer a new realization on the whole working.

With cabbalistic workings you should study with great care the Hebrew
letter associated with the path. Study its shape, its meaning and its
numerical value and, in the case of the final letters, the different number
and meaning. For instance, when travelling Path 15 on the Tree of Life,
you milestone will show the letter HEH. The usual image given for
this is a *window*, but its actual translation has a more subtle meaning
that loses much when put into English; the nearest we can get to it is,
incoming light. The word 'window' simply implies something that frames
a hole in the wall and lets light through; the word HEH means the
actual *light* coming through the window – illumination, realization, truth.

Knowing this will put a whole new slant on the path you are treading.
Half-way into your journey the milestone is telling you that the latter
end of the path will reveal something to you if you watch out for it.
But you are not yet finished with HEH. This letter is one of a group
that symbolizes nine archetypal functions; the function of HEH is *life*,
so your milestone is saying that this path can offer you a deep realization
about your life or about life in general.

Cabbalists hold that each Hebrew letter is much more than just a black squiggle on a page. It is a living force in its own right. HEH goes one further, because it is the symbol for creative life (it was not until the creative HEH was added to their respective names that Abraham and Sarah were able to have a child). It holds great power and even more so when it comes at the end of a letter. When HEH is spelled out it becomes HEH-HEH final, so the 15th Path on the Tree of Life, when experienced as a pathworking, holds more than is at first apparent. There are times when no milestone is seen, at least not openly, in which case look around at the environment or the characters within the working. It is probable that they will supply the missing letter or its equivalent. It is this sort of data that you must have at your fingertips if you wish to master the ancient art of pathworking.

It is only when you are new to journeying that the marks are made very visible. As you progress they become more and more withdrawn, for you are growing in your ability to walk between the worlds and the need to pause half-way has gone. Nevertheless they are still there, inherent in the scenery and symbols around you on the path. It is often a good idea to go back and do some of the early pathworkings every once in a while as it helps you to keep things in perspective.

Many other kinds of symbols can be found as markers and all will have something to add to your working, so always make time to look at them when they are presented to you and see what you can deduce from them and, in many cases, from their situation. It is possible for you to come across Greek letters as well as Hebrew, so it is worthwhile learning the Greek alphabet as well so you can decipher them, or at least memorize their shape and record it when you return.

There will be times when you may come across the Tarot cards, both Major and Minor Arcana, acting as milestones halfway through a working, in which case, unless you are familiar with the Tarot, remember the card and when you write out your records take the meaning of the card, and if it was reversed or not, into consideration. In this way you will be getting far more out of your journeys than those who simply have a nice walk from one end to the other and back. A pathworking is not an evening stroll!

When you are building a working of your own, for the first year at least always put in a half-way marker. At first use either a letter or a symbol that you *know* has some meaning for the path itself. Later on, however, you should use one of two methods: either meditate on the goal or aim of the working and allow a symbol to present itself and use that as a marker, or allow a symbol to appear when you are actually in

Both ways have much to offer. Later still you will find ᵣmatically build themselves into the working, but when ᵤuilding them for anyone else, especially when training ᵣewcomers, always see that they are there and that they work in with the symbolism of the path.

The symbols or markers at the other end of the pathworking are equally important. Often there is a quite definite goal – a mountain, a castle, a tower, or something of that nature. But it could just as well be a person, someone whose symbolism, if a god-form, or mythic qualities are part of the meaning and aim of the working. Occasionally it may be something like a stone circle or a *menhir* with symbols or runes carved on it. Whatever appears or whatever you choose to symbolize the furthest point of the working, stick to it and do not go beyond that point. Only in the passive workings can you allow yourself to wander on until a natural barrier becomes apparent. Most of the time such points are placed there for your own protection, since even inner level strength has its limitations at times, especially for those new to the deeper workings. Keep in mind that a good pathworking channels as much power as a high level ritual, and don't overstretch yourself.

When working with a group make sure that everyone knows the route of the pathworking and has had time to study it and prepare their mind by collecting images and data. In this way you will not have people saying afterwards that they got very little feedback because they had no back-up material. Make sure the group gets on well socially as well as in the context of a working group. Stand back from them mentally and see if you can detect any underlying friction. Someone unable to take direction from the Narrator or Leader and who goes off at a tangent in the middle of a working is someone you can do without.

You will often get people who seem to fall asleep throughout the working. This can be a problem but it has two main causes. Either they are going so deep that they are touching one of the seven levels of meditation, in which case let them be; they are following the working on a different level and, although they may say they 'saw' nothing, they will have made the contact in a different way. The other cause is usually because they are physically tired and cannot maintain the alert relaxation that this work requires, or they are putting up a subconscious barrier for some reason; either one is going to call for a lot of tact and diplomacy on your part.

Do at least six months of solo work before you set up a group, unless you have done a lot of such work beforehand, or you have received proper training from a teacher. For a while work from a set of reliable pathworkings such as those in *Passages*, or *Mind Games*, or *The Shining Paths*. Keep with active workings for a while, for passive ones tend to need more confidence and your group should be allowed to build this gradually. When you reach a point where you are mixing both kinds, remember, if the working is active be sure everyone *keeps with* the Narrator and doesn't go wandering off on their own. If it is passive, be *very sure* of your ability to cope with unexpected intrusions.

Every group, as well as solo practitioners, should have a set of pre-selected phrases that will bring you back immediately should anything untoward arise. No matter what precautions you take, emergencies can arise, from a fainting fit to an attack of asthma, or an urgent call from family, etc. Talk it over with your group and arrange a signal whereby everyone knows they are to return at once. Make sure they understand that they *must* walk around, touch objects, hold hands, anything to ground them as soon as possible. Make sure you always have several flasks of hot beverages and some biscuits on hand. It helps to earth you very quickly. As for the signal, it can be anything you choose but I use the old, well-tried one of '*Red Alert*', spoken several times, but *not* in panic-stricken tones. Say it firmly but quietly and it will cause less shock. It is a good idea to 'sound the alarm' every once in a while as a practice run and tell them that you intend to do this at intervals, but never tell them when. In this way they will learn to respond at once.

A working group should start off with no more than one working every two weeks. Keep to this for between three and six months, or until you are certain that everyone has adjusted to the mental demands of pathworking and that the group is well integrated. After that you can try once every ten days for a while and from then on you should be able to cope with one a week with no trouble. *Never* allow any of the group to fall into the glamour of doing them solo, one or more times a day; there are some who are daft enough to try it.

Appoint a recorder who will be responsible for collecting reports, typing them out and keeping them in a special file. This way you can keep an eye on the group's progress. Every six months call a meeting and discuss the past work and the future plans. The most important thing to remember is this: do not be deceived by the ethereal quality of pathworkings, they *always have an effect on the physical world, usually within forty-eight hours*. They may feel like dreams, but they are *not*.

Taking in new members when a group has already built up a rapport can be tricky. Rather than put a novice in with experienced people, you should try starting a beginners' group which can then join up with the main group after, say, six months. During that time you might build some low-key workings that can occasionally be worked all together to give the newcomers something to look forward to and to bring them into full contact with the others. Forming a group to do pathworkings can be just as rewarding as forming a group for ritual work. It is also less demanding in time and effort, for the building of a temple and the need to keep to a calendar of ritual work can be very tiring and expensive.

Unless you have several members who possess good speaking voices and who do not mind taking it in turns to be the narrator, invest in a good-quality tape recorder and pre-record all workings. It must be taken reasonably slowly, with the pauses marked in the script, so that those listening have time to build the images. You will soon get to know the right amount of time, but remember that not everyone needs the same amount of time so you will have to learn by trial and error. Alternatively, each member can take a turn to read; the only trouble with this is that some people have irritating voices when reading aloud, and they are often the ones who fancy themselves as budding Oliviers!

If the group grows to be fairly large, say ten people or over, then you may have to appoint one person at each meeting to be Guardian, that is to be ready to deal with outside emergencies should they arise. If you are using the passive method of working then there should be a signal that will let everyone know it is time to return, and allow another five/eight minutes for them to make their way back. A wristwatch alarm is good for this as it is not as loud as a bell or a gong. Some people use a metronome to set off the working. I am not a fan of the idea as it can lead more to a form of self-hypnosis than the state of deep inner awareness required.

Make sure that your group fully understands the difference between the role of observer and that of participant. Make them use each method in turn with every working so that they get used to both styles. It also fully balances these inner journeys and one can often gain extra insight by first observing and then taking a full part in the working. Warn them also that when participating it is sometimes very difficult to prevent oneself from sliding into the observer mode. They will have to keep checking on themselves throughout the journey.

In an earlier chapter the role of the day-dream was discussed, but we can use the power of night dreams as well to further our exploration into the art of pathworking. Much research has gone on into the phenomenon of lucid dreaming in the last ten years or so and among many other discoveries we have found out that mankind *needs* to dream, that it fulfils a basic need and eases the stress that builds up during the day. In this it has much the same healing power as does the day-dream and the pathworking. It is also possible to share your dreams, quite literally, and to pick up where you left off if you are woken suddenly from a dream, and to control the content of your dreams and, in a sense, choose the subject you want to dream about.

In her book *Creative Dreaming*, Patricia Garfield, PhD, tells the story of the Italian author, Giovanni Guareschi, and his young wife who was suffering from deep depression. This was so bad that it was manifesting in her dreams as well as troubling her during the day. She dreamt of walking endless dark streets and complained to her husband that her feet were 'so tired'. He suggested, much to her annoyance, that she get a bicycle. However, a few days later the bicycle duly appeared in her dreams. From then on each time she came across an obstacle in her dreams Guareschi made her face up to the situation during the day. Invariably the solution to her problem turned up in a dream until finally she was able to sleep without fear of her dreams. I recommend this book for your reading as it gives some fascinating clues to our night-time world of dreams.

The Senoi Indians live their whole lives by the power of their dreams. Each morning every member of the family will relate the dream they had during the night. The father or oldest member will help to interpret them or, if they show signs of being very important, they will go to the priests and elders of the tribe. This sharing of dream experiences is a vital part of the whole tribal existence and an integral part of their religion.

We too can share our dreams with another person for it will give great satisfaction and help, for they are reflections of what troubles or sustains us during the day and, by talking them out, we learn how to cope with stressful or potentially hurtful situations. When you undergo occult training one of the basic disciplines is to recap on the day before you go to sleep. A lot of students regard this as a bit of a bore, but there are several good reasons for doing it. It clears the mind, itemizes the day's events in order of importance, and paves the way for a dream either to offer a solution or, at the very least, give a different slant on the problem. By looking at each day in retrospect we keep a check on the Law of Cause and Effect. We can remedy any act that is less than charitable, correct something that we can see is going to lead to trouble if we allow it to go on, or occasionally feel satisfied that something has turned out well. This keeps the Scales of Justice more finely balanced by a daily cancelling out of the little bits of karma that would otherwise keep adding up.

Anyone who has established a pattern of pathworking can move on into creative dreaming. It follows a somewhat similar preparation. First

you choose what you want – or need – to dream about, then you build
the first part of a storyline similar to a pathworking, but only so far.
After a while it peters out and leaves you perhaps standing by a roadside
waiting for someone you have selected to meet in your dream, or you
are walking through a garden on your way somewhere. This small
fragment you 'pathwork' over and over again in your mind as you drift
off to sleep. It helps if you stay up until you feel nicely tired, and could
sleep as soon as your head hits the pillow. But stay awake long enough
to do that little piece of pathworking once or twice. It may not happen
right off but, with very little practice, you will find yourself inside the
dream and finishing off the working, bringing in the chosen dream
subject. The hardest thing is remembering it in the morning; that is
something you will have to train yourself to do. Recall is very important.
Keep a small notebook and pen by your bed or under the pillow. You
can get pens that are also flashlights and this will help you see what
you are writing if you wake in the middle of the night. Never tell yourself
you will remember it all in the morning, because you won't. I have lost
many good dreams like that and not only dreams but whole chapter
layouts of books simply because I felt too tired and sleepy to write it
down there and then.

To start with, the best time to try creative dreaming is at the weekend
when you are more relaxed and have a little extra time. During the day
keep thinking about the subject of your dream. If possible, put a picture
either of the actual subject, or something resembling the subject, by
your bed and look at it last thing at night. Fill your mind with it and
build up a feeling of pleasant anticipation. All this will help to set the
scene.

All the ancient traditions used this kind of dream healing or dream
communication. If you think back to the Old Testament you will find
that Daniel, Joseph, Samuel, Tobias, and many others benefited greatly
from the use of dreams. For thousands of years such methods have been
used until the days of modern science. However, things are changing
and once again the art of dreaming is being explored and used to good
purpose.

You can use many different techniques in creative dreaming. You can
ask questions and demand answers from your dreams, you can hold
conversations with them and find out more about your inner, secret self
than you would have thought possible. You can start to teach children
from quite a young age to cope with their dreams and especially with
nightmares. There are certain rules that the Senoi Indians teach their
children as soon as they are old enough to understand.

1. Never run from anything dangerous or frightening. Stand your ground and face it, it is only a part of yourself that you have not yet learned to face up to during the day.
2. If you have a nice dream try to prolong it in any way you can.
3. Never allow your dreams to end on a bad note. Always make yourself come out on top in your dream.

If you are faced with someone or something that threatens you, fight it. Call for help from your guardian spirit, your favourite god-form, an archangel or even a large English bobby. When you have conquered it, demand something from it, something positive, and take careful note of what the gift is, what it is like or what it represents. It need not be an object, it can be an idea, a way to create a much-needed situation, the strength of will to break a habit, anything, but demand it and get it. By the same token, if people or animals in your dreams are helpful, give them something as a gift. Since you can create anything from astral matter this presents no problem.

Learn to look about you in your dreams and observe in as much detail as possible. I have already explained that in pathworking the power of observation is a key element. It is the same in dreams. Write down everything, even the most trivial things, for they are all part of a pattern. Read back over your dream records once a month and compare them. When you have become reasonably adept at dreaming to order try the following. Build a beautiful room with open french windows; outside you can see only stars. The room is empty but one wall is covered with large mirrors. Start to dance, use all the space you have and sing to yourself as you dance. Now dance over to the windows and look out. The room seems to hang in mid-space. Float out into this space and keep on dancing. Tell yourself you are going to dance a beautiful world into being, like Shiva. The planets will provide the music and you will dance . . . let the dream take over from there. Record your success or not, as the case may be, in the morning as usual.

For the next exercise meditate on the Tarot Trump of The Lovers, and sleep with the card under your pillow. For the path into your dream create an island and cover it with trees and flowers. Fill it with wildlife and give it your choice of climate. Add water, fruit trees, etc. . . . then wait and see who turns up to share it with you.

You will soon find that dreaming and pathworking follow similar patterns. Both are controllable, both can offer ways of talking to the inner self, of spiritual growth, and increasing mental awareness. The study of one will help the other.

One question I am often asked is, 'Where do you find material for your pathworkings?' By now I must have written well over a hundred and they still keep coming, but it comes back to the collection of data. I have lived all my life surrounded by books, pictures, and people who talked *to* me and not *at* me during my formative years. In this I have been blessed but anyone can write a pathworking, or create one in their mind for their own personal use. The material is all around you. At first you will find most of what you need in myth and fairy-tale. These are archetypal stories that stimulate both a need and an answer from within. They can be played out within the mind in many different ways and with many different endings. Real life can provide a startling amount of situations that can be used as a foundation, and I have already shown you how to utilize poems and books. Do not let yourself be bound by set stories, change the endings and the beginnings and transpose them into different settings. In one of my own pathworkings ('The Castle of Merlin'), written for the 1986 SOL Conference, I took the Island of Avalon and made it into a piece of Atlantis which, in turn, was a piece of Paradise. I explained that the ancient Priests of the Sun and Priestesses of the Moon had taken the isle out of time and space and set it between the worlds so that, in time to come, the Heroes of Albion would be taken there instead of dying, to serve their race when the time came. The subconscious mind works in strange ways and it was only several weeks later that I realized that I had carved Avalon, the Apple Island, out of a bit of Paradise where the Apple started all the trouble!

It is in such ways that you must learn to bend and curve old tales into new settings. Read, read anything and everything you can lay your hands on. Look at pictures and set what you have read into the frames of the pictures. Take extraordinary characters and place them in new settings, change the shape of history and play the game of 'What would it be like now if .... had/had not happened?' Look for ideas outside your normal racial groups. Try the Hindu myths and the Chinese. Look into shamanism and try drumming as a lead-in to a pathworking. The usual way into the inner world of a shaman is through water, a cave mouth leading into the earth, or climbing a tree that goes up beyond the clouds. The legends of the North American Indians offer many ideas; so too, does the Tibetan Book of the Dead, making a change from its Egyptian equivalent.

Museums and archaeological digs can give you many ideas. For instance, many years ago when uncovering a death pit filled with the bodies of slaves and courtiers who had gone into the Land of Shadows with their Queen, the workmen came across a row of bodies, all of young girls who, in life, had been dressed in identical dresses and wore a silver ribbon fillet around their heads. One girl did not have one, the ribbon was still wound up into a neat roll just by her hand. The poignancy of it has never left my memory. Why did she not have the time? Was she saying goodbye to her parents, or a lover, a husband? Was he too buried there? All these questions are still unanswered, but they could be built into a pathworking where you stood watching as those who had elected to die with their ruler went serenely to their deaths. You may even see why the little maid did not have time to finish her toilette. I have said many times in this book that you must cultivate your creative imagination so as to be able to experience pathworkings. You also need it to write them.

Go to history and relive the great moments. Slip inside the forms of those who helped to make the world we live in and see what they saw, feel what they were feeling. Go to sport and win Olympic gold medals, take chunks out of Edgar Rice Burroughs' book *The Princess of Mars*, still a darned good adventure book after fifty years. Look, and keep on looking, and once your subconscious mind sees what you are looking for it will give you more ideas than you can use in a lifetime.

When you find a theme and start to build an inner journey, break it down into three parts, the beginning, the middle (which should contain the aim of the working), and the return journey. Unless you are an experienced traveller in the otherworlds always return the way you came. Select a Door, Gate or Opening of some kind in harmony with the general layout. If you are going to use the same Door all the time personalize it with a key and a symbol over the lintel. Always allow a pause as you set foot in the otherworld to let those with you take in their new surroundings.

As far as possible, do not allow a character to disappear in a puff of smoke or similar circumstances. Make it as normal as possible because you want this inner world to become normal to you whenever you are here. Do not over-people it at first; keeping track of two or three is fine for a start. If you must have crowds of people keep them in the middle to far distance. Don't worry if their faces keep changing. It is very hard to keep astral matter in one place and one form for more than a few minutes. If you can keep it 'fixed' for just a few seconds then it will be established on this level until you dismiss the whole working at the end. Try always to have an aim in mind, be it to find or fetch something, to see somebody and talk with them, to go to a location and experience some realization there. Anything, but let it be definite. Use any means of transportation, feet, horse, chariot, car, train, plane, spaceship, but try not just to 'appear' in places. Methods of getting about should be as normal as possible – though of course in this world only you know what is considered normal. An eagle with a forty-foot wingspan capable of carrying a man may be quite normal. Don't get too elaborate with clothes; stick with a plain hooded robe and sandals for a while, add a cloak if it is cold. If you select a location in ancient Greece and it begins to rain, please do not conjure up an umbrella; keep your time location as close to the original as possible.

When you have achieved your aim, pause for a while to allow the whole working to shift into a departure mode, then start the return journey. If you find something in your working that is nasty, or someone you don't like, never accept anything from them, especially food and drink. If someone is kind to you offer them a gift, even if it is only a flower. Deities should always be offered something – flowers, perfume, fruit, cakes, wine, or an ornament, but never anything of you – no hair, no blood, no bits of food from your own lips.

You may find yourself observing the scene from some strange angles, such as from the top of a tree; don't worry, the mind plays tricks like this. Sometimes you actually watch yourself going through the working. Again don't worry, you will find it easier as you do more and more. If you find yourself slipping out of your mental body, try looking down at your feet or hands, and the front of your body. This will help you to focus on your imaginary body and keep 'inside' it.

It may be of interest to some readers that a way to measure the imagination of people has been developed by a Professor Murray of Harvard University. 'TAT', or Thematic Apperception Test, is the name given to this set of measurements. The idea is to have people make up stories pertaining to ambiguous (their word not mine) pictures. The report states that 'one can measure the transcendence [?] of these stories as an indication of imagination.' This seems to me to be a very long-winded way of going about things. Why not have a competition for the best, or most enjoyable pathworking instead? The winner would surely be either a trained student of the occult or a writer of science fiction – on that I would be willing to place a bet. But it does go to show that even Harvard University is willing to acknowledge the fact that day-dreaming 'has a use'. They even give that use a name – 'a rehearsal for future events'! Not a bad description!

Always keep a copy, clean and unused, of every pathworking you build. Keep them all in a file along with the dates they were worked and the reports given in by the group or, if you are working alone, your own reports. These are important documents for they represent a window on to your inner life and, as such, they should be kept away from prying eyes. Make arrangements for them to be either destroyed or handed on, unopened, to a person selected by you as a fit and worthy person in the event of your death. This is not being morbid, it is being sensible, for every occultist should make provision for such papers to be passed on for safe keeping to a chosen successor.

Newcomers to the occult often worry overmuch about protection. There seems to be a very unhealthy fixation among a certain type of student that they are being 'physically attacked'. I have explained in *The Ritual Magic Workbook*, (Aquarian Press, 1986) that a real one hundred per cent attack is extremely rare, firstly because very few magicians have that amount of power to spare or the physical strength to keep it going; secondly because most students, as soon as they enter a school, come under the protection of the Eggregore of that school, not to mention the Presence of the Teacher. That, in itself, when you are working under such guidance, constitutes all the protection you will need for your ordinary day-to-day work, including anything you may do in the way of extra-curricular work, provided it has been sanctioned by your tutor. Thirdly, such attacks have a nasty tendency to return to those who sent them with a double force. Most magicians with any sense know this and all have, at one time or another, tried it on – and in weathering the resulting storm have learned a valuable lesson.

However, we still get a lot of people writing in complaining of such interference. Ninety per cent of the time it is either their imagination working the wrong way, i.e. building up the images and imbuing them with their own negative force or, and this is the more likely, they are consciously or subconsciously seeking to impress to make themselves appear important. It only makes them a darned nuisance and unlikely to impress anyone. In the rare cases of real psychic attack, whatever has attached itself to that person will leave 'traces' of its presence on them to such an extent that it will permeate the paper they use to write on and this can be picked up by a competent psychic. However, a lot of things can actually be coming from the person themselves, albeit unconsciously. We all store up in our lower selves a great deal of very nasty thought matter. When you enter occult work of any kind, be it learning the Tarot, sitting in a development circle, or entering a school for serious all-round training, this is bound to get stirred up and may even seep out into your conscious level and take shape in the form of vague feelings of unease, nightmares, bouts of illness with no apparent cause, and even the sense of seeing things from the corner of your eye. All these things will gradually melt away if no notice is taken of them.

Mr Butler's advice was usually to 'go and see a good comedy film . . . nothing like laughter to dispel such things.' He was right. In fact, laughter is one of the best forms of exorcism there is. It will dispel a great deal of such annoyances. Remember also that the hidden name of the Devil in the Major Arcana is Illusion, and the best way to dispel all illusion is with laughter.

Having said all this, there are some protections you can use if you are working outside the influence of a school, or feel the need for something extra in the way of defence. The first is to use the Cloak of Mirrors. This is just what it says; a cape made of thousands of tiny mirrors is placed about the body in the mind's eye before beginning the meditation or the pathworking. Pull the hood right over the head and imagine yourself covered in the reflective light coming from the surface of the cloak. This will reflect anything directed towards you back to where it originated. It can be used in most ritual or similar cases.

The next most effective way of protecting your physical self whilst engaged on deep meditation levels is to use the 'Star of Isis'. This is a five-pointed star (*not* a continuously drawn pentagram) with an Ankh in the centre. Place this either just above the head or on the forehead and, at the same time, put a circle of blue light around the body, starting from the middle of the back, going over the head, down below the feet and joining again at the back. From the same point, a second circle encloses the body at right angles to the first circle. This is a most effective protection and one I often place around those I love when they are travelling. To this can be added the enfolding wings of the Goddess herself, enclosing the whole thing.

If you are out of doors a circle of salt around you will keep most things at bay, and as I have already intimated when talking about stone circles etc., there can be influences out in the wild that are just as baleful as anything you may encounter elsewhere. There are quite a few of our ancient sites that are not places to linger in for too long and especially after the sun has set. For a very simple and quick method of protection in the older (pre-Druidic) places, two household pins crossed on your sweater or shirt will give enough protection to get you out of harm's way, or an iron nail in your pocket. The old tale of the hero sticking his knife into the lintel of the door to fairyland was not altogether without a base. Iron has strange properties which are not always apparent on this level of being. If you insist on working within a rath, or a stone circle about which you are less than certain, leave an unsheathed knife between two of the stones, to keep the way open.

One of the things that most catch the imagination in this work is the art of shape-shifting. In the early days of man's emergence when the physical body was much less dense than it is now, it may indeed have been possible for the atoms of the body to metamorphose into another shape, and another species. But now that is past and, unless you get a throwback to those times, the only way to shape-shift is to use the imaginative abilities. I know this will come as a shock to some who fervently believe it is possible, but one of the things you have to come to terms with in magical work is that most magic takes place within the mind on a different level of existence. This does not make it anything less real *on that level*. Disney type magic begins and ends with Disney. When you accept that, you are on your way to becoming a real magician.

If you train your mind to a sufficient degree you can shape-shift within the imagination to such a degree that to all intents and purposes you *are* the shape you have chosen. But before you can achieve such a feat you must master one of the first lessons spoken of in this book: the art of observation. It is no good expecting to shape-shift into a bird if you do not know exactly how a bird's body works, or an otter's, or a wolf's or a whale's. In *The Ritual Magic Workbook* I have said that the knowledge needed by a working magician exceeds in variety almost any other profession (yes, I *did* say profession, for it is just that, no matter what pseudo academics have to say). To get to grips with shape-shifting you should begin with just two or three forms, no more. Later, you can add to these but for now this is more than enough to cope with at this stage of your training.

Visit a zoo and study the shapes you have chosen at first hand. Watch the bird or animal at rest, at play, in movement and asleep. Take your time, write notes, take photos. Practise curling up like a wolf with a tail over your nose. Look at things with your head held to one side, using just one eye at a time as a bird would do. Stretch first with front paws and then with the back like an otter waking from sleep. Gradually think yourself into the part. The longer you spend on preparation the easier and more successful your first shift will be. If you have a video that has a slow motion mode use it to study how animals move and birds use their wings. Look for the little details that will give you an authentic mental link with a species, the way an otter will use a back leg to scratch, the way it shakes itself after emerging from the water, the way a deer lifts its head to test the wind in short delicate sniffs.

When you have assimilated all this, then you can take your first try at shifting. It is most important that you are not interrupted. More than any other kind of meditative work this requires privacy, and freedom from interruption. Think about your intended shape, build it up in your mind's eye then shift it down to your solar plexus and hold it there as a template. Now let the change begin. Start either from the feet or the head to begin with, let the hands and feet change first, then let it flow up the body, feel the feathers or fur growing from the skin, the ears lengthening, the teeth changing and the wings or tail emerging. *But remember*, it will all take place in your mind and you must *never ever* allow the change to include your mind or your personality. When the change is complete, make the usual door in the wall and go through into the inner world. You should find less difficulty in maintaining an animal shape on the inner levels than your normal human shape. Don't ask me why, I have no idea, but I personally find it much easier. One more note of caution: don't shape-shift too often. Once you have mastered the technique make it an occasional thing rather than doing it every time. Too much and you can find certain elements of the most often-used 'shift' will begin to seep through into the physical level, and a taste for raw liver, or the tendency to perch on the bedrail with your head under one arm does not go unnoticed by your nearest and dearest!

If you are of an adventurous turn of mind you might like to try interdimensional Gateways. Take a two-foot-long piece of ribbon and twist it once, then sew the two ends together. This is a Moebius Strip. If you run your finger along the outside edge you will find that edge will lead you into the inside edge without changing sides. This little phenomenon has played havoc with scientific minds for a long time. It is also a gateway to other dimensions as it forms a half-way house between us and them. When the idea and shape of the Moebius Strip is fixed in your mind, build a much bigger one, as broad as the street outside your house, in your imagination. Then on either side of it, at neatly spaced intervals, build doors or gates or just irregularly shaped holes filled with multi-coloured fog that forms strange shapes and patterns. If you are inclined to try it out, these entrances can be used to enter other dimensions, but take a few precautions. Always provide yourself with a large ball of string, tying one end round your waist and paying it out as you go through the entrance. The mind is a strange animal and has certain basic fears, one of which is getting lost in strange places. The string leading you back home is an idea the mind can hold on to and will lessen any tendency to panic. This is about the only time when you will not need to keep any records. If you have built the gateways correctly you will never be able to describe or write down what you see, you will only experience feelings, colours, sounds, scents and tastes that are indescribable. Don't try, just enjoy.

Time travel is another possibility in pathworking but there are two kinds. In one, the most often encountered, you will need a lot of data with which to work. This will prime the imagination and you can make a good educated guess as to how it must have been, but sometimes what starts out this way turns into something quite different. Suddenly the scene can change from the way you have built it into the real thing. All that you see and feel now is as it was in that time. This means that you have, by accident, touched a time, place and location that coincided with a former incarnation. Everything clicks into place, time of year, time of day, the street or house or garden, and old memories are revived with almost frightening clarity. Don't be afraid, you will not be trapped there, your physical body in the present will pull you out of it with little or no trouble, but it can be very startling when it happens. If you can keep your wits about you take notes, look for something, anything, that can be verified by research later on. Again, the only danger here is a tendency to try again and again hoping that all this will happen. Don't; let it occur of its own accord, not your will to make it happen.

Science fiction can provide endless situations for personal pleasure pathworkings and this, in fact, is what has happened in the case of Star Trek. People found this series such an open door into inner experiences that they would not let the series die. There is no hour in the twenty-four when Star Trek is not being shown somewhere in the world. I have seen it and heard it dubbed in Dutch, Spanish, Hebrew, Greek and even in Malay and Hindi, the last in Singapore. Spock speaking Malay is really something!

In the early thirties and forties the old *Amazing and Astounding* magazines attracted a readership with an interest in science fiction that has never lessened. Those who once read those marvellous old mags now have grandchildren and even great-grandchildren who are just as eager to 'get out there'. This being so, modern science fiction is as much a part of the art of pathworking as any based on myth, alchemy or hermetic beliefs. Like them it expands the mind, opens it wide to new horizons that are slowly beginning to turn into reality. I am not ashamed to say that I still love science fiction. My father has a collection of the old magazines to which I return every now and then. Nowadays they are collectors' items and deservedly so for the breadth of imagination that gave them birth has pointed man to the stars within a startlingly short space of time. You can learn a great deal from them, even from the earliest of all, *20,000 Leagues under the Sea* and *The First Men in the Moon*. Leonardo Da Vinci was indulging in science fiction when he drew blueprints for helicopters and submarines. If one of the greatest names that ever lived can indulge in some wishful thinking, I'm certain it can do modern men nothing but good.

Some people find pathworking in the mental sense is not enough and take it further. This has brought into being such things as the Sealed Knot, jousting tournaments and, in America, the Society of Creative Anachronisms. This last is a truly amazing flight of fancy on the part of those who belong to it. It has Kingdoms, Kings and Queens (decided by a frighteningly real hand-to-hand battle once a year, the victor and his lady occupying the 'throne' for the next twelve months). Everyone has a name and a coat of arms. There are knights, courtiers, heralds, barons, earls, ladies, bishops and champions. The costumes are authentic in style, colours and, as far as possible, material. People get married in their costumes and are preceded by heralds carrying their personal banners. After the ceremony another banner, now displaying the quartered arms of the newly wedded couple, is paraded for all to see. It is an amazing sight to see and to take part in, for the group mind built over a long period of time overshadows the proceedings and, for a while, it is impossible not to believe that you have been transported back in time.

There are many who would sneer at this, but uphold traditions like Trooping the Colour. One is part of the other to my mind, for it shows that people hold a reverence for the old ways and the old pageantry and seek to hold on to it in any way they can. Use such things in your pathworkings and in this way you will help to keep alive the colour and the richness that once belonged to us and which the drabness of modern life has hidden from view.

CHAPTER ELEVEN

Examples I

In this chapter and the next you will find examples of pathworkings of most of the types described in this book. All have been specially written for this book. They may be safely undertaken by newcomers to this kind of occult work. Please observe the precautions usually given before pathworkings, i.e. choose a time and a place when you are unlikely to be disturbed. Let someone know that you will be unavailable for a certain length of time so they can answer the door/telephone. Alternatively, take the phone off the hook. Work in a soft light rather than complete darkness and choose a comfortable but preferably upright chair to support your back. Make sure your clothing is not constricting in any way. Take your time in getting quite comfortable. A small cushion or footstool beneath your feet will raise your legs just high enough so that the sensitive blood vessels beneath and behind the knees are not irritated, causing the legs to jump and twitch. The room should be warm enough for comfort but not overheated. If you have recorded the working have the recorder within easy reach, and allow a minute or two on the tape for you to make yourself ready. Have a flask of hot tea and some biscuits ready along with your pen and pad to record your experiences. All this may seem tedious at first but it will soon become a habit and take only a few minutes to set up. At the end of the working allow yourself time to 'come back'. Let your eyes pick out things in the room, repeat your name softly to yourself several times. Then get up and have a good long stretch and stamp your foot on the carpet as a sign to yourself that you are fully conscious.

THE ORPHIC PATHWORKING

The Sleeping Gods
From where you sit you can see forming on the opposite wall a darker misty patch. It grows in size and darkens until you are looking at a fairly

large hole in the wall through which you can see a night sky. It looks cool, almost frosty and the stars are very bright and clear. One seems brighter than the rest. As you watch it gets bigger and bigger and you realize that it is coming towards you. Fascinated, you move from your chair and walk towards the hole in the wall. As you do so, you notice that just above the hole on the actual wall there is a symbol outlined in gold. It is the symbol of the caduceus, a staff around which twine two snakes; just below the top of the staff is a pair of tiny wings and surmounting it, a silver pine cone.

The bright star is now very close and so bright that it hurts to look at it directly. You close your eyes for a moment and, when you open them again, standing before you is a young man. His smile is as dazzling as the star itself and his eyes dance with secret amusement. You are a little taken aback to find that, but for a pair of silver sandals and a broad-brimmed hat, both furnished with lazily flapping wings, he is quite naked. This does not seem to bother him in the least. He is tall and slimly built yet gives the impression of great strength if it were needed. His skin gleams with a faintly silver sheen and his hair clusters in short curls over his head and slightly pointed ears. His eyes are grey and very keen, but they also give you an impression of slyness quickly hidden. He holds in his left hand a larger version of the symbol on the wall above, the right he holds out to you, inviting you in a soft persuasive voice to go with him. You ask by what authority he comes, and where he wishes to take you, and to whom. Stand your ground and demand that he answer, firmly but with a slight deference due to his godhood, for this is Hermes, son of Zeus, messenger to the Olympians.

His manner changes and he becomes more the herald and less the impish youth. His authority comes from his father, Zeus, who asks for your presence on Olympus. He again holds out his hand and this time you take it in yours and bid Hermes understand that he is under pledge to return you safely to this place when your journey is accomplished. He takes the pine cone from the caduceus and gives it to you, telling you that this is the token of his promise. Put it into the pocket of the robe you now discover you are wearing and step with the young god over the threshold and into the starlit night. He bids you place your hand now on his shoulder and the two of you rise swiftly into the night air.

You feel no cold nor any kind of apprehension as you climb up in a long spiral until you are high enough to see the beginning of the earth's curve. Below you the land is laid out like a tapestry, its colours night-washed, silvered by the moon which now comes into view. Hermes guides you over the landscape and a kind of exhilaration grips you as you begin to pick out shapes and outlines as they glide beneath you. The sea looks dark and cold with faint glimpses of white as waves break on dark and unseen shores. Lights glimmer here and there from houses, towns, harbours, and ships at sea.

Now you are passing over tall mountains with snow-capped summits. The sense of humour and mischievous nature of your guide prompt him to swoop downwards taking you with him and racing round the highest peaks, flurrying the snow with the speed of your passing. After the first gasp of fear, you find your breath again and enjoy the sensation as your Olympian roller-coaster takes you on a joy-ride amongst the alpine peaks. Then, with the same suddenness, you veer off towards the east and soon the mountains are behind you and small towns and villages pass below, sleeping and dreaming in their valleys and plains.

Another sea, then more mountains. This is an older, more rugged land, there are few lights to be seen and the peaks look harsher, colder and slightly forbidding. You start to descend in the same long spiral that took you up, Hermes explaining that this is to allow you to become accustomed to this level of the astral plane. You seem to be heading straight for a wall of ice, but as you get nearer, it becomes a palace of white marble pillars opening into a vast hall. Although you have passed through a snowy wilderness, here it is warm and full of the scent of summer flowers. You are set down gently and Hermes allows you time to look about you and adjust to the pressure presence of Olympian power.

Your eyes take in the muted pastel colours, the mosaic flooring and delicate wall tapestries, the centre fountain and the glimpses beyond of blue sky and fleecy clouds. In and out of the pillars there strut fantailed peacocks, their high-pitched screaming echoing in the empty vastness. But soon you realize that it is not empty. At intervals around the great hall stand thrones of coloured marble cushioned in scarlet and purple and gold, and on them, sitting as if in stone-encompassed sleep, are the gods.

Hermes crosses to the centre throne raised above all the rest and kneels before it, head lowered, hands touching the feet of a beloved father. For a moment you are startled to see those feet washed by tears as Hermes weeps for the lost greatness of his sire. You join him, placing a hand on his shoulder, a mortal offering comfort to a god. From above you there comes a voice, faint and thin, yet still with a note of authority. Zeus speaks.

'Welcome to Olympus, child of earth. My son has done well to bring you to me. You see around you all that is left of the glory of the gods of Greece, for we exist only so long as mankind has need of us. As he forgets so we decrease and, maybe, like others before us, we shall melt away like snow in spring. Only Hermes resists the change for his attributes are those needed still by man. Cunning, stealth, swiftness of travel, acumen and communication, a silver tongue made slippery with guile, and yet withal the gift of laughter and the heart of youth. We need to be needed else we shall go hence into the night of time and be no more. I have sent Hermes forth time and again searching for one who will breathe life into us once more that we may still serve as was decreed from the beginning by the Great One of the Night of Time. How many disappointments this has meant, always the one that came promised and then allowed the mists of forgetfulness to cloud the mind and we drifted once again into the state in which you see us now. Only I, Zeus, have retained just enough power to help the Messenger to seek out those who might help us. We do not seek to rule mankind as once we did when he was young and needed our wisdom and judgment. Now we seek to fulfil our own destiny as beings created as you were created for a purpose. You seek your divinity, we seek the way back to that which created all things. Can you, will you help us?'

They both look at you and you realize that father and son share the same grey eyes. You also realize that you have a decision to make, but you have to be cautious. You ask how you may help, what will be required of you? Zeus smiles and answers.

'Ah, truly has mankind imbibed the foresight of Prometheus. I know what is in your mind. No, we do not ask for worship or for sacrifices as of old. We never asked for blood to be shed, that was the demand of the priests that they might net our powers in the sight of men. All we ask is that you know, understand, believe that once we lived, that you cast your mind back to the days when the earth was young and learning to be wise. Read what was told of us, but do not believe all you read, for poets have always clothed the truth in their own words. Yet the kernel of truth was always there, look for that, look, search, ponder and allow us to come back to life within your thoughts, not as gods, but as elder brethren who once led you by the hand. Look deeply into each one of us and allow us to tell you what we stood for. We are asking for *love*, Child of Earth, if you have a little to spare it will save the gods from extinction. We wish, as all who live and breathe do wish, to leave some mark behind when, finally, the road opens before us and we depart as did the Old Ones before us. We want what we leave to be a feeling of kinship. You will understand that in every exchange such as this there must be something given on both sides. I will give to you, in the fullness of time, your heart's desire. You may not recognize it when it comes;

it may be not until you prepare to depart that your mind, drifting back in thought, discovers that it was given and experienced. What your consciousness thinks of as the heart's desire is not always what the heart itself desires, but it will be given. I, Zeus, give my word. Now, if you have what we need within you, begin; Hermes will guide you.' The god falls silent and you stand and think over his words, while Hermes waits impatiently at your side, watching you with sidelong glances, the wings on his sandals flapping irritably as if wanting to be off. He taps them sharply with his staff and they subside.

Think long and deeply on what has been said. If you do not wish to offer your love then tell Hermes and he will guide you back to your own place and leave you safely there. If you decide to help the gods make sure you understand the words of Zeus. He has asked that you study each god and goddess in turn and try to understand what lay behind their form, symbols, and legends, that each had a good and a bad side as you do, above all that they existed, loved, fought, quarrelled, and had their own god to whom they turned at the last. Tell Hermes of your decision and watch his face light up. It has been lonely for him with all his companions helpless and frozen. He lays down his staff and takes you by the hand to stand before Poseidon, brother of Zeus and god of the sea and all that lives in it. Encouraged by Hermes you place your hands on the cold feet of the seeming statue and think of the sea in all its moods, fierce and wild, warm and gentle, of seabirds calling in the early dawn and the laughter of children playing on the shore. You think of the moon reflected on the still water at midnight and the golden path of the sun as it rises over the oceans of the world. You think of the creatures of the deep, the giant whales, so few in numbers now, the gentle fun-loving dolphins always a friend to mankind. Slowly the feet beneath your hands grow warm, you double your efforts and think of the love that man has always felt for the sea, the cradle of all life on earth, of tall ships and the men who have sailed them for thousands of years seeking new shores and new horizons. A great laugh sounds above you and you look up into the eyes of Poseidon, eyes of changing blue and green, a bearded face of great strength. He places his huge hand on your head and suddenly you are mentally one with him, sharing all the secrets of the sea, feeling the kinship with those whose world it is. Then Poseidon rises from his throne and walks from the hall to take up his place in oceans of the world. Now he will be able to help his creatures fight extinction and fight against the pollution of earth's waters.

Now you move to Hades, the dark-browed god of the Underworld, and again you place your hands on the marble feet. The same oneness occurs and you plumb the depths of the so-called God of the Dead only to find in those depths a light and a warmth you had never dreamt of finding. Far from being a figure of dread, Hades is the guardian of the deep earth where unseen riches have their existence, where the forgotten rivers feed the far-down depths with nutrients and minerals. Here the core of the earth keeps the planet from becoming an ice ball. The mighty caves and caverns, filled with the lace of frozen waters, delight the eyes of their Lord and you learn also that he is part of the hidden depths in the mind of men. Startled, you discover someone you would never have recognized from the legends, and you know now what Zeus meant when he said, 'Do not believe all you read.' The hands on your head are gentle and the voice of Hades is deep and resonant. 'I will remember you with love when it is your time to go down into the seeming dark; with me beside you, you will have no fear and you will learn the greatest of all secrets . . . that there is no dark . . . only a new and more beautiful light.' Then he is gone.

Now you come before Hera, wife of Zeus, and you feel a niggle of unease. She has not the best of reputations . . . Her feet are firm and strong beneath your hands and you are reminded of the women you have known that have cared for you in your life. The discipline, the strictness, but also the love beneath it and the determination that you should be able to stand upon your own feet. A contralto chuckle sounds above you and you look into the warm brown eyes of Hera. 'Truly did my Lord Zeus warn you . . . Is there not a saying in your world concerning "a bad press?"' You both laugh and her mind flows into yours and you become one with all that nurtures and upholds the family. You feel every bruised knee and lost tooth. You know, too, the closeness of the marriage bond and, with a shock, you plumb the meaning of the words *matrimony* and *sacred rite*. You feel the strength of every wife and mother living again within you and know the joys and the despairs that have been shared with this great goddess. She bends over you and places her lips on your brow. Its imprint flows through you like a benediction and, impulsively, you hold up your arms to her and she embraces you. Then she is gone to walk the earth once more and Hermes is urging you towards another throne.

Hephaestus, first-born of Hera and Zeus, the mighty Smith of Olympus. You have heard of him and his ability to create beauty in metal and jewels, and of his lameness. His feet warm quickly beneath your hands and an answering fire rises in you for the core of your body heat leaps to match the forge fire of the god. His eyes are tawny brown and gold and flames leap within them. Your link with him brings more surprises for he is far more than just a craftsman. In him there is a connection with the gods of fertility for the fires he controls and uses to shape form are also those of man's sexual nature. He has a booming laugh that reminds you of his uncle, Poseidon, and he leans low to whisper in your ear. 'Are you so shocked to learn of my hidden powers, Child of Earth? Remember, do not believe all you read.' He rises and pauses to place in your hand an exquisite pendant of gold and precious jewels. It depicts twelve tiny rings interlaced together in an intricate pattern, each carrying a different stone. You know from your mental link with him what it represents; each ring is one of the gods and, together, they make a united wholeness of Love, Power, and Wisdom. Hephaestus strides away to begin the work among men, and Hermes urges you towards the next throne. The feet are small and slender, high-arched delicate ones, they warm with life as you touch them and Hermes laughs. 'The Goddess of Love is always quick to warmth.' A silvery laugh echoes his and the scent of flowers and the fluttering of doves tell you that Aphrodite has once more come among men. Her link with you is swift and causes an instant rise of sensuality within you. But, again, you discover depths within depths and soon comes the understanding that the Goddess of Love is more than just a symbol of sexual love, she is also the laughter and the sharing of self among those who come together. She is the first love of every man and woman, then she hands over her powers to Hera who takes them further. The Love Goddess draws man to maid and buck to doe, and all creatures come to their mating because of her. You find within her the love for her smith husband denied by the poets. She is bound to him by the fires of love, but her love for Ares is also permissible and the link is the forge fire that builds both forms of beauty and of weapons. She presses a rose into your hand and glides away, her dove fluttering around her golden head, her sea-blue eyes dancing with anticipation.

You move to the throne of Ares, looking up into his red-bearded face as you place your hands on his feet. The link tells you of his role as protector of the weak and the oppressed, but also of his own weakness that allows him to be used by man's greed for power. This causes him shame and he is silent as you plumb the depths of his mind. He is asking that you control within yourself the powers that are his, those of temper, rage, desire for revenge, and the lust for power over others. With your help he can control the imbalance within himself, and you can teach others. He rises and salutes you with his sword, and asks that you forgive him for the way his power has been misused in the world. Then he strides away leaving you for the first time with the feeling of heavy responsibility that you have brought him back to the earth. But you cannot release some and not others, you cannot deny the free will of mankind to follow its own desires. Hermes watches you a little anxiously, then smiles with relief as you pass on to the golden-haired Demeter and take her stone-white feet in your hands.

She stirs and places her hand on your head and you fall into her mind like a ripe pomegranate falling from its tree. For long, breathtaking moments you know the earth in her full glory as the giver of food and shelter, you know at last your own oneness with all that lives and moves. You feel the unending patience of the great trees as they stand in their appointed places, you know the uprising of the seed in the winter ground searching for the sun and the light above. You endure the urges of the great herds as they migrate across thousands of miles. You are the corn and wheat, the rice and the barley, you are the lamb and the child, the eater and the eaten, the sacrificer and that which offers up its life. Shaken by the power you have glimpsed you will never be free of this moment, you are forever part of earth and she is part of you. Demeter rises and walks away to sow her seeds of life.

Apollo next and the first indication that he is with you is the music of his lyre. Its notes tumble into your mind and form patterns that teach and reveal, entice and lead until your head is full of whirling notes that form symbols and whisper of events yet to happen. From the centre of the notes a light appears and grows until it is too bright to look upon. It comes towards you and enters your body, passing through but leaving some of its substance within. You are left with knowledge concerning the image of a sun behind the sun, of the ordered precession of season and time. Of limitless light and music forming and creating and bringing new things into ordered time. The music stops, the light fades, but the inner knowledge will stay. Apollo bends to you and breathes his own life force into your body, you feel its healing fire flow through you and mutely thank the god for his gift. He laughs joyously and, for a brief moment, places his hand in that of his half-brother, then departs leaving behind a shaft of brilliant sunshine that lights the Hall. Hermes watches him go with affection, then takes you to Artemis.

Her coolness takes some time to warm, but soon you feel her stir. Leto's slender daughter, the huntress of the night forests, lifts one of her silver arrows and with it wounds your right hand. The blood flows and you understand her role as the huntress, that all things flee their ending and must be gently hunted to their destiny. As the Moon Goddess, she gives dreams to mankind and orders the tides in both oceans and women, for both are mothers, one of the past and one of the continuing future. Artemis now cuts her own hand and presses her blood to yours, a coldness runs through you in contrast to the heat of Apollo, but you know that it is a balanced force now that leaps within you. You understand the meaning of ebb and flow more clearly now. The goddess rises, taking her bow, and runs from the Hall, leaping into the night and calling to her hounds to follow her.

Hermes takes you now to the oldest of all the gods. His shaggy limbs and cloven hooves have terrified men down the ages. His curving horns and mocking bearded face have been made the image of evil by the ignorant. But as you touch the hooves of horn the voice above you is gentle and sad. 'Do you call me back to crucify me again, my brother?' Your shock is soul deep. Images swirl and form within your mind, you watch them sick at heart that something you have always looked up to as a faith of love washes its hands in the blood of innocents. Back in time you are taken to the beginning, seeing Pan as that which was before all things, for he *is* all things. 'I am all that was and is and will be again. I am the animals that have gone, never to be seen again. I am the plants and the small lives that shall never come again. I am the ruined forests and the oil-choked seas. I am the One who lives in every heart, I am life itself. I do not choose to be recalled who have been defiled by those I loved.' You start to plead but Hermes stops you. 'Let it be, come again in a little while and try again.' You pass the throne and come at last to Zeus once more. Gently you touch his feet and water them, as did Hermes, with your tears for the thought is in you that you have failed.

'No, not failed, none has failed that has done their best; Child of Earth, you have learned a deep and lasting lesson, not everything turns to the hand and bidding of man, but my son is right, return when you can and try again. Maybe some day you will persuade great Pan to live again. Now let me touch your mind and heart and dwell within you for a space of time.' He touches you and draws you towards him, melding you together. You know a complete oneness with him, and through him, with all the gods. You know things on a level you cannot put into words, you reach an understanding that will, in the days to come, seep through into your conscious mind little by little. Then, as suddenly, it is gone, so is Hermes and you are alone. You walk to the entrance of the Hall and look into the night. There is a faint light breaking; dawn is coming. Within the gods laugh and you laugh with them, you stretch out your arms and let the dawn winds carry you from Olympus over the mountains and the plains, over seas and lands to your own place, just ahead of the first rays of the sun. You alight before the hole in the wall through which you stepped aeons ago. Above it you see the caduceus sign and hear deep within you the silver laughter of Hermes, 'We are all one, Child of Earth, we live again in you.'

Suddenly tired, you move towards your chair and take your place, allowing weariness to overtake you. For a moment in time you sleep, then wake again with the knowledge of your journey safe within you, the first of the new Olympians.

THE HERMETIC
You will probably be relieved to know that this pathworking is not as long as the previous one – well, not quite anyway. The Hermetic type of pathworking takes in as subsidiary types the Magical, the Cabbalistic and the Alchemical. The Magical type includes the Egyptian, Chaldean, and Geometric or Pythagorean; the Celtic school, because it belongs more to the feeling/emotional type, belongs with Orphic. The following is Cabbalistic in type. The same rules of preparation apply to all workings.

The Castle
Meditate upon the glyph of the Tree of Life, build in the mind then project it outwards on to the wall opposite your chair. Keep it there and increase its strength until it glows with power. Around it there forms a door that opens slowly to reveal a pathway leading into a landscape of fertile fields and forests. You rise and walk towards the door, stepping through into the country of the mind. The path leads away and down into a pleasant valley; you meet no one and there is a feeling of emptiness about the land; animals and birds are in profusion but no human beings, or indeed, beings of any kind. Nor do you see any houses or farms. You press on through the little valley and up onto the higher ground. From here you can see a vast forest ahead and, just seen above the thick green of the trees, the top of a tower. From its turret flies a pennant bearing the Tree of Life symbol. You follow the path down the forest and enter its dark-green half light. The path becomes a mere track that winds from side to side deeper and deeper into the forest. Gradually your eyes become accustomed to the dim light and you start to notice the life of the forest around you. Rabbits scuttle across your path, deer, magnificently antlered, stop to stare at you with a golden gaze before disappearing into the deeper reaches of their green realm. Birds sing loudly from every tree and the mosses and flowers carpet the whole floor of the forest with colour and scent. Then you hear the first faint notes of music. At first you think it is the wind blowing through the branches, but then it gets louder and more insistent, calling you further into the

leafy heart of this magical place. Soon you are following eagerly, almost running as the liquid harp notes beckon you onwards. Then, they stop.

You move forward into an open space. Before you is a ruined castle; the steps leading to its massive rusting gate are broken and misaligned. The Gatehouse looms darkly against what little can be seen of the sky overhead, and the whole place smells of a silence long observed. Between the bars of the gate you can see beyond into a courtyard with grass and weeds growing in between the ancient flagstones, then further on, the dark outline of the castle itself, the great oaken door shut tight.

In your heart you know this place holds some adventure for you, and that here you will find the source of the music you heard in the forest. With a fast-beating heart you climb the broken steps and push open the rusty gate. The scream of its mouldering hinges in the heavy silence makes you jump, but you go on into the courtyard. Looking about, you see the massive walls towering above you with the small window slits offering only minimal light to the interior. But above and beyond you can just see glimpses of turrets and small towers, balconies and larger windows that must surely give on to bigger rooms. You walk across the courtyard and try the door to the Great Hall. It seems locked and there is no key that you can find. But above the door in ancient script you can read the words, 'Knock, and enter'. Set into the middle of the door is a dirt-encrusted door-knocker shaped like a woman's head. You lift it and knock three times. The mouth of the knocker moves, and slowly, as if it had forgotten how to speak, the mouth says, 'Who knocks at the door of the Castle of Images?'

Surprise makes you silent, so the knocker repeats the question somewhat testily, then, recovering, you give your name and the door swings open allowing you to enter the Great Hall. In the middle of the floor is a huge fire pit, the iron roasting spit still in place. Around the walls are wooden tables with benches on both sides and at the far end of the Hall, raised on a dais, another table with a richly decorated cloth now tattered and covered in dust and cobwebs. Behind the table stand three high-backed chairs, beautifully carved. Around the walls hang tapestries and banners and here and there great war-shields with crossed spears behind them. On the walls around the Hall are iron torch sconces and at one side a staircase leads up to a gallery with one door in the centre. You now see other doors leading from the Hall, one on the right and one on the left, and one small one half hidden by a curtain directly behind the centre chair on the dais. You walk around the Hall and begin to look more closely at the tapestries and carvings. There are four main hangings and they depict the four seasons of the earth. Each one shows ordinary people working at their tasks of sowing, ploughing, reaping and threshing. Around the edges are shown the symbols of the four elements and the four winds of heaven. The carvings on the chairs and stairway are of fruit, and wheatsheaves, animals, and flowers. The hanging behind the chairs shows a young girl walking through a forest with an armful of flowers in her arms, and in her hair; clustered about her feet are the wild creatures of the forest. Her smile is warm and sweet and woven into the edge of the hanging is her name, Kallah, the Bride.

You pause for a moment to reflect on all these things and to realize that you stand in the Hall of Malkuth, the place of the Earth Mother, with all around you the symbols of her fertility, yet it is cold and uninviting, damp and drear. You go out into the courtyard and look for the woodpile, finding it in a corner. With some effort you carry enough into the Hall to fill the pit, then holding your hand over the logs and reaching down into your own inner core of body heat, you contact the Ashim, the Souls of Fire. 'Burn!' . . . and the wood leaps into life, throwing warm shadows onto the walls and ceiling. You go to the sconces and give the same command. 'Burn!' . . . and the long-dead torches flame into life. The spit begins to turn above the fire and now it holds a side of beef slowly roasting over the logs. Voices of long-forgotten revellers sound within the Hall and soon it rings to the noise of happy people feasting and enjoying the benefits the earth has provided. The Hall of Malkuth has come alive once more.

You take a torch from the wall and open the small door behind the dais. It opens on to a narrow passage lit only by the daylight coming from a slit window and leading to another door with big iron hinges. You open it and see steps leading down into the darkness beyond. Holding the torch high you climb down. At the bottom you stumble over something and looking down you see a skull lying among a heap of bones. For a minute you stand there contemplating the pitiful remains and thinking that this is what all men must come to in the end. You bless them and pass on. The path slopes downwards and becomes a winding passage with a rough, uneven floor. You pass doors heavily barred, from behind which come strange and fearful noises. Each door is sealed with a symbol, some you know, others are new to you, but you are aware that you must not open these doors until you have more knowledge of yourself and your abilities.

Now the passage starts to go uphill again and the way is easier. Ahead there is a door that must lead back into the castle but, before that, there is another door, like the others barred and sealed with a small grill set into it and written below it is your own name. You are about to open it and look when a rough voice behind you whispers, 'Do not open the door.' You look back and see an armoured figure behind you. It kneels before you explaining that it was once the knight whose bones you blessed and gave rest to. For this he has taken shape one last time to warn you. 'That door holds back all that is degenerate in your own self. Do not seek to open that which you cannot withstand, or like Pandora you will let loose your lower nature. Take heed and pass on.' The knight disappears and you pass on to open the door leading back into the castle.

You enter a room small and circular with windows all around; like the Hall below its walls are covered with hangings, but these show the star patterns of the night sky. In one window bay stands an old-fashioned telescope, and above you the ceiling has a glass dome. In the very centre of the room stands a stone font filled with water and around the edge is written, 'Only the wise man or the fool can safely look into the waters of the moon.' For a while you stand and think about which of these categories is yours, then you remember that the Hermit and the Fool are of equal importance and represent every human being that searches for truth. You step forward and look into the dark water. What you see there is only for you to know. When you are ready go through the door opposite the one through which you entered and find yourself standing on the gallery above the Great Hall. To one side a small passage leads away from the little Hall of Yesod and further along joins a larger passage lined with banners, shields, carvings and tapestries that glow with all the colours of the rainbow.

Along this corridor you hear once more the silver sound of the harp. It seems to be coming from the big double doors ahead of you. The doors are carved with many ancient symbols and the handles are formed like circlets of roses. You take hold of them and push them open.

You come into a Hall much larger than the one downstairs and far more beautiful.

It has three windows; that facing you has been cut from crystal and has many facets which colour the light entering. The other windows have pictures inset into them. On your left it is that of a bull, on your right a lion, behind you a carved eagle sits over the lintel of the great doors. But the most breathtaking sight of all is the huge round table that takes up most of the Hall. Seated around it are many figures but they are not easy to see for they seem to be made of pure light. Dimly you perceive knights, and ladies, but also others of many kinds and forms, not all of them human. In the centre of the table lies a sword; it is plain and simple with just a single ruby set into the hilt. The figure directly opposite you stands and takes the sword in its hand. It speaks.

'You who have penetrated to the Hall of Excalibur know this, that all who come here must prove their worth in the outer world. When you return you will start upon the search for that which men call the Grail, but which, in reality, is your own heartself. When you have proved yourself to those who sit here, then will you be recalled to take your place among us. Now go on and behold the veiled image of that which you must seek.'

You bow and walk towards the door behind Arthur's seat. As you open it you hear again that sound of the harp drawing you onwards. You see before you a winding stair, its treads made of mother of pearl. As you climb up you can see through the tiny windows that you are very high up, you can see the forest and the enclosed gardens of the castle below you. You hope that one day you can explore the castle further and search out its secrets. Before you the music grows louder until you come before an arch filled with light. It seems to you that you can see the ground below you, that this opening is a deception leading you to destruction. Yet the music urges you on and, placing your trust in the unknown, you step forward . . . into a small chapel. There is only one thing in it: an ancient wooden box fitted with carrying poles, at each corner of which a carved seraphim kneels with hands and face uplifted. Symbols are carved around the four sides of the box and it is closed with a lock of pure gold.

As you stand before this wonder it begins to open and you cover your eyes against the light that it contains. The harp music quivers to a halt and all is silence. Through your protecting fingers you feel the light dim enough for you to see and there, standing within the ancient casket, is a veiled chalice. The music begins again and now you know, it comes from the Grail itself. The music pours out, enfolding you and healing you, filling you with strength and love and peace, but it also brings self-knowledge and you weep, for you know how far you stand from what was ordained for you. But the Chalice sings of hope and light and the promise of support. Now it sings of sleep and dreams and you curl up before the Ark and sleep, protected by these two eternal symbols.

In your dreams you see the castle from above and now you can see that it has the outline of the Tree of Life. Its topmost turret lies within the reach of clouds and is illuminated with the sun. You know that you may return to this place whenever you wish to explore and search out all its secrets, but you know also that what you find may not always be pleasant, for this is the castle of your inner self and you must be prepared to face all the facets of your personality.

You wake slowly to find yourself in an empty room with no sign of its former glory. You descend the stairs and retrace your steps back to the Hall of Excalibur. This too is empty, only the great table remains. You return the way you came, finally coming back to the Hall of Malkuth where there is still a lingering warmth. You promise yourself that you will return, soon. The door shuts firmly behind you and you cross the courtyard, pausing to look at the weeds . . . maybe you could start to tidy it up. With plans already beginning to form in your head you find yourself back in the forest with the sounds of birdsong and the wind all around you. You turn for a last look at the castle, then make your way back through the forest, singing as you go with an unseen harp accompanying you.

At the entrance to your own world you stop and think about what you have seen and heard and learnt. This place is yours now, you can bring the castle - your inner self - back to its former glory and make it beautiful again. It will not happen in one or two visits, but then you have all the time you need. You step through into your own world.

★   ★   ★

When using Bible stories as pathworkings it is advisable to do the working as an onlooker rather than a participant, at least for several months. The power built up by actually participating in them is considerable and can be very disturbing, especially to newcomers to the art. Try New Testament stories first; they are easier to cope with than the Old Testament. When you feel you can cope with any power surges that may come, you can start 'being there'. The parables and the teachings, like the Sermon on the Mount, are the easiest to work with. Much later you can try taking on the role of a follower, disciple, or one of His friends. I must caution you against taking on the persona of any who were cured of illness or any complaint as related in the New Testament. This can be extremely dangerous and can end with you being caught up in that persona and, consequently, with a copy-cat form of the same illness or symptoms.

The same applies with the Old Testament. Be careful what you choose to work, read the part through with great thoroughness before trying it out. A book called *Everyday Life in the Bible Lands* will be useful for gathering details about dress and everyday things like pots, footwear, food, etc. There are some that lend themselves to pathworking very well, like David dancing before the Ark, or singing his psalms to the music of his harp. The story of Esther, or Deborah or Susanna can be used because there is a wealth of detail in them. Remember, too, that the Apocrypha contains some truly beautiful passages that were cut from the Bible as we were taught it but which repay reading. The Acts of John contain the wonderful Lord of the Dance ritual which makes a marvellous working. You may even copy it as a ritual in its own right.

Even if you are not a practising Christian you should try one or two workings in this style as, indeed, you should try some in the style of other faiths and religions because it will give you a much deeper insight into their teachings. You don't have to practise a faith to understand it or grant it the right to exist . . . remember that the United Nations Charter grants to all men and women the freedom to worship in their own way and according to their beliefs . . . something that is conveniently overlooked by some people. Tolerance is the hardest of all virtues to acquire!

THE MYSTICAL

The Mystical pathworking is akin to what is sometimes called the Practice of the Presence of God. As has been mentioned in a previous chapter, the spiritual exercises upon which Ignatius de Loyola based the training of the Society of Jesus are in every sense similar in make-up and application to the occult pathworking. Today, being an occultist does not mean giving up one's orthodox faith, far from it, occultism merely opens up deeper levels of whatever faith one practises and gives a different viewpoint of its teachings. This being so, I have included in this chapter a Christian Mystical pathworking in order to show those who delight in abusing the occult movement and labelling it as un-Christian that we are not as 'black' as we are painted – though criticism coming from a faith whose priests have possibly the bloodiest hands in history has always seemed strange to me. Jesus of Nazareth, I am sure, would not have advocated the wholesale slaughter of primitive people because they believed differently, nor would He have lit the pyres of the Inquisition. As one of the greatest of initiates He had love enough for all people, including tax-collectors, thieves, whores, and those who professed other faiths and beliefs.

One of the most relaxing of all guided workings is to regress in age and become a child once more. One experiences again the feeling of being able to rely on someone older and wiser than oneself. This is the feeling aimed for in this pathworking, though having said that do not be lulled into thinking it has no power.

The Children's Parable

Build the symbol of the Star of David on the wall and let it enlarge until it forms an entrance into the world beyond the world. Step through

into a hot dry dusty day full of chatter and noise and the bustle that
only comes when a lot of people are living and working close together.
You look down at your feet; they are much smaller than before, smaller
and rather dirty and bare. Thin brown legs and a rough homespun tunic
or dress girded with a bit of the same material. Over your head is another
piece of cloth as protection against the fierce heat of the sun. You are
conscious of an empty stomach but you are also conscious that this is
nothing unusual. Many people in this village are hungry at least some
of the time.

A group of children about the same age as yourself run past and you
join them. They accept you as one of them and show no curiosity; you
are known and friendly to them. The main gathering place is the well
and you all sit around listening to the gossip of the women, giggling
and pointing at the young girls who, only a few months ago, were running
as wildly as yourselves. Now they are promised in marriage and have
to learn the work of women.

You are enjoying the more juicy bits of tongue-wagging when one
of the women looks up and, with a frown, shoos you all away. Like a
flock of dusty birds you set off down the little street, the only street
in your village. You tumble in and out of every shop and stall, peering
into houses and chasing the goats that roam everywhere. You play hide-
and-seek among the narrow entrances and yards of the flat-roofed houses
until you find a shady place and sit together chattering and laughing
among yourselves, gradually quietening down as the sun climbs higher
and grows hotter. Soon most of the children are asleep but you remain
awake, a feeling of excitement running through your veins. There is a
sense of waiting for someone, someone you know, and yet have never
met. Deep within you can feel this tremendous something drawing nearer
and you watch the dirt road that leads out of town, watching and waiting
for someone to come into sight.

As you wait you look about you carefully, storing up memories and
making mental notes of the little village and those that live in it. There
is a sense of familiarity about it all. As the day wears on the sun gets
a little cooler and the children begin to wake one by one and they too
begin to watch the road. Finally you all walk up the road to the well
and watch the women drawing the evening water. The children are thirsty
and the women take turns in drawing cool water from the deep well
so that they can drink. When your turn comes, it is a sweet-faced woman
that offers you her pitcher. Her smile is gentle and warm and she seems
different to the others, wiser, more caring, more motherly. You look up
at her and she smiles and nods her head as if the two of you shared

a secret. Then she lifts her eyes, looking down the road into the sun-hazed distance and her whole face lights up. There is joy in her face and a terrible sorrow underlying it. For a moment it chills you and you clutch at her hand seeking to comfort her. She looks down and quickly runs her hand over your head as if in blessing, then she lifts the pitcher and walks gracefully away towards her own house fronted by the carpenter's shop. The children are jumping up and down yelling and laughing and with you among them run off down the road towards a group of dusty figures trudging up the road. Fathers, uncles and elder brothers are greeted with delight and the children are hugged and cuddled, swung up on to broad shoulders that, although weary, still have the strength to bear the slight burden of a beloved son or daughter. Only you hang back, conscious that you do not belong here, that you have no claim on any of these laughing bearded men. You feel lost, and very alone, and turn away.

Then you feel a hand upon your shoulder and look up into a pair of dark gentle eyes. A smiling bearded face speaks your name, and its alien modern sound seems utterly natural on his lips. *He* takes your hand in his and you walk together into the village.

The women gather round to pour water over tired feet and hands and to offer the day's news to the menfolk. Then they drift away to start the evening meal and the men settle down to rest and talk. Only you and your friend sit apart, silently at first and then he begins to talk, pointing out the tall cedars growing on the hills around, telling you how trees like this were used to build King David's great temple. He draws you a plan of the huge building in the dust and tells you that he was there when he was young and about the richness of the furnishings inside and the golden Menorah before the altar. You listen contentedly to the sound of his voice. When it stops you look up and meet his gaze and say in the time-honoured way of all children, 'Tell me a story please.' His smile holds all the love that any child could wish for and he lifts you into his lap and holds you close. You can feel the warmth of his body and hear the beat of his heart. He is real, as real as you are and the story begins, your story told only for you.

Once long ago when the earth had just been made and it was as bright as a newborn star, the Lord God walked upon its green hills and valleys and loved His creation. He looked upon the animals and the birds, the trees and the flowers, the oceans and the mountains, and then He looked upon mankind and He loved them all, and they loved Him. But after a while the Lord God became sad and the Bright Ones who walked with Him were troubled and asked Him why He wept. The Lord God said, 'I have looked upon mankind and seen his love for me, but that love is there because I am the only one of whom he has knowledge. He loves because there is nothing else to love . . . I wish to give mankind free will to love where he will so I may know that when a man or woman says "I love the Lord God" it is because they have chosen to love me. To do this there must be one who shall oppose me and tempt mankind to deny me, that he may choose of his own free will to turn to me alone. Say, which of you my Bright Ones, will do this for love of me, who will depart from my Presence until time shall run its course? Who will deny me and seek to turn mankind against me that he may choose from his own heart who to serve?'

Then did all the Bright Ones turn away their shining faces and weep and the Lord God went among them saying to each one, 'Will you do this for me? Who will set his face against me for my sake and be cast out of Paradise? Who? Who?' But they all wept and said, 'Not I, O Lord God, not I, do not ask this of me', and they turned away.

And the Lord God sat upon the tallest mountain and was troubled in His heart. Then there came to Him the brightest of all His Lords of Light, the best beloved of His heart, the Archangel Lucifer, whose name means He who brings the Light. The mighty Archangel knelt before the Lord God and placed his hands in His and wept, and through his tears he offered to be cast out from Paradise and until time ran out to tempt mankind away from Him that man might know free will.

'Is there no other one who will go from me?' asked the Lord God, 'No other than you, my Beloved? Must I lose you for all time?' And there was no answer from the other Shining Ones. Then up rose the Lord God and made this decree, that Lucifer should be cast out of Paradise and banished until time was no more. That he should tempt mankind away from God that he might know free will. And God spoke saying of Lucifer, 'And Man shall revile you and cast a shadow upon thy brightness and shall know it not for what it truly is, and thou shalt tempt every man and every woman, yea, even the One I shall send to man in my stead shall you tempt, and none but the wisest of the wise shall know of this sacrifice; but to ease the pain I give thee one wish, name it.'

For the last time Lucifer, the Morning Star, looked upon the unknowable face of the Lord God and asked that every time a man or woman turned away from him and towards God that he would be granted one hour to stand at the Gate of Paradise and hear the singing of his brethren about the throne of God. And this was granted. Then Lucifer took his leave of his brethren. Dark-eyed Uriel and silver-winged Gabriel, gentle Raphael wept and embraced him and then Michael, the warrior

angel, cried aloud in despair at his task, then took the Bright One and
cast him from the sight of the Lord God. And from the tallest mountain
on the earth in those days he fell for a day and a night like a shooting
star burning brightly as he fell. Since those ancient days he has kept
the promise to his God and has tempted mankind against Him. But
every time they deny Him he sits for one short hour at the great Gate
of Paradise and his brethren gather there and sing for him.

The voice dies away and you bury your head in his shoulder, not
wanting the moment to end, but he puts you away from him and tells
you, 'You must learn to be strong so that, when the time comes, your
strength may grant my brother an hour of bliss at the Gate of Paradise.
Can you do this for me?' You look up into his face, not the pale fair-
skinned face on school-room walls, but a strong, dark face with a curving
nose and a slightly crooked tooth and eyes that hold a pain too deep
for you to understand. Your voice when it comes is stronger than you
thought you could make it. 'I can do this for you, Yeheshua. I will be
strong when the time comes.' He smiles and takes your hand and together
you walk up the street in the gathering dusk to a strange hole in a wall.
Looking through you can see your own room. You turn and hug him
one last time, then tumble through the hole into your own world and
your own time.

CHAPTER TWELVE

Examples II

We have been through examples of traditional types of pathworkings. Now we should look at the more abstract types, for they are just as valid in what they can offer and what they can teach. The easiest to start with are paintings, for they offer an already built-in scene. The choice is vast, it simply depends on your taste. However, I would warn you against going for the works of Michelangelo, Da Vinci and Botticelli, etc. as starting-points, simply because the mind of the Renaissance artist overshadows his works and you are quite liable to get caught up in the person rather than the subject he was painting. Rather you should choose the gentler English painters like Constable, Turner, or the contemporary artists who are sometimes looked down upon for turning out 'mass-produced' paintings. But although they may not have the haunting quality of Turner, nor the almost three-dimensional detail of Constable, yet they do provide the eye with what it needs in the context of pathworking, which is – a subject that invites you into the picture.

In Hawkwood College in Stroud there used to be a painting that I coveted more than all the great names put together. I do not know the name of the artist, but it was perfect. The eye was looking from the edge of a wood down a narrow path towards a house all but hidden by its surrounding wall. The door, an old wooden affair looking to be in need of a coat of paint, had swung half open and one could just see the hint of a beautiful cottage-type garden. That picture held a promise of peace, tranquillity and beauty that I will never forget. I can recall it in detail and use it frequently as a relaxation exercise when I am tired and tense. There are many similar modern paintings and even posters that can be bought or studied in a gallery. A second-hand shop often has a pile of dusty pictures tucked away in a corner that can be bought for a few pounds. It may take a time but you can eventually find a favourite that will become your mainstay and which you can use as a starting-point for many pleasant workings. For while the traditional pathworkings are used as teaching aids, a picture, a piece of music or a poem is used mainly for pleasure or for total relaxation of mind and body, something that is needed more and more in this day and age.

All but the avant-garde artists tell a story with their painting, whether or not they intend to do so. The surrealistic schools are not suitable simply because contemplation of their work induces tension rather than dispelling it. It is up to you to try out variations and explore the inner depths of the picture. I have 'seen' the inside of my walled garden in every season, helped with the planting and the weeding, picked summer flowers and autumn fruits and put out crumbs for the birds in winter. The house is known to me and I have spent many happy visits there. I have others of course, and you will come to yours if you look and anticipate the finding.

These are very personal workings and are best kept to oneself or used with someone with whom you are very close. We all need a hidden place of our own where we can be at ease, and as we have already seen, such a place can become the starting point of the greatest adventure of all, the journey into that far country 'from whose bourne no traveller returns'.

Pictures have always been magical things for, in many cases, they depict scenes from within the mind of the artist and so are already part of the inner world; in just looking at them you are half-way there. Paintings have always held a fascination for us, and writers have been quick to exploit this theme. *The Picture of Dorian Gray* is probably the best-known example. Many television plays have taken the idea of entering a picture and living within its painted landscape as a very successful theme, and some years ago I saw a play that like the picture at Hawkwood has remained with me. The picture, showing a simple landscape of hills and woods, had at its central point a thatched cottage with a lovely garden. One of the two main characters, an elderly and lonely office cleaner, often visits the art gallery where the picture hangs and dreams of living in the old cottage. She makes friends with one of the attendants, like herself old and lonely, and they sit before the picture together, dreaming. One day they make the discovery that they can enter the picture and find that the cottage has been waiting for them to arrive. Two or three times a week they visit the place and come to think of it as their home. Then the gallery is sold and the pictures packed up ready for the auction room.

The old lady manages to enter the picture before it is packed and promises to wait for her friend who has to say goodbye to his son. When he arrives at the gallery only a few of the packaged paintings remain. Frantically he tears at the packing cases looking for the right one, and all the while the carriers are removing them one by one. Finally, he finds the painting of the cottage, only now the old lady is standing by the gate waving. He makes the transition and they walk together into the house, from the chimney of which there now rises a plume of smoke. Simple it may have been, but it has impact enough for me to remember the play for over twenty-five years.

This is the kind of feeling one should look for when choosing a painting to work with. One modern mass-market reproduction shows a vivid autumn landscape of trees in many shades of gold and russet; the ground is covered with leaves and there is a pathway leading away into the middle distance. The colour and the composition make this ideal for a working.

When you have made your choice, spend quite a while just looking at it and thinking about it before you attempt a working. Try to work out a possible route, or even several; think ahead to what might be hidden just out of sight. In your imagination extend the edges of the picture gradually until, in your mind, it covers the whole wall giving you a much wider view. Then, when you are satisfied that you have prepared as much as you can, make the first pathworking. Do not go beyond the actual scene for the first few times, explore the scene as it appears and make yourself familiar with it and with all the nooks and crannies that you have been looking at for several days. Make those first times quite short, just five minutes or so, and slowly extend it to ten. Then there will come a time when you stand at the edge of the picture and you *know* it is time to go further and deeper into that part of the picture that, as yet, you have not visited. Fix your internal clock to bring you back after fifteen minutes and never allow yourself to extend beyond twenty at the most. Pathworking for pleasure can become too pleasurable and this will, in time, disrupt your everyday life. Remember what was said in the first chapter about the dangers of Dungeons and Dragons. This type of working can become addictive. It should be a way of ridding yourself of tension and not allowed to become a way of escape.

When using a painting as a jumping-off point for a *group* working, care should be taken that the subject is agreeable to everyone concerned. If not, you will get one or two people hanging back in their visualization and that can invalidate the whole working. I have written in *The Ritual Magic Workbook* about the power of the group mind and it must be thoroughly understood that when you are doing a group pathworking a group mind can snap into existence with great speed. The power of the group mind depends upon the closeness of the group and the way they feel about the subject chosen. If they all like it and there is no dissension, the group mind will provide a lot of power to the actual working and much may be gained. If, on the other hand, there is no great enthusiasm, the whole thing will fall flat.

If you intend to form a Pathworking Group, choose your people carefully. Sharing the inner landscapes of the mind with people you do not like will slowly but surely build up blocks and you may find it harder and harder to enter the inner world, even when on your own. Compatibility is top priority when selecting your group. It is far better to have people who are not expert visualizers but with whom you feel comfortable than to take in experienced members who irritate you or any of the others.

Make one person responsible for organizing and working out the mundane problems *before* you start any work at all. A good reliable recorder should be used, preferably with a built-in stereo, or equipment that links in to a stereo system. That is ideal, but good results can be obtained with a simple common or garden recorder. Use high-quality tapes and make certain that everyone chips in towards their cost. Do not jeopardize your potential group mind with hidden animosity because you always seem to be buying the tapes or providing the coffee and biscuits. Make a small sum payable each week from each member and take it in turns to buy the refreshments, and make a written rota so that everyone knows in advance whose turn it is this week. It is best, however, to stick to the same location each time, and the same day and date if possible. This helps the group mind to form more quickly and, as it grows stronger, it becomes 'aware' of the timing and begins to build up a day or so ahead of time.

Don't go straight into the working; allow at least twenty minutes of socializing before the work starts, and then begin with a five or ten minute period of inner quiet. Then, when everyone has slowed down and relaxed, you can start. You might like to read out some of the reports sent in about the last meeting and discuss them, or you might like to end the evening with such a discussion. Whatever you decide, make the atmosphere pleasant and free from tension.

Because of the effects of pathworkings it is best to start with no more than one every two weeks for at least six months. This is quite enough for a group to handle. Remember, when you work on your own you are dealing with just your own power sources, with a group you are going to intensify that by as many members as are gathered together. When you have become used to each other and to the group mind you can increase that to one a week, but groupwise it should never be more than that. If you select a working that is fully guided there should be few problems; if you choose a passive working – and most workings with

a picture as a focal point are passive – then make sure you have a signal
to call everyone back. A small bell can be used, but make sure its sound
is sweet and not strident. I have found that a small travelling alarm clock
with a buzz rather than a bell suits me better as it can be set for whatever
time is being allowed and no one has to keep one eye open to ring the bell.

Set your picture up where everyone can see it clearly. Remember you
are going to use it for several sessions, and discuss its points and make
certain they all look at it very carefully. If it is a piece of music, they
should all have had the opportunity to listen to it by themselves at least
once before meeting to use it as a working. It is best to refrain from
discussing the music beforehand because it tends to put pre-set ideas
into the head. With a picture the image is half-way there; with music
it should be allowed to build its own mind pictures. It should be
mentioned here that in the case of music, and perhaps poetry too, the
time must be elastic. One cannot confine a musical piece to twenty
minutes, or cut down a fairly long poem. This is where one's own
common sense comes in and you must make your own decisions. Always
allow your group time to 'come back' fully; some people take longer
than others. Wait until everyone seems to have their feet back on the
ground, and then bring in the refreshments. I have found personally
that it is a good idea to have the coffee/tea ready-made in a flask and
a tray laid so that little time is lost in getting the group closed down
psychically. Until they have had this, do not allow any discussions. When
everyone has something hot inside them, then you can let them loose.

It is up to you as to whether you ask for written reports later in the
week, or if you prefer to discuss the working there and then. Whichever
you choose make sure there is a record of what is said. Records are vital,
not just for you, but for those that come after. You may find yourself
growing as a group and, if this happens, inevitably you will grow too
big and have to divide into two groups. If this happens, don't feel sad,
you have achieved something very important.

Where you choose a poem the format should be that a selection is
offered to the group and a choice is made in this way. That done, the
poem should be recorded and, as with the music, each member of the
group should both read the poem themselves, silently and aloud in their
own homes, and listen to it as they will hear it at the meeting. If one
of your number has a good reading voice you are lucky; if not then may
I suggest that you go to the local drama group and ask one of their star
members if they would record a series of poems for you.

In my experience they will jump at the chance. Alternatively, your
local library, if it has a record section, will probably have or be able to

obtain a record of some famous voice reading poetry aloud. They are often made for blind people and most of the famous poems have been recorded in anthologies or by the author.

Poems as workings are not everybody's cup of tea. A pity, since they offer a key to the inner world that has unique properties. A painting is often taken from life or from an amalgamation of several memories of similar places. A piece of music is inspired by a feeling, an emotion, an event, or a place, and shared with those who listen to the finished product. More often than not, a poet writes for himself alone and, therefore, you are eavesdropping in the mind of a stranger.

People have very varied tastes in poetry; some loathe it, some love it. You will have to find out if you are running a group what their tastes are in art, music and writings. If you are friends it is possible that you will share similar tastes, but don't bank on that. I have friends who go into raptures over the music of Benjamin Britten. I cannot stand it, but will listen to Sibelius and Delius by the hour. You will soon find that running a group, any kind of group, is by no means easy, whether it be for a twice-monthly pathworking or raising money for the local hospital. You will need patience, tact, and more understanding of human nature than you ever knew you possessed.

At your inaugural meeting draw up a list of poetry or poets, music or composers and ask for ideas about paintings. Alternatively, ask each member to submit a list themselves. You might organize a trip to the local art gallery, or to one in a nearby city. Concerts also will give you many ideas, as will listening to programmes like the Proms or the recitals given almost every day on the radio.

You will soon find that some composers are more visual than others; the same with poets. Elgar, Vaughan Williams, Borodin, Mussorgsky, Prokofiev, Grieg, Sibelius, Wagner, Shostakovitch, Delius, Dvorak and Debussy all offer music that is extremely visual. Elgar's 'Enigma Variations', and Vaughan Williams' 'Fantasia on Greensleeves' and 'Fantasia on English Folk Songs', are made for pathworkings. A lovely piece called 'On the Steppes of Central Asia' will repay listening, as will Delius' work 'A Walk to the Paradise Garden' and 'Summer Song' and Dvorak's 'New World Symphony'. Gershwin's music is not to be overlooked. He wrote serious music as well as light musical comedy, and Percy Grainger's 'Country Dances' suite will delight you with its springing rhythms. There is another suite of three pieces called 'The Three Elisabeths' that offers a great deal, and do not forget the overtures, 'Aida', 'The Pearl Fishers', 'Fingal's Cave', and even that which introduces 'The Yeoman of the Guard'. You will discover many delights in searching for musical pathworkings, some new and some old favourites. Don't be put off by the fact that some have been a little overplayed, like 'Clair de Lune', and 'La Mer' or 'Le Bateau' by Debussy; remember that he was an occultist himself. For inducing a memory of summer and long hot days in the sun, when the actual temperature outside is zero and snow is forecast, I suggest you play 'L'Après-midi d'un Faune'. For the invocation of sheer heat it is unsurpassed. Nijinsky's interpretation of this piece caused a near riot in Paris when it was first performed in public. Its sensuous rhythms and erotic overtones as danced by Nijinsky were too much even for the sophisticated Parisians of that era, and an apopletic Diagileff screamed at the dancer, 'Do you realize you have masturbated in front of the whole of Paris!'

The medieval poets offer some very visual pieces, most of them being actual stories that can be followed easily in the mind. The eighteenth- and nineteenth-century poets also returned to the more evocative telling of tales and drew very near to the ancient way of the bard and the troubadour. Byron's *Childe Harold* and Tennyson's *Idylls of the King* have already been discussed but I would urge you, if you are thinking of using them, to make certain the recording is adequate to the occasion. Nothing is worse than trying to build inner visions images when the voice of the narrator is totally unaware of rhythm or inflexion, or has a grating voice.

At the end of this chapter you will find a list of music and poetry all of which will be found eminently suitable for your purposes. The paintings you will have to search out for yourself, although in the following example I have used a fairly well-known painting as a guided working just to give you an idea of what can be done. With regard to poetry, do not forget the works of St. John of the Cross and Teresa of Avila. They can offer a deeply spiritual experience for those who follow the orthodox side of Christian Mysticism. As regards music, do try to watch the televising of the last night of the Proms. It offers a superb example of a musically invoked group mind.

THE PICTURE WORKING

Constable painted Flatford Mill many times, but instead of using *The Haywain*, the picture I have chosen is almost the same one, but without the horse and cart, showing simply the mill, the river with a distant view of meadows and a small boat carrying two people. The picture is entitled *Willy Lott's Cottage*.

First let us look at the picture more closely. In the foreground is the river and part of a rocky outcrop that seems to protrude from the water causing small eddies of water. To the right we see a brick wall built against the overflow of the river and the late sunshine is just catching it, making the bricks glow with warmth and beauty. Leaning over the wall is a figure. It looks to be that of a young girl. She is fishing and such is the artistry that one could almost see the place where the line has landed. Beyond the figure a series of trees rises in height and forms a cluster about a tiny cottage structure almost lost among the overgrown vegetation of the bank. To the left, we see on the river itself a boat carrying two people, a man and a girl. She is looking down into the water as he poles the craft along. Behind and just above them rises Flatford Mill itself with a wooden jetty easing out into the river. Again a series of trees takes the eye back to the centre of the picture where the trees on both sides of the river form an archway of green framing the distant water meadows. The whole scene is one of quietness and tranquillity.

First let us imagine the scene as if we were the figure with the fishing rod. You are walking along a very narrow path leading to the wall; you are carrying the rod and line and perhaps a small basket in which to put your catch. The sun has not yet set. It must be about half-past-four or five and you can still enjoy the warm sunshine. Reaching the wall you pause and look across at the mill. You can hear the hum of the wheels and the murmur of voices, and louder still in your ears is the hum of bees as they take their fill of the flowers crowding the river bank.

You prepare your line and cast it out into the lazily moving water, hearing the faint plop as the bait settles and sinks. Now you settle down to watch and wait. The water makes small eddies around the rocks and there is a constant chattering sound as it makes its way through the meadows; you can almost hear what it is saying. From further downstream comes a small boat poled along by a young man, probably a farmer's son from downriver. He draws near to the wooden jetty and he and his companion, a girl, maybe his sister, unload the heavy sacks. A call from the young man brings the miller himself, and between them they carry the sacks up into the mill. In a few minutes they reappear carrying the flour, already ground, back to the boat. In a short while all is safely stowed away and there is the clink of coin as payment is made, then the man climbs back into the boat and, after casting off the rope, guides the heavily laden boat back into the middle of the river.

You feel the pull of your line and reel in a plump fish; quickly you put the fish into the basket and reset the line. You are quite content here to fish and watch the water, and listen to the distant hum of summer insects. You look down the river and imagine what the far-off meadows are like, what the inside of the mill is like. Perhaps you will see next time you come here. Perhaps you will call to the young man and the girl in the boat and ask them to take you across, or better still to take you on down the river. But for now you are quite happy to pass the time fishing and enjoying the sun.

After a while longer you pull in another fish. That is enough for tea. You wind in the line and cover the dish in the basket with some large dock leaves to keep them cool. Before you leave you look across at the mill. The miller himself is standing on the little jetty. He sees you and waves cheerily. You wave back, then turn and walk down the little path and into your own world.

Each time you visit the picture make sure you start off with the scene as it is painted, then go on from there. Make a note of what you see and hear, even down to the smallest detail. You will find this builds up the inner life of the picture, the one that was actually going on as it was painted. Always make the first move when working inside a picture, do not let the figures initiate any event at all. To do so is to run the risk of allowing them to become too real for comfort. Play safe and make sure you always have control of all that happens within the framework of the painting.

THE POEM

Possibly one of the most descriptive poems is Alfred Tennyson's 'The Lady of Shalott'. With its subtle rhythms and delicate images it is ideal for a pathworking. Tennyson, although outwardly the ideal Victorian family man, had a strong inner vision that showed clearly in his writings. He was fond of meditating upon his own Christian name, something that comes close to modern day transcendental meditation with its personal mantra. There is no doubt that this practice would have induced some form of altered state and, like Coleridge, he used this heightened perception as a source of inspiration.

The poem is full of half-tones and lightly drawn touches and, though to ears used to a modern metre it can sound overly Victorian, it still has the power to move if read by someone who cares about the imprisoned Lady. If we think back to Chapter 2 and recall what has been said about the Sleeping Princess in her hidden tower, then this poem seems to take on a new and far deeper meaning. The Lady becomes the bright inner self, condemned to sit alone and weave just what she can see in a mirror, another magical symbol for the soul. She sees in this mirror a knight with whom she falls in love (the conscious self). For him she is willing to give up all, including her life. (The inner self dearly wants to join forces with the outer self so that they can become a whole person, and for this it will risk all.) She does the forbidden thing and emerges from her tower unbidden and tries to contact her chosen one, but he is not ready for such a mating and the Lady dies alone as she had lived.

The Lady of Shalott

The poem is far too long to copy entirely so it is my intention simply to indicate those stanzas which in particular serve to enhance the pathworking. The poem should be read once or twice silently and read aloud at frequent intervals prior to actually using it as a working. If one of the group has a good voice, a 'live' reading does much to enhance the effect. You will find the poet's description of the scenes so vivid that there should be little difficulty in building the images. The first part sets the actual scene describing the island and its immediate surroundings. The first five lines establish the reading rhythm.

> On either side the river lie
> Long fields of barley and of rye,
> That clothe the wold and meet the sky;
> And thro' the field the road runs by
> To many towered Camelot . . .

We are already there, looking at a small islet in a river with ripening fields on either side. This is countryside but Camelot, with its spires and towers, is not far away.

> . . . Four gray walls and four gray towers,
> Overlook a space of flowers,
> And the silent isle embowers
> The Lady of Shalott . . .

Now we know what her prison looks like, foursquare and of grey stone, a rain-coloured landscape that fits in with the many tears shed by the imprisoned maid, and to add to the cruelty of her fate, there is a small garden of flowers, blooms that she will never see. This one picture adds to the poignancy of the story the tension is increased by the word 'embowers' a word that implies a place of flowers for the use of lovers.

> And by the moon the reaper weary,
> Piling sheaves in uplands airy,
> Listening, whispers, 'tis the fairy
> Lady of Shalott' . . .

With these lines we know the season. It is autumn and the harvest is being gathered. We learn also that the Lady is not of mortal blood but is, in fact, one of the Fair Folk, a fairy.

Part two begins to explain her punishment and the way in which she has spent her time for many long years. This is made worse because as a fairy she is immortal and thus condemned to such a life for eternity.

> There she weaves by night and day
> A magic web with colours gay.
> She has heard a whisper say,
> A curse is on her if she stay
> To look down to Camelot.
> She knows not what the curse may be,
> And so she weaveth steadily . . .

We know she is a skilled weaver, that like Penelope, the wife of Odysseus, she works a magical web, and that she will suffer a curse if she looks out upon the world, but she does not know what form the curse will take. Cruelty upon cruelty; she does not even know what her fate will be, or even if it will happen at all. Yet she has found a way of looking out:

> And moving thro' a mirror clear
> That hangs before her all the year,
> Shadows of the world appear . . .

> . . . And sometimes thro' the mirror blue
> The knights come riding two and two,
> She hath no loyal knight and true . . .

The lady watches all that goes on in her mirror but that is merely a shadowland, and how she envies those ladies of Camelot who have knights to whom they may give favours and upon whom they may call when in need. The Lady has no one.

> 'I am half sick of shadows,' said
> The Lady of Shalott.

Clearly the Lady has a limit to her patience with her fate.

Part three is the longest and is devoted to a description of the knight for whom she dares the curse. Only when almost to the end of the part do we get to know his name; the description builds up gradually, first his horse and armour:

The gemmy bridle glitter'd free,
Like to some branch of stars . . .
. . . And from his blazon'd baldric slung
A mighty silver bugle hung,
And as he rode his armour rung . . .

This is no ordinary knight. He is wealthy and can afford to hang his
horse's bridle with gems, he has a blazon - a coat of arms, and so is
highly born, and he is wearing full armour so he is returning from some
knightly quest.

All in the blue unclouded weather
Thick jewell'd shone the saddle leather,
The helmet and the helmet-feather
Burn'd like one burning flame together,
As he rode down to Camelot.
As often thro' the purple night,
Below the starry clusters bright,
Some bearded meteor, trailing light,
Moves over still Shalott . . .

This is descriptive poetry at its best. One can see the magnificent figure
of the knight with his jewelled saddle and the flame-red plume in his
helmet flickering in the sunlight as he rides. Truly he must have seemed
to the Lady as brilliant as a 'meteor trailing light . . .' She has never
seen anything like him; now we come to the knight himself . . .

His broad clear brow in sunlight glow'd

. . .
From underneath his helmet flow'd
His coal black curls . . .
. . . Sir Lancelot . . .

The Lady has fallen in love with 'the best knight in all the world', the
peerless Lancelot. Now we, the readers, are ahead of the tale for we know
that, even had she not been under a curse, her love would have been
refused, for Lancelot has love only for Guinevere. We know now that
the Lady is doomed come what may and this colours the poem from
now on. We come to the most dramatic stanza in the poem and, when
reading it, it should be given full value and taken slowly.

She left the web, she left the loom,
She made three paces thro' the room,
She saw the water-lily bloom,
She saw the helmet and the plume,
She look'd down to Camelot . . .

Now the die has been cast. She has seen for the first time the space
of flowers below her tower, and she has seen Lancelot. Now comes
payment.

Out flew the web and floated wide;
The mirror crack'd from side to side;
'The curse is come upon me,' cried
The Lady of Shalott.

The first sign of the curse, the breaking of the web and the cracking
of the mirror, has occurred. In all magical tales the rending of the web
or veil is the forerunner to disaster, as when the veil before the Holies
of Holies was rent in the Temple of Jerusalem, when mourning in the
ancient lands the women rent their clothing and wept. The cracking
of the mirror foretells death, for the mirror is the symbol of the soul
and being cracked that soul is now released. She knows the curse now:
it is death.

The last part carries the tale to its bitter end and the Lady waits until
the evening tide. What did she do in those last hours? Did she spend
them looking out at the real world from her window? I think she did.
I also think that seeing Sir Lancelot was the culmination point of the
desolation that must have been building up for many long weary years.
At that moment she decided to dare the curse and take the consequences,
half knowing what they would be and, perhaps, glad of an excuse to
end her lonely days and nights.

In the stormy east wind straining,
The pale yellow woods were waning,
The broad stream in his banks complaining
Heavily the low sky raining.

Clearly the scene is being set for the tragedy on a grand scale. The storm
and the rain are symbolizing the tears of the Lady as she leaves her tower
for the first and last time.

> Down she came and found a boat,
> Beneath a willow left afloat,
> And round about the prow she wrote
> The Lady of Shalott . . .

Even the willow, the weeping tree, is here being used to heighten the effect for which the poet is now striving. She looks down to Camelot with 'a glassy countenance . . .'

> And at the closing of the day
> She loosed the chain, and down she lay,
> The broad stream bore her far away . . .

The linking of the close of day and the close of life is emphasized here and adds to the next stanza for, lying in her white robe, the Lady sings her last song, her Death Chant, her Rite of Departure. For her, an erstwhile immortal, now only too mortal, the last adventure is approaching. Is she to be pitied, or has she been granted what all the fairy folk seek according to tradition – death, and through death, a soul? If the latter, was she really cursed or was she afraid to take the plunge into humanity until she saw and loved Lancelot? Now the end is very near.

> For ere she reached upon the tide
> The first house by the water-side
> Singing in her song she died . . .

The adventure has overtaken her and she is at peace. Now we are given a brief look at the fair town of Camelot.

> Under tower and balcony,
> By garden wall and gallery . . .

The people of the town come out upon the wharf to see this strange sight: a beautiful woman dead upon a floating bier, the unknown Lady of Shalott. Their questions are hurried and fearful. What might this portend? Even in the palace the feasting stops and the knights and their ladies come out to see what is happening. Perhaps Lancelot intuits something, for of them all, it is he who pronounces her epitaph. He looks on her serene face for a moment and says:

'She has a lovely face;
God in his mercy lend her grace
The Lady of Shalott.'

In asking a blessing upon her he finalizes her completion into human state and she is set free as a pure soul. The tale is ended.

Relaxing and building pictures to music is probably something everyone has done from time to time - the rapt faces on the audience of a London promenade concert speaks for itself. Disney did it and, on the strength of his musical visions, brought Fantasia to life on the cinema screen. The popularity of screen background and theme music proves that the most ordinary people realize, even if subconsciously, that such music brings back vivid memories of the film. It is taken for granted these days that everyone knows that each major character has his or her own musical theme that is played whenever they are on screen.

Unlike a painting or a poem it is not possible to go into detail about a piece of music and the working aligned with it, therefore all I can do is to give you the piece of music and tell you what I see when I hear it. The piece is Vaughan Williams' 'Fantasia on Greensleeves'. This is, in fact, a combination of two English traditional songs perfectly matched together, one blending in where the other leaves off with such skill that you cannot 'see the join'.

The piece begins with the sweet piercing note of a solo instrument, and follows with a descending cadence that is possibly more English than any other piece of music ever written. Then the harp chords introduce the first gentle strains of Greensleeves. For me nothing else can bring to mind an English forest in summer so clearly and with such mind-shaking atmosphere. Somewhere at the back of my mind it has become synonymous with the ancient Nottingham forest, nowadays a mere fraction of its former glory, and with it a vision of Robin Hood and Maid Marian.

As those first notes ring out I see a group of men and one woman riding along a path leading into a dense forest. As the harp comes in they enter the first really dense stretches of green and ride on. I can hear them laughing and talking back and forth and seem to follow them in some way, drifting through the trees in their wake like woodsmoke.

They pass along narrow tracks and hidden ways, sometimes they dismount and lead the horses. Once they pause while the girl gathers flowers and makes a garland for her hair. All the while I can hear their voices though not the actual words. As the music draws to its close I see them arrive at the very heart of the forest to be greeted by others.

Although this may not seem much to go on, playing the piece yourself and following these or your own images, you will perhaps feel something of the ambience of the Greenwood that gives *me* so much pleasure. Music also has other uses: for instance it has been proven that studying whilst listening to any kind of music with a sixty-beat-a-minute rhythm will improve your ability to remember what you are studying by as much as 60 per cent.

You can develop an inner ear in just the same way that you develop an inner eye, or an inner nose, an inner touch, or an inner taste. It is merely a matter of patience and application to the task. All five of the physical senses can be used in altered states and to invoke memories of foods, scents, sounds and touch that you knew long ago. This kind of talent fully developed is of enormous use in the art of pathworking.

Below you will find listed music and poems that I have found useful when teaching and demonstrating pathworking to students. No doubt you will have favourites of your own, but these will give you a basic list from which to work immediately. There are many recordings of each piece of music by different orchestras and conductors so I have not entered any one in particular. The *Oxford Book of Mystical Verse* is a useful thing to have and a good rummage through a second-hand bookshop or two will provide the collected works of Tennyson, Whitman, Longfellow, Wordsworth and Coleridge, along with many more. Nowadays few take poetry seriously and it is a great loss to our children. I shall let you into a secret regarding my choice of *The Lady of Shalott*. Long ago when I was still at school, if someone chattered excessively in class the whole class were kept after school until the offender had learnt a poem well enough to recite it aloud before the class. Needless to say the shortest poem possible was chosen. It happened one day that I was accused of talking when, in fact, I was quite innocent. Highly incensed at the injustice of the accusation I waited until the end of lessons and then, with the entire class fidgeting around, I set to work to learn by heart the longest poem in the poetry book we always used . . . *The Lady of Shalott*! It took me from a quarter-to-four to just on six o'clock. The teacher could not go back on her word, and the guilty one would not own up . . . at least not then. When we did get out it was a free for all and the real culprit arrived the following day with several bruises and a sorry expression. I still know the poem by heart. Childish anger and resentment provided the emotion needed to engrave it on my mind permanently. The anger has long since gone and now I love the work for itself alone.

MUSIC

For assistance in improving memory use almost anything of Vivaldi's: Concerto in F Major; Concerto in D Minor for Viola; Concerto in D Major for Guitar and Strings; The Four Seasons. Or Handel's Concerto number 3 in D and Concerto number 1 in F; or Telemann's Double Fantasia in G Major and Concerto in G Major.

For pathworkings: Beethoven's Pastoral Symphony and the Ninth Symphony; or Debussy's 'La Mer', 'Le Bateau', 'Clair de Lune', 'Pelleas and Melisande', 'L'Après-midi d'un Faune'.

Recommended too are the overtures to most operas. In this category include all of Wagner's, Bizet's *Carmen* and Puccini's *Turandot*, and those preceding *Pagliacci* and *Cavaleria Rusticana*, and with the latter also the beautiful Intermezzo. Many marches offer good visualization images including 'The March of the Priests' from Aida, and that of the Toreadors. Also, 'Thus Spake Zarathustra' (Strauss); 'Nights in the Garden of Spain' (De Falla); The Concerto de Aranjuez (Rodrigo); 'Night on a Bare Mountain' and 'Pictures at an Exhibition' (Mussorgsky); 'The Nightingale' and 'The Fire Bird', 'Les Sacrés du Printemps' (Stravinsky); 'El Amor Brujo'. To these add: most of Vaughan Williams, Elgar, Percy Grainger, Delius, Sibelius, Grieg, some of Berlioz, and a very little of Bartok and Dvorak. Don't forget John Williams; as a composer of film themes he is unsurpassed. Try the music from *The Lion in Winter* with its superb invocation of twelfth-century England. *Star Wars* music can be used as well and the 'Thunderbirds March' is still one of the best. Look around at ethnic music, especially that from South America - in short, explore.

POETRY

Tennyson: 'The Mystic', 'The Kraken', 'The Hesperides', 'The Sea Fairies', 'The Merman and The Mermaid', 'The Miller's Daughter', 'New Year's Eve', 'Le Morte D'Arthur', 'Locksley Hall' (an amazingly accurate vision of the future and the world wars of the twentieth century), 'The Charge of the Light Brigade', 'Idylls of the King', 'The Coming of Arthur', and 'The Passing of Arthur'.
T. Gray, 'Elegy written in a Country Churchyard'.
W. Blake, 'Jerusalem', 'The Divine Image', 'The Tyger'.
W. Wordsworth, Most of his poems are worth using.
T. Coleridge, 'Kubla Khan', 'The Rime of the Ancient Mariner'.
Lord Byron, 'The Vision of Judgment', 'Childe Harold'.
D. G. Rossetti, 'The Blessed Damozel', 'Goblin Market'.
A. Swinburne, 'The Garden of Proserpine'.

To these add: Gerard Manley Hopkins, John Donne, John Milton, Alfred Houseman, John Masefield, Robert Browing, W. B. Yeats, R. Kipling, W. De La Mare, D. H. Lawrence, T. S. Eliot and Carlos Williams.

CHAPTER THIRTEEN

The Star Traveller

We all look forward to the future - every day we think about the next day, the week, the year and so on. The mind is a highly efficient time-traveller and gives us a reasonably good view of what we can expect up to a point. But as we have already discussed in this book it can be used to programme future events into a required pattern. For many people this poses a few questions.

1. Have we any right to 'alter' our future?
2. Can we alter our future?
3. Should we try to alter the future for others?

Firstly man was given free will. It is the greatest of all gifts from a Creator to His created ones. It means we are trusted to do what *we* think is best for us . . . all right so we fall on our faces with monotonous regularity but we are just beginning; potential gods we may be but we still carry L-plates. It is a hard fact to face, but we learn only by making mistakes, which is why we learn so much when we have a war. Dreadful but true. Plastic surgery for birth defects, accidents, and industrial injury was born out of the work done on the fire-scarred Battle of Britain pilots. We have medicines, surgery techniques, safer air travel, better engines, computers, and space travel because of what we learned during the war years. No one wants wars or conflicts, but the sad truth is that every time it happens man learns a bit more. What he does *not* learn is how to live in harmony. There is in him a total inability to allow other people and countries to live in the way they choose and not to interfere and force upon them other ideologies, other religions, and other ways of living. Missionaries, both political and religious, have caused more harm and desolation than anything else in history. Zeal is all right in its place, but its place is *not* in another man's mind.

Yes, we *do* have the right to alter our future whenever and wherever and however we can. We alter it when we decide to stay on another year at school, to take an Open University course, to have another baby that we really cannot afford, to try our hand at writing a book, take up a new hobby or fall in love. We are altering our futures every day of our lives. Man controls his own destiny, God waits patiently for the day when he finally makes it all the way.

Can we alter it? Of course we can, by the ways listed above and by the use of the techniques set out in this book. Yes, they work, and work well. What they do not do is work instantaneously. One of the greatest of human faults is that of impatience (unlike God!). Since the invention of instant coffee mankind as a whole has expected everything to happen in the same way - one spoonful and add hot water. With coffee it works well, with things like pathworkings/rituals all forms of occult training - forget it. If there is one basic piece of knowledge every occult student *must* learn it is that all occult studies take effort (lots of effort) and dedication. I spend a lot of time every year trying to convince would-be students that the advert in the *Magician's Herald* promising the degree of Magister Templi in three months is a ploy to get their money. Sometimes they listen.

If you take this book seriously you *can* alter your future. If you read and practise what is written in Maxwell Maltz' book *Psycho Cybernetics* you will change it even more quickly. However, it will take time and effort and it will not happen overnight even with Mr Maltz' book. The important thing is you must *want* to change your future, and you would be surprised how many people dream about it but, at heart, simply do not have the real desire to change. They prefer to grumble and hope that it will come all right by itself. Dreams can come true, I promise you they can. But they can only use the material at hand - you! It is your desire, your effort, your determination, your detailed dreaming that will make it happen.

Should you alter the future of others? We do it all the time. With our children, shall we send them to a private school, or the local comprehensive? Shall we take out a policy that will help send them to university? We do it with ourselves: 'Darling, will you marry me?' 'No.' We do it when we work with and therefore change others. Doctors change the lives of those they treat, teachers do it every working day of their lives. Forty years ago a much-loved and respected schoolteacher told me, 'You should think of writing as a career.' I laughed all the way home that day but the idea had been set deep into my mind. I was still set on becoming an opera singer, but my love of words grew stronger than my love of music. It took many long years and a lot of encouragement from others but I did write. Lester Robilliard was a born teacher. To him I owe more than I could ever repay. He knew me, as he knew all his pupils, better than we did ourselves. Yes, alter the future of others, but take the responsibility for your own actions. You will alter their futures simply by living, working and speaking with them. But altering such futures because of a whim of our own, because you think you know better than they what is good for them, *that* carries a heavy karmic debt. Politicians do it all the time, religious leaders when they leave the pulpit and start meddling in other areas do it, scientists do it, newspapers and TV do it, and very few of them have any compunction about what may come of their interference. *Always* look, think, and think again when you try to alter someone's future deliberately. Ten to one you will do more harm than good. This last question holds many paradoxes; one could say yes, do it, and no, leave it alone, and both would be right. It comes down to the first question and man's free will. We will always meddle in the lives of others; just try and think about the consequences and the responsibilities of what you are doing.

What about the past? We can use the techniques of pathworking here as well as the future. Where the occult is concerned it is mostly used in the talent of far memory. However, I personally have reservations in some areas. I am not happy about regression unless there is a very, very good reason for it. Simply using it as a form of analysis is, to my mind, dangerous. Let sleeping lives lie. At this moment you are the sum total of all your lives and experiences. To return to the past for the sake of curiosity, or just for the hell of it, is not good occult practice. There are rare occasions when it is useful. There are occasions when it comes up all by itself due to circumstances, or mental trip wires, then it has meaning and use. Trying to find out if you were an Egyptian priestess of Amun Ra or a soldier in the army of Charlemagne, a witch who was burnt in the thirteenth century – for some weird reason being burnt as a witch holds some kudos in modern occultism; it was a horrific and terrible death and most of them were totally ignorant of witchcraft and died for nothing – is a waste of time. Much better to say, 'Here I am, this is what I am now, I will go on from here.'

What does it matter what or who you were when you have such marvellous things ahead of you? Regression can bring up memories that are better left alone, and I speak from experience, having been through it. It took me many years to recover and left me with a lifelong aversion to certain people. Some years ago a book called *The Christos Experiment* was published. I tried its methods with a group of trained initiates as companions. We all ended up with depression, insomnia, and recurrent nightmares, and I might add, one of the people concerned had worked with the author. We were not going it alone.

So when can we use the past? We can use it to explore history and open areas of the world memory thereby gaining intuitive knowledge that can be used in other areas of occult work. Most writers of historical novels do it unknowingly, though Maureen Peters, a highly successful novelist with over a hundred titles to her name, uses it consciously and with great effect. It helps that she is also a trained mediator and an initiate. Both her historical novels and her occult writings (R. Hale Publishers) show the results of her far memory talents. She also writes as Catherine Darby and Sharon Whitfield.

Far memory is a talent that most people have in small amounts. Some people, however, seem to have a quite remarkable talent for it, like Joan Grant. For most of us, however, it comes and goes, switched on by locations, colours, situations, or objects. I have a friend who will go to great lengths to avoid passing the Sekmet statues in the Egyptian gallery of the British Museum because it triggers off things she would rather not remember. But another friend has the most wonderful memories set off by the same figures. We all have moments when we seem to half recall things we did and said in some far-off time. We all have longings to visit certain places. Strange as it may seem, I have no desire to visit Egypt . . . after all, it has changed a great deal since I knew it! But mention the Aleutian Islands, or Tierra del Fuego, or certain half-forgotten villages in the Pyrenees and my mind goes into top gear and presents me with image after image.

Far memory can be trained up to a point but, unless the real talent is close to the surface, it will never be more than just occasional flashes. The kind of training needed means working closely with an expert who can steer you away from the pitfalls and give you graded exercises that will slowly stretch your memory. You can work by yourself but it is long and tedious and you have no one to make you check on your memories continuously.

Pathworking through the past can be used to make children aware of history in a way that is far more exciting than just learning dates by heart. Experiencing the Battle of Trafalgar as a powder monkey or a midshipman, or acting as a Lady in Waiting to Anne Boleyn at her coronation, may not be the education authorities' way of doing things but they will give a child the ambience of the period in a way nothing else can. There is a flavour to it, a sight, scent, and sound that floats up from the world memory banks to which we are all connected mentally that stimulates recall of that era. Unless he be an exception a small boy in a history class is not too interested in the Battle of Waterloo, but if he imagines himself as a young soldier, a runner say between the Iron Duke and one of his generals further afield, then he is part of the whole experience. After all, he plays at 'make believe' almost every day like most small boys. Then he starts to become interested in what those despatches he is carrying actually said at the time.

Geography lessons could be made far more interesting if the child were encouraged by the parents to sit down and pathwork his way around a certain area of the world. And what of mathematics? Numbers are simply symbols for gatherings of things. They can be seen as things in their own right; from then on they become more approachable and more understandable. Think of them as little creatures from another world visiting our world. Their funny shapes and qualities make it an enjoyable game to play in these circumstances. It is time some genius made numbers into something akin to the Mister Men on children's television instead of the terrible stuff that is meted out daily. Children hate being talked down to, yet most presenters of children's programmes adopt a hearty 'let's all pretend we are rubber balls' approach that does more for apathy than Question Time in the House of Commons.

It is in the present that we can use pathworking to the fullest advantage. We can roam the universe in our minds and let our dreams run free. If you have ever bought a magazine called *Omni* you may well have seen some of the superb illustrations of the other planets in our solar system. They are usually headed 'An artist's impression', but what else is this impression but the result of a mental visit to the place combined with whatever factual knowledge is available?

Jules Verne did it in *Twenty Thousand Leagues Under the Sea* and predicted the hi-tech submarine almost half a century before it happened, then did the same thing with rockets in his *Journey to the Moon*. Da Vinci thought up the submarine and the helicopter even before Verne. Even dear old Victorian Tennyson told us in Locksley Hall . . .

For I dip't into the future far as human eye could see,
Saw the Vision of the world and all the wonder that would be.
Saw the heavens filled with commerce, argosies of magic sails,
Pilots of the purple twilight dropping down with costly bales.

Heard the heavens filled with shouting and there rained a ghastly dew
From the nations' airy navies grappling in the central blue.

That is vision of high quality from a man who has pathworked into the future and brought his vision back into his present. What he and others did we can do. We too can peer into the future and bring back images of what we see there - an artist's impression of what lies ahead.

Indeed, Tennyson tells us quite clearly in the same poem, 'ancient founts of inspiration well thro' all my fancy yet . . .' Clearly he was aware of and used some form of Mystery teaching. Locksley Hall well repays reading, though I should warn those ladies who are fiercely feminist that certain stanzas will raise their blood pressure. But, if you can grit your teeth and remember this man was writing in a far-off age with very different ideas about womankind, and just look at the depth and breadth of vision almost amounting to prophecy, you will understand a great deal.

The past can offer the advice of experience, the future can promise as yet undiscovered delights. The present is where they both meet and meld. That is also where we should be for most of our time. The ancient art of pathworking can give us much, can open many doors, but in the end this, the present, is where it happens. A fleeting moment, for yesterday is now as much in the past as is Imperial Rome and Golden Greece. Tomorrow is as much in the future as will be 2300, but here and now is where all three meet, and where we stand at the crossroads of Time.

BIBLIOGRAPHY

Astral Doorways, Herbie Brennan (Aquarian Press, 1986)

The Book of Lilith, Barbara Black Koltuv (Weiser, 1986)

The Book of Mysteries, Edited by Colin Wilson & Christopher Evans (Robson, 1986)

Children at Play, Heidi Britz-Crecelius (Floris Books, 1979)

Consciously Creating Circumstances, J. W. Plummer (Derek Ridgeway, 1953)

The Cult of the Black Virgin, Ean Begg (Arkana, 1985)

Dancers to the Gods, Alan Richardson (Aquarian Pres, 1985)

Daydreaming and Fantasy, Jerome L. Singer (Allen & Unwin, 1975)

Dragons of Eden, Carl Sagan (Coronet, 1979)

Dream Body, Arnold Mindell (Routledge, 1982)

Dream Sharing, Robin Shohet (Turnstone, 1985)

Dreams and How to Guide Them, Hervey De Saint-Denys (Duckworth, 1982)

The Dreamwork Manual, Strephon Kaplan Williams (Aquarian Press, 1984)

The Egyptian Book of the Dead, Wallace Budge (Dover, 1978)

Experiments in Aquarian Magic, Marian Green (Aquarian Press, 1985)

Frankenstein's Castle, Colin Wilson (Ashgrove Press, 1980)

The Gods Within Us, W. T. Palmes (Aquarian Press, 1961)

The Golden Bough, J. G. Frazer (Macmillan, 1975)

Imagery in Healing, Jean Achterberg (New Science Library, 1985)

Inner Vision, Nevill Drury (Routledge, 1979)

The Interior Castle, Teresa Avila (Sheed & Ward Ltd., 1974)

The Inward Arc, Frances Vaughan (Shambhala, 1985)

Judaism, Isadora Epstein (Penguin Books, 1966)

The Kabbalah Trilogy, Carlo Suares (Shambhala, 1976)

Larousse Encyclopaedia of World Mythology (1965)

Magic for the Aquarian Age, Marian Green (Aquarian Press, 1985)

Magical Thought in Creative Writing, Anne Wilson (Thimble Press, 1986)

Meditation and the Kabbalah, Aryeh Kaplan (Weiser, 1985)

Mind Games, Masters and Houston (Turnstone, 1972)

My Mother, My Self, Nancy Friday (Fontana, 1979)

My Secret Garden, Nancy Friday (Virago, 1975)

New Dimension Red Book (Helios Book Service, 1968)

Passengers: A Guide for Pilgrims of the Mind, Marian Anderson and Lewis Sadary (Turnstone, 1974)

Psychocybernetics, Maxwell Maltz (Pocket Books, 1978)

Return to the Goddess, Edward Whitmont (Routledge, 1982)

The Right Brain, Thomas Blakeslee (Macmillan, 1980)

The Ritual Magic Workbook, Dolores Ashcroft-Nowicki (Aquarian Press, 1986)

The Shaman and the Magician, Nevill Drury (Routledge, 1982)

The Shining Paths, Dolores Ashcroft-Nowicki (Aquarian Press, 1983)

Spiritual Exercises, Ignatius Loyola (Anthony Clark, 1973)

Suggestion and Autosuggestion, Charles Baudouin (Allen & Unwin, 1922)

Superlearning, Sheila Ostrander and Lynn Schroeder (Sphere Books, 1981)

Table of the Grain, John Matthews ed. (Routledge, 1984)

Waking Dream, Mary Watkins (Interface Books, 1976)

Way of Perfection, Teresa Avila (Sheed & Ward Ltd., 1974)

The Western Way - 2 vols, Caitlin and John Matthews (Arkana, 1985)

INDEX

SERVANTS OF THE LIGHT is a school of occult science founded by the late W. E. Butler. For details of its correspondence course of instruction, apply to the Director of Studies, S.O.L., P.O. Box 215, St Helier, Jersey, Channel Islands, Great Britain. Please include S.A.E.